EMBRACING THE WITCH AND THE GODDESS

Embracing the Witch and the Goddess is a detailed survey of present-day feminist witches in New Zealand. It examines the attraction of witchcraft for its practitioners, and explores witches' rituals, views and beliefs about how magic works. The book provides a detailed portrait of this undocumented section of the growing neo-Pagan movement and compares the special character of New Zealand witchcraft with its counterparts in the United States, Great Britain and Australia.

Kathryn Rountree traces the emergence and history of feminist witchcraft, and links witchcraft with the contemporary Goddess movement. She reviews scholarly approaches to the study of witchcraft and deals with the key debates which have engaged the movement's adherents and their critics, and ultimately presents what Mary Daly declared was missing from most historical and anthropological research on witchcraft: a 'Hag-identified vision'.

Based on fieldwork among witch practitioners, *Embracing the Witch and the Goddess* is an important contribution to the emerging profile of present-day witchcraft and Paganism.

Kathryn Rountree is Senior Lecturer in Social Anthropology at Massey University. As well as publishing widely in academic journals on aspects of feminist witchcraft and Goddess spirituality, she has written texts on academic writing and a series of educational books on New Zealand prehistory.

EMBRACING THE WITCH AND THE GODDESS

Feminist ritual-makers in New Zealand

Kathryn Rountree

Routledge
Taylor & Francis Group
LONDON AND NEW YORK

First published 2004
by Routledge
11 New Fetter Lane, London EC4P 4EE

Simultaneously published in the USA and Canada
by Routledge
29 West 35th Street, New York, NY 10001

Routledge is an imprint of the Taylor & Francis Group

Typeset in Garamond by
The Running Head Limited, Cambridge
Printed and bound in Great Britain by
Biddles Ltd, Guildford and King's Lynn

British Library Cataloguing in Publication Data
A catalogue record for this book is available from the British Library

Library of Congress Cataloging in Publication Data
Rountree, Kathryn
Embracing the witch and the goddess : feminist ritual-makers in New Zealand
Kathryn Rountree
p cm
Includes bibliographical references and index.
1. Witchcraft—New Zealand. 2. Magic—New Zealand. 3. Goddess religion—New Zealand.
4. Neopaganism—New Zealand. I. Title.
BF1584.N45R68 2003
133.4'3'0993—dc21

ISBN 0–415–30358–3 (hbk)
ISBN 0–415–30360–5 (pbk)

FOR HER

CONTENTS

PREFACE

Since the earliest days of the fledgling Goddess movement, New Zealand women have eagerly consumed a stream of books about the movement, virtually all published in the United States and the United Kingdom and almost all referring to spiritual ideas and practices circulating among American and British witches and Pagans. As well as the deluge of popular titles dealing with ancient goddesses, modern Wicca, magic, women's alternative ritual-making, Paganism, indigenous spirituality and so forth, scholarly interest in these areas has grown too, and a body of academic literature is developing. The bulk of this material also focuses on the beliefs and practices of American and British witches and Pagans.

Meanwhile small groups of New Zealand women and many individuals in all parts of the country have, since the late 1970s, been using the ideas in these books to piece together a vibrant local variant of feminist spirituality, one which nonetheless owes a great deal to the immediate New Zealand landscape and socio-religious context. This very loose community of several thousand women has a relatively low profile within New Zealand society generally, and so it is perhaps not surprising that they have not registered in scholarly discussions of the Goddess movement's global demographics, let alone in discussions about its adherents' spiritual beliefs, worldviews and ritual practices.

In 1997 anthropologist Lynne Hume's excellent *Witchcraft and Paganism in Australia* provided the first detailed examination of Paganism in the Antipodes. My book focuses attention on their Kiwi sisters in an attempt to remedy New Zealand's invisibility in the global profile of the Goddess movement and, more importantly, to show as clearly as possible what these women believe, how they conduct their spirituality and what it means to them. I should emphasize, however, that I deal here only with feminist witches and women involved in Goddess spirituality, not with New Zealand witches and Pagans more generally. This is because, when I went looking for witches to study for my doctoral research 13 years ago, feminist witches were the first ones I came across. At that time they formed the largest and most visible sub-group of Pagans in New Zealand – they probably still do, although other branches of Paganism have grown up around them. Focusing on feminist witches also fitted in with my desire to carry out feminist anthropology.

The thesis which emerged as a result of the first three years of my research was completed ten years ago. Since then, I have continued to consort with witches and those in the Goddess movement, and quite a lot of my academic writing has been related in some way to this research area. It has been fascinating to watch the movement grow up as well as to expand, to observe important and heated debates arise, to see witchcraft achieve a degree of normality, or at least acceptance, within the liberal quarters of mainstream society.

Pagan scholars are not so rare and less of a peculiarity than they were 13 years ago when I went tramping the corridors of my university (the University of Waikato) looking for someone who would agree to supervise my research. I will always be grateful to Dr Patrick Day for taking me on, despite my dubious topic; he was as fine a supervisor as any doctoral student could wish for. In April 2001 I attended the annual conference of the British Sociological Association's Sociology of Religion Study Group in Oxford and, for the first time, experienced being one of a company of Pagan scholars – almost enough to fill one whole dinner table! This was wonderfully stimulating (as well as reassuring) and it was one of these colleagues, Dr Graham Harvey, who kindly introduced me to Routledge's commissioning editor who suggested I write this book.

The purpose of the book is to present an ethnography of New Zealand feminist witches – to colour one small space in the global picture of Paganism – and to engage with a number of issues and debates which concern the feminist spirituality movement as a whole. I have also compared New Zealand witches with those in places where the movement is much better known, chiefly the US and UK. The first part of the book deals more with global concerns in relation to the study of witchcraft and the Goddess, while the second part is a close-up study of feminist witches and women involved in Goddess spirituality in New Zealand. Chapter five, which discusses my methodological approach as a feminist anthropologist, introduces the New Zealand ethnography. Because the readership for books about Paganism and witchcraft is wide – including scholars and witches, and readers who are both and neither – I have tried to write in a way that will be useful and accessible for this broad readership.

Over the relatively long period that I have been researching this area, I have become indebted to an enormous number of people who have taught, influenced, helped and supported me in innumerable ways. My first and greatest debt is to the hundreds of women ritual-makers with whom I have worked over the past 13 years. Their honesty, wisdom, generosity, hospitality, good humour and love have been remarkable. Above all, I thank the women who belong, and have belonged, to the ritual group I joined in Auckland in 1990, and those whom I interviewed: Juliet, Lea, Noreen, Sybil, Kez,

Galadriel, Joy, Scarlett, Bonney, Joan, Megwyn and Alex. The ritual groups I belonged to for shorter periods in Hamilton and Wellington also provided precious support and friendship.

Juliet Batten and Lea Holford have made enormous contributions to women's spirituality in New Zealand and to my research, and I am deeply grateful to both for welcoming me as a researcher, for inspiring and teaching me, and for reading my dissertation. I also wish to thank Céline Kearney, who very generously sent me a copy of her book about New Zealand women's spiritual lives, *Faces of the Goddess*, when she knew I was working on this book. Over the years Gillian Marie has been a wonderful friend and tireless champion of Goddess spirituality, facilitating numerous formal and informal opportunities for New Zealand women's healing and empowerment. My dear friend, Clotilde Mifsud, has facilitated the sacred journeys of women from many parts of the world during her 'Goddess tours to Malta', and I am thankful for all the help she has provided during my recent research in Malta.

I wish to thank my colleagues in the School of Social and Cultural Studies at Massey University, particularly the staff and postgraduate students in Social Anthropology, for years of lively engagement and for helping to provide a stimulating and supportive environment for research. My Head of School, Associate Professor Mike O'Brien, has been entirely supportive and encouraging, offering institutional assistance for me to attend international conferences and to take a period of sabbatical leave to complete the writing. The librarians at Massey's Albany campus have been extraordinarily helpful, not only fulfilling, but also anticipating, my research needs. I am also very grateful for the support given by anthropologists at the University of Waikato where I was a doctoral student in the early 1990s. I am especially indebted to Dr Judith Macdonald at Waikato and Dr Tricia Laing at Victoria University of Wellington who, along with Dr Pat Day, supervised my thesis.

In writing some sections of the book I have drawn on previously published articles. Chapter four draws on material from two papers (Rountree 1999 and 2001). An earlier version of chapter 11, titled 'How magic works: New Zealand feminist witches' theories of ritual action' was published in *Anthropology of Consciousness*, volume 13, number 1, 2002, published by the American Anthropological Association. Aspects of this work have also been presented at a number of national and international conferences, and I am indebted to all who have offered insightful and provocative feedback and encouragement, especially at several meetings of the Association of Social Anthropologists of Aotearoa/New Zealand and at the British Sociological Association's Sociology of Religion Study Group's conference in 2001.

I owe a special debt to my amazing son, Sam, much of whose infancy was spent bouncing on bean-bags or building tunnels in the corner of a room while I participated in Goddess workshops, and whose five-year-old's definition of a witch as 'a wise, magical, healing woman' is one I love to quote. His first-hand education about witches has instilled in him a healthy respect for and scepticism about all religions and spiritual paths. My parents, Iris and Brian Rountree, have supported all my academic endeavours and helped in many practical ways during the years of my doctoral fieldwork: their love and pride have sustained me. So, too, has the magnificent friendship of Jo Colyn over many decades. I am indebted to Yon Ankersmit for her consummate care and expertise in photographing the cover image for the book: it is a joy to see the result. Finally I should like to thank, with much love, my husband and colleague, Dr Joe Grixti, who read every word of several drafts of the manuscript, helped check the bibliography, and offered numerous perceptive comments, questions and editorial suggestions. His astonishing fortitude and generous-spirited engagement with my work have been an invaluable blessing, and my gratitude to him is inexpressible.

1

INTRODUCTION

> I always associated the witch with magic. I was always very curious about how the gingerbread castle got there. What skill, expertise, or mastery did she have to work things like that? I read *The Lord of the Rings* quite young, and I really identified with the Elven women there. That was my image of 'witch' – woman of power, prestige and magic.
>
> (Galadriel)[1]

> You say 'witch' and there's an image that comes to mind. Until that image is dispelled, it's going to be a constant dilemma for women. Identifying as 'witch', I feel more fulfilled in this time of my life than I have in any other.
>
> (Sybil)

> We must learn to dis-spell the language of phallocracy which keeps us under the spell of brokenness. This spell splits our perceptions of our Selves and of the cosmos, overtly and subliminally.
>
> (Daly 1979: 4)

I met my first witch at the age of three in a children's fairy story. She was a warty, black-clad old hag who lived alone in the depths of a forest, snared and dined on juicy children, and turned those who displeased her into toads. She presented an image of menace, cunning, pure evil. My story books were full of mothers who turned out to be step-mothers who made children's lives hell, grandmothers who were wolves in disguise, and godmothers who cursed the infant in rage when not invited to the party.[2] Witches could *seem* attractive and enticing in these stories, but would turn out to be cannibals.

What the story books did not tell, but what the European witch-hunters of the fifteenth to eighteenth centuries claimed, was that this wicked witch also had sexual intercourse with the Devil, suckled demons and her familiars, stole and ate penises as well as babies, and participated in orgies with fellow witches. The image of 'witch' incorporated both the hideous hag and the irresistible seductress.

I met my first goddess at primary school during a study of Greek mythology. She glows in the memory as an image of marvellous beauty and power. She had long golden hair and wore flowing white robes; she combined sexual desirability with moral goodness, superhuman strength with supernatural power. As an image, she represented the polar opposite of the wicked witch.

But both images – the witch and the goddess – produced a kind of awe. Both were female, but they existed outside the range of images acceptable or even imaginable for 'normal' women – the goddess so far above ordinary women that she inhabited the realm of the supernatural, the witch a terrifying inhabitant of the margins of the social world. Both were images of independent female power which was designated off-limits for 'normal' women. In any case, neither witches nor goddesses were 'real'.

After the scary fairy stories and childhood romance with Greek myths, I had nothing to do with witches or goddesses until I went to university. There I learnt about the victims of the European and Salem witch-hunts and about witchcraft in distant, exotic places – mostly in Africa. Whereas the evil-doing hag of childhood stories had evoked fear and later ridicule, these scholarly accounts of witches engendered pity or disbelief. Nonetheless, as an anthropology student, I was fascinated with other peoples' belief systems, especially their religious beliefs however bizarre or irrational they might seem, and how they governed peoples' lives.

Years later, after I had returned to university and was casting about for a topic for doctoral research – something that would remain fascinating for at least three years – I was listening to a lecture on cross-cultural ideas about illness and wellness, medicine and magic, when the idea of studying witches suddenly came to me. I knew witchcraft was quite an orthodox topic for anthropological study, but to my knowledge Western anthropologists' research on the topic had always been conducted in 'other cultures', rather than in their own. I wanted to study witches 'at home' in New Zealand, despite the fact that I knew no witches personally and had no idea how I might come to meet some. I had heard vaguely about people who met in graveyards at midnight to perform unsavoury rites, but was inclined to doubt the truth of such stories. I imagined it would be difficult to find witches, and more difficult, not to mention dangerous, to gain their permission to study them. I had never heard of 'feminist witchcraft' or 'Goddess spirituality'.

When I excitedly told people what I hoped to study, most responded with smirks, serious doubt about whether the topic was substantial or serious enough for doctoral research, or genuine alarm about what might become of me. Witchcraft, it seemed, was a legitimate topic for study only so long as it was witchcraft in an 'other culture'. One woman, however, a student in one of my anthropology tutorials, responded by cheerfully telling me that she was a witch herself, and that I should read Starhawk, an American writer, if I wanted to find out more about contemporary witchcraft. I borrowed Starhawk's first book, *The Spiral Dance*, from the university library and read it in an evening.

Another friend passed on a newspaper clipping she had saved about a local woman artist which described her as a 'modern day witch'. In the clipping I learnt that a number of women's ritual groups met in Auckland and that the artist, Juliet Batten, had written a book called *Power from Within: A Feminist Guide to Ritual-making*. From this book I learnt that the author taught courses on ritual through the University of Auckland's Department of Continuing Education. (I later discovered that Juliet called herself a ritual-maker rather than a witch, as the newspaper had described her.) I checked out the university's publicity brochure and found two courses offered: a weekend workshop taught by Juliet and a second – due to start in a few days time – called 'Rites of Passage for Women' led by another facilitator. There was one place left on this course so I enrolled and, with some trepidation, took the course. Two weeks later I attended the first of many workshops on ritual with Juliet Batten. That was 13 years ago.

Most of the women I met in those early workshops, and hundreds like them I have met in the years since, are involved in a movement known in New Zealand both as 'feminist witchcraft' and as 'Goddess spirituality'. At first I baulked at the idea that these two names referred to a single phenomenon. I was used to thinking of the hideous hag and the divinely beautiful goddess as polarized images. But the women I met were re-examining the witch and the goddess as images of womanhood and deconstructing their stereotypical meanings. They claimed that far from being opposites, the witch and the goddess were one. Moreover, they claimed that 'ordinary women', like themselves, could legitimately self-identify both as 'witch' and as 'goddess'.

Most of my early research focused on trying to understand how and why these women should want to do so. Why would any feminist, with the knowledge that many thousands of women had been victims of the European witch-hunts, embrace a label which epitomized the misogyny of patriarchal cultures, not to mention the terrors of childhood? Wasn't it presumptuous, even heretical, or at least unnecessary, to call oneself a 'goddess'?

In the course of the research I came to see the women's self-identification as 'witch' and 'goddess' as having dramatic symbolic value. In their view, the reason for the traditional designation of the witch and the goddess as illegitimate models of 'normal' womanhood is that both constitute images of female power which lies outside male control: hence their appeal to this group of feminists (but not to all feminists, as we shall see in chapter four). By self-identifying as 'witch' and as 'goddess' the women I studied symbolically lay claim to the independent female power which the two symbols represent: they image themselves as strong and autonomous, as having the right to choose and direct their own lives. Identifying in these ways is a symbolic act of self-empowerment by which these women permit themselves to connect with and legitimate both the sacred, strong and the dark, dangerous aspects of themselves. They are attempting to re-member themselves, to reclaim aspects of themselves to which they believe they have been denied access. By re-membering the witch and the Goddess and assigning them with new meanings and values, women are re-membering and re-valuing themselves.[3]

By employing the symbol of 'goddess', they are recalling a time when, they believe, Europe was peopled by societies whose religions centred on female divinities, especially various versions of a 'Great Mother' Goddess who was responsible for the fertility of crops, animals and human communities. This period of 'pre-patriarchal religion', the evidence for which they say stretches from 30,000 to around 4,000 years ago, is claimed to correspond with a period of pre-patriarchal social relations when women were valued as highly as men and both sexes participated fully in society. Modern followers of Goddess spirituality trace a direct connection between the demise of the Goddess and the demise of women's position in society. The shift to patriarchy and patriarchal religions in Western societies, with the eventual dominance of Judaeo-Christian monotheism, they argue, meant that women were alienated not only from social and political power but also from powerful parts of themselves. Gadon (1990: xiv) writes:

> When the balance changed, the dark side of the feminine was also suppressed. The Goddess had been a model of women's nature in all its fullness. The irrational, the chaotic and the destructive, which had been acknowledged when the Goddess reigned supreme, were split off from divinity and became feared. Women could no longer express their complete psychic reality.

It was this 'dark side of the feminine' which, they claim, was distorted and eventually came to be imaged as the witch (Walker 1985). I discuss the historical development of the witch stereotype in more detail in chapter two.

While many women in the Goddess spirituality movement see the early goddess-worshipping societies of Europe in a utopian light with respect to gender relations, they do not yearn to turn back the clock several millennia, advocate de-evolutionary cultural change, or idealize everything about ancient societies. They would not, for instance, wish to embrace Stone-age technology, carry out animal sacrifices, or endure high infant-mortality rates; nor do they imagine that goddess-worshipping societies were free of injustice or cruelty. They do believe, however, that the past offers different models for more balanced gender relations and for a more sustainable relationship between humanity and the earth. In recalling the religions of ancient societies they also want to point out that patriarchy and god-worship are not normative and that 'goddess' can be a useful symbol for women today (the best known article on this topic is Christ 1982, originally published in 1978 in *Heresies* 5).

It must be noted, however, that throughout its history (a little over 30 years) the modern Goddess movement has come under fire from many feminist and other scholars in relation to, among other things, what are regarded as romantic, utopian and plain false beliefs and claims about goddesses and ancient societies. The Goddess movement is accused of mythologizing and misrepresenting the past to serve a contemporary socio-political and religious agenda. The debate became extremely heated in the wake of the publication of Cynthia Eller's book *The Myth of Matriarchal Prehistory: Why an Invented Past Won't Give Women a Future* (2000). The movement has also been savagely criticized by some feminists for re-invoking unhelpful essentialist ideas about 'woman as nature' and nurturer. I discuss these debates in chapter four.

By creating and embracing a spirituality in which the primary image of divinity is a goddess, feminist witches are not only re-conceptualizing the nature of the divine, they are also re-conceptualizing the nature of the feminine. They reject the image of the feminine as inferior, weak and passive as an oppressive legacy of Christianity.[4] The symbol of 'goddess', on the other hand, is seen as opening up a great range of images of the feminine: virginal maiden, enchanting seductress, nurturing mother, warrior, protector, creator, death-dealing crone, and so on. The Goddess, feminist witches say, has a thousand faces.

Collapsing the witch/goddess dichotomy is one aspect of a much broader challenge these women are making to the worldview which has long been dominant in Western societies, one founded on dualism in which women come off worse than men, Blacks come off worse than Whites, the body is subordinate to and in conflict with the spirit, and the natural world's value is measured in terms of exploitable resources. Instead they prefer a holistic worldview which emphasizes connection, balance and cyclic processes. This alternative worldview is explored in detail in the following chapters.

Of course feminist witches are not the only ones who have been challenging the dominant worldview in Western societies. In the past three to four decades, feminists more generally have been challenging the hegemony of Western patriarchy, the hegemony of Western colonialism has taken a further battering, the civil rights, gay rights, environmental and peace movements have become increasingly vociferous, active and effective. The call for a more holistic worldview is coming from many diverse quarters: eco-feminism, psychotherapy, alternative healing, the New Age, self-help and 'human potential' movements, scientific theories such as James Lovelock's 'Gaia hypothesis', and so on. Feminist witches see themselves as part of this larger amorphous 'mood' or 'movement' abroad in contemporary societies which is challenging the 'dominator model'[5] which has framed social relations with regard to gender, ethnicity, age, class and other social distinctions, as well as human relationships with the rest of the natural world.

While feminist witchcraft is broadly connected with the diverse movements listed above, its closest relationships are with two umbrella movements whose own constituencies are large and diverse. Feminist witches form a subgroup both within feminism and within modern Paganism. The latter is known also as 'neo-Paganism', a name which draws attention to the fact that this is a newly created religious movement (although some Pagan traditions, like Druidry, extend back to the late eighteenth century). Paganism, which the 'Introduction' to *Paganism Today* says is 'fast developing as the new religion of the twenty-first century', incorporates Wicca, Goddess spirituality, Druidry, Shamanism, Heathenism, Sacred Ecology and a number of other traditions (Hardman 1995: ix). Griffin (2000b: 14) quotes sources which estimate that there are up to 500,000 in the American Goddess community and between 110,000 and 120,000 in the United Kingdom.[6] While numbers of Pagans are greatest in the US and UK, there are also Pagan communities in continental Europe, Scandinavia, Canada, South Africa and Japan. Many branches of Paganism are also active in Australia (see Hume 1997).

Essentially Paganism today consists of a group of modern Earth religions whose first principle is love for and kinship with nature, and reverence for the life force and its continuous cycles of life and death (Hardman 1995: xi).[7] 'Paganism is a religion at home on Earth'; for Pagans 'every day is sacred and all the Earth is holy' (Harvey 1997: vii, 1). The word 'pagan' comes from the Latin *paganus* meaning 'country dweller', and of course it came to be associated with those who followed older religions which Christianity sought to replace. While there is no codified set of beliefs and practices, most Pagans acknowledge the concepts of Goddess and God (and often many gods and goddesses) and follow the ethic: 'Do what thou wilt, but harm none', which stresses individual freedom alongside responsible concern for all other beings and for the planet. Most Pagans celebrate a series of eight seasonal festivals (two Solstices, two Equinoxes and four others) within an annual cycle called 'The Wheel of the Year'. These are discussed in chapter nine. There is now a substantial and growing literature on various forms of Paganism, a small proportion of which is academic, almost all of it referring to the United Kingdom and the United States.[8] An excellent introduction to Paganism, covering a range of traditions, is Graham Harvey's *Listening People, Speaking Earth: Contemporary Paganism* (1997).

Under the 'Pagan' umbrella, witches are probably the most numerous group.[9] Although most witches assert that their Craft stretches back millennia before 'The Burning Times' of the European witch-hunts, most scholars credit Gerald Gardner, a British civil servant, with being the originator of the specific practices of modern witchcraft, or 'Wicca' as it is known.[10] In 1954, three years after the Witchcraft Act was repealed in Britain, Gardner published *Witchcraft Today* wherein he set out the beliefs and ritual practices of witchcraft which, many have since argued, he largely invented, or at least creatively assembled from a variety of sources, himself. Gardner claimed to have discovered an ancient coven in the area of the New Forest into which he was initiated in 1939 by one of its members, Dorothy Clutterbuck. Scholars and Pagans alike have long debated the truthfulness of Gardner's story.[11]

While Gardner's name is the one associated with the founding of modern witchcraft, its origins can be traced to various philosophies and experimental groups active in the nineteenth century, the most relevant of which was the magical group called the Order of the Golden Dawn, formed in 1887 by three dissident Freemasons, which in turn spawned the Society of the Inner Light in 1922. But the important ideas and rituals of modern witchcraft have much older heritages within the Hermetic tradition of the Renaissance, neo-Platonism, old European folk-beliefs, magical practices and seasonal festivals, various polytheistic mythologies (for example, Greek, Egyptian, Celtic and Near Eastern), pre-Christian 'pagan' religions and European Shamanism.[12]

Just as witches form the most numerous group within Paganism, most literature in the field by both practitioners and academics (a number of authors fall into both categories) is about Wicca. Wicca differs from feminist witchcraft in significant ways: while both share a holistic worldview, revere nature, use the same basic ritual structure and are polytheistic, Wiccan covens are mixed and stress gender polarity and complementarity in the working of magic, and embrace gods as well as goddesses (although the Goddess is thought to be pre-eminent). There are many books introducing Wicca and witchcraft: the first I read (also the first book many witches read), *The Spiral Dance* by Starhawk, is an excellent introduction. (By 2000 sales had exceeded 300,000.) Feminist witches, on the other hand, usually meet in women-only groups and focus exclusively on the Goddess and a wide range of goddesses from ancient and living religious traditions. Their feminist politics determines a strong emphasis on women's self-empowerment and healing during rituals. Their beliefs and practices, especially those of New Zealand feminist witches, are explained in detail in the following chapters.

Historically, on the global scene, feminist witches (or 'Dianic witches' – after the goddess Diana – as they are sometimes called in the United States) are generally seen as an offshoot of Wicca and as a relatively small component of the neo-Pagan movement generally. However the situation is rather different in New Zealand. Here, until very recently, feminist witches have had a much stronger presence in terms of visibility and numbers than other witchcraft traditions or forms of modern Paganism. Undoubtedly, as was the case in Australia, followers of other witchcraft and Pagan traditions were practising their religion well before feminist witchcraft emerged on the New Zealand scene in the 1980s, but they kept a very low profile and continued to do so into the 1990s. This has changed only in the last few years, helped by the growth and increased public profile of Paganism and New Age spirituality globally, the development of a local 'critical mass' of Pagans and witches, and the internet.

In the 2001 New Zealand census 5,862 people, out of a total population of 3.7 million, identified themselves as some variety of Pagan, of which 2,196 said they were Wiccan.[13] In September 2000 a Federation of New Zealand Pagans was established and in 2002 the first New Zealand Pagan Festival, attended by 160 people, was held (although many festivals focusing on alternative spirituality had previously been held, some attracting several thousand). The opening ritual was led by Janet Farrar, a well-known British author of practical books about witchcraft.[14] Festival-goers spent their time listening to lectures and music, swimming and bush-walking, shopping for crafts, watching a medieval fighting re-enactment and telling late-night stories about elves and fairies by candlelight.

A string of groups and covens practising a variety of traditions – Gardnerian Wicca, Heathenism, Druidry, Shamanism, Fellowship of Isis and others – now meets up and down the country. The Universities of Auckland and Otago, the country's two biggest campuses, have Pagan networks. One city's Wiccan Association hosts a 'Witches' ball'. All New Zealand cities and a few large towns have shops catering for Pagans selling everything from candles, incense, crystals and herbs to organic menstrual cloths, individually crafted wands and freshly mixed potions. Workshops on topics such as 'Introduction to magick', 'Dream-sharing', 'Drumming', 'Belly-dancing' and 'House clearing' (recommended for real estate agents in particular) are on offer, and there are the inevitable web-sites and publications.[15]

While the pace of Pagan activity has recently picked up in New Zealand, it is clearly far from being as well developed or on the scale one sees in the United Kingdom, the United States or Australia. This is unsurprising given New Zealand's much smaller population. Interestingly though, despite their much lower numbers in New Zealand, Pagans form a percentage of the total New Zealand population which is only a little lower than their percentages in Britain and America. Indeed, they may well be similar, given that one can probably assume that the New Zealand census figures under-represent actual numbers of Pagans because of the wariness of some about declaring their religious affiliation on the census form.

The relationship between feminist witches and other witches or Wiccans differs from one local context to another. Greenwood (2000a: 165) says that in Britain 'there is an uneasy tension between feminist magical groups and the wider subculture' because the feminist groups do not work with the central Wiccan idea of gender polarity, and because of their overt feminist politics. In the United States, where feminist witchcraft first developed, there is usually a happier relationship with Wicca (Eller 1993: 50), with writers like Starhawk apparently sliding across the two. Hume mentions no tension between feminist witches and other witches or Pagans in Australia, although there Dianic Wicca seems to represent only a very small portion of Paganism as a whole (Hume 1997: 88). In New Zealand there is no animosity between Wiccans and feminist witches, but they know little about and have little to do with each other, apart from perhaps patronizing the same Pagan shops. Feminist witches here, as I have noted, have had a more open public profile than other witches and have always been more closely affiliated with the women's movement and the ecology movement than with Paganism as a whole. There seems to have been less strain (although there certainly has been some) between so-called 'spiritual feminists' and 'political feminists' in New Zealand than has been evident in some quarters, particularly in the United States.

Although I have said that the names 'feminist witchcraft' and 'Goddess spirituality' both refer to the one movement in New Zealand, women in this movement identify in a variety of ways: as 'feminist witch', 'witch', 'feminist ritual-maker', or as 'involved in the women's spirituality movement', 'feminist spirituality', 'Goddess spirituality' or 'the Goddess movement'. Some will say they practise Wicca, although they have probably never heard of Gardner, have never been initiated or trained according to strict Wiccan protocol, and may well be ignorant of its existence. In this case 'Wicca' is used simply as a synonym for witchcraft. Not only do different women define themselves differently from one another, but one particular woman will define herself differently in different contexts for reasons which I discuss in chapters three and seven. Within a single group whose members share the same beliefs and practices, there will be some women who call themselves 'witches' and the group a 'coven', while others say they are 'involved in women's spirituality' and refer to the group as a 'ritual group'.

In the literature about the movement, the labels 'women's spirituality' and 'feminist spirituality' are frequently used. I find these terms problematic to use in this book because of their vagueness and broadness: sometimes they are used elsewhere to include Christian and Jewish feminists and neo-Pagan women generally as well as feminist witches. 'Women's spirituality' may also be taken to refer to an ill-defined spirituality which all women possess whether they think about it consciously or not. I use the terms 'feminist witchcraft' and 'Goddess spirituality' synonymously to refer to the movement I have studied because of their greater precision and because they are the names with which most women in the movement are familiar and comfortable. I frequently abbreviate 'feminist witch' to 'witch' for the sake of economy when it is clear that I am talking about feminist witches. The women themselves make the same abbreviation.

I also had to decide whether to write 'goddess' with a capital or lower-case initial letter. I follow the practice of using a lower case 'g' when referring to specific goddesses – for example, the goddess Demeter or the goddess Kali. I use a capital 'G' when referring to 'the Goddess', an overarching term embracing all goddesses and used by women in the movement to refer to the sacred feminine, the life source, ultimate reality, the Great Mother, the divine being of women and the creative energy in the universe at large.[16] This Goddess, as we shall see, should not be taken as the Pagan counterpart of the God of monotheistic religions like Judaism, Christianity or Islam.

Another decision was whether or not to capitalize 'witch'. According to one line of thinking, 'Witch' should be capitalized in the way that the names for adherents of other religions are. However, I see feminist witchcraft as leaning in the direction of being a social movement; it is the spiritual wing of feminism. I would not capitalize 'feminism'. A woman's decision to identify as 'witch' is conditional upon her mood, context and shifting ideas; it is fluid and often politically-motivated. Capitalizing 'Feminist Witch' would seem to fix and formalize women's identity more than many would want to do. Moreover feminist witches in New Zealand very seldom capitalize 'witch' themselves. However I do capitalize 'Paganism' and 'Wicca', because their members clearly see these as names of religions.[17]

When I chose witches as a subject for doctoral research I was looking for an exotic, risky topic. I have spent almost 13 years since then explaining to people outside the movement that witches are not exotic or risky. They are mostly middle-class, well-educated, liberal-minded feminist women with whom, in fact, I have a great deal in common. They are good mothers and devoted grandmothers, lesbian and straight, married and single, old and young women who are socially responsible and deeply concerned about the environment. Since I began this study the neo-Pagan movement globally has grown enormously, and so has the literature about it. Among the academic writing on the subject, a handful of ethnographies has been produced by anthropologists, sociologists and scholars in religious studies who, although I did not know it, were conducting fieldwork among witches at more or less the same time as I was. It has been fascinating to compare witches in New Zealand with their siblings in the US, UK and Australia, although studies in these places have almost all focused on witches more broadly, rather than on feminist witches in particular.

Of course New Zealand witches have much in common with witches elsewhere, especially as many of their ideas derive from books produced in the UK and US. But the New Zealand variant of the movement also has some unique characteristics. These have to do with New Zealand's diasporic location, the personalities who have been influential here, the manner in which the movement began and developed in the country, and various socio-historical factors concerning the relationship between feminist witchcraft and movements such as feminism, eco-feminism, Christian feminism and the New Age.

It seems to me that there is also something unique about New Zealand witches which relates to what New Zealanders see as the 'national character' (although I am wary of reifying that term to any great extent). New Zealanders see themselves as possessing a 'D-I-Y genius' which derives from their relatively recent pioneering roots.[18] Kiwi blokes pride themselves on being able to fix anything with 'a bit of 4x2 and some number 8 wire', and New Zealand children grow up being told stories about heroic great-grandparents who, with minimal fuss, established homes in the bush and transformed flour bags into curtains and children's clothing, dripping into soap, and kerosene tins into baby-baths and bush toilets. New Zealand witches are mistresses of improvisation: when the British ritual manual requires snow, the Kiwi witch (who lives in Auckland where it never snows) chips ice off the freezer and pulverizes it in the food processor. New Zealand witches cheerfully make do with improvised or invented ingredients, tools, rituals and spells. The celebrated creativity of New Zealand witches' rituals also has a lot to do with the fact that many participants were introduced to feminist ritual-making through workshops run by artists.

Compared with Luhrmann's (1989) and Greenwood's (2000a) descriptions of British witchcraft, feminist witchcraft in New Zealand is less institutionalized, formal or secretive. (However, such comparisons are not straightforward because British ethnographies have not focused primarily on feminist witchcraft.) Compared with Wiccan and Dianic covens in the United States, New Zealand feminist witches' groups have fewer formal trappings – for example, titles like 'high priestess', 'initiate' and 'apprentice' are not used, and methods of initiation are usually made up for a particular occasion. Feminist witches are a much more significant component of the Pagan scene in New Zealand than they are in Australia. Comparisons between feminist witches in New Zealand and their better known counterparts in other parts of the world will be explored in later chapters.

My broad goal from the beginning of this research was to discover and understand feminist witches' beliefs, values and ritual practices and the reasons why women find them attractive and compelling. I wanted to understand how women come to identify as 'witches', why they choose a label long associated with the mythical evil hag and with woman-killing. I was interested in how women saw the relationship between their spirituality and the political goals of feminism. I wanted to find out how they thought their 'magic' worked, and about their relationship with goddesses. This book is largely preoccupied with what I discovered in pursuit of answers to these questions.

As an anthropologist I have tried to look at witchcraft through an insider's eyes, to give what Mary Daly (1979: 216) says is sorely needed in scholarship on witchcraft: 'a Hag-identified vision'. This has not been difficult. When I sat up half the night reading *The Spiral Dance* before I embarked on this research and before I knew feminist witchcraft existed, I discovered that witchcraft was not the dark, dangerous or titillating phenomenon I had more or less expected it to be. I found a worldview which embraces the earth, this life, a sacred current which runs through all beings irrespective of gender, ethnicity, religion or even species, one in which there was room for the imagination and mystery. Although the ritual trappings of witchcraft seemed rather outlandish at first, its worldview was not too far from my own.

During the years in which I conducted doctoral research and in the decade since, I have never encountered anything sinister in my experiences with witches or their rituals. Indeed at least some of the intrigue and suspicion which has surrounded witches in the public's eye seems to have dissipated.[19] In my university classes there is no longer the collective holding-of-breath when I begin a lecture about witches, many students have some knowledge of the movement: a mother, daughter, friend or girlfriend is a witch, or they have attended some kind of ceremony or celebration – a birthday, baby-blessing, wedding or funeral – which had Pagan overtones. Paganism has not become commonplace, but neither is it any longer regarded as particularly bizarre. The aim of this book is to make it less so.

2

APPROACHES TO WITCHCRAFT

> One mustn't be silent about certain wicked women who become followers of Satan (I Tim. 5: 15), seduced by the fantastic illusion of the demons, and insist that they ride at night on certain beasts together with Diana, goddess of the pagans, and a great multitude of women; that they cover great distances in the silence of the deepest night; that they obey the orders of the goddess as though she were their mistress; that on particular nights they are called to wait on her.[1]

When I first told people that I had chosen witches as the subject of my doctoral research, a friend suggested that I might ingratiate myself by taking along 'a nice plate of bats' wings or a dish of jellied newt'. My mother fretted that I would 'discover too much' and that 'they' would retaliate by kidnapping my baby. Other people joked about midnight orgies in graveyards and New Age spiritual masturbation. I received impassioned lectures on the irrationality of witchcraft, requests for spells to despatch a troublesome lover and an employer, and a generous offer of some old Black Sabbath records. When I was away from my university department attending rituals, I was said to be 'off on my broomstick'.

From these responses we could construct the contemporary popular concept of a witch: a malevolent or ridiculous hag inclined towards Satanism, cannibalism, illicit sex, levitation and lunacy. This image parallels remarkably closely the image of the witch popular in sixteenth-century Europe at the height of the witch-craze.[2] Drawing from writers of the fifteenth and sixteenth centuries, Jeffrey Russell, in his *History of Witchcraft* (1980: 37), describes what was almost universally believed about witches at that time. Each Sabbat,[3] witches, who were mostly women, sneaked out of bed, rubbed themselves with an ointment which enabled them to levitate, and flew off on animals, fence-posts, pitchforks, bread paddles or broomsticks to meet with fellow witches in caves or cellars or on deserted heaths. Novices were required to kill a young child and bring its body to a subsequent meeting.

Each witch had to renounce Christianity and worship the Devil or his representative at the Sabbat by offering him the obscene kiss on the buttocks. After the ritual was completed, the feasting and orgy began. Children's bodies, stolen from good Christian families, were boiled up and consumed in a parody of the eucharistic feast. At the conclusion of the Sabbat, the witches flew home and slipped back into bed beside their sleeping spouses.

I begin this chapter by drawing attention to the strength and resilience of the historical image of the witch, because I think it significant that Western academics of any discipline who study witchcraft have also, unavoidably, grown up with this image. The 'wicked witch' is a well-established, highly consistent and evocative image in literature from Shakespeare to the Grimms to Roald Dahl. Because the image of the glinty-eyed, warty-nosed hag cackling evilly over a cauldron brimming with plump children is obviously fictional, it has been taken as given that 'real' witches do not and never did exist.[4] They did not become carnate during the witch-craze, nor had they ever been. Witches are 'cultural constructs, not existing in any biological sense,' writes historian Willem de Blécourt (1999: 150). The witch is only as real as the witch belief.

Academics' beliefs – or disbelief – about witches have had an important role in underpinning their theoretical approaches to the study of witchcraft. Because witches are believed to live only in stories and in our minds (but not among us), scholars have looked for social, psychological, political and economic reasons – but seldom religious reasons – to explain why societies, including our own, construct witch beliefs and witch stories, why they label people 'witches', and why they hate and persecute the objects of such labelling. Thus, the academic study of witch beliefs has not been the study of witches' beliefs, but rather the study of beliefs about witches.

In her introduction to *Witchcraft: Confessions and Accusations*, a collection of papers by anthropologists and historians from a conference to mark 30 years since the publication of Evans-Pritchard's *Witchcraft, Oracles and Magic among the Azande*, Mary Douglas (1970: xxxiv) notes this tendency of academics to focus on the society which holds witchcraft beliefs, rather than on the witches themselves:

> Anthropologists have usually approached witchcraft from the point of view of the accuser, always assuming that the accusation is false. This has made it hard for us to interpret witchcraft confessions. Threats to practise witchcraft against an enemy, these we can interpret as empty boasting. But the idea that a person may sincerely believe himself a witch and go to a diviner to be cured of his state is difficult to understand within the terms of our analysis.

Again, in *Natural Symbols*, Douglas (1973: 165) writes: 'The ethnography of the world seen from the eyes of the accused sorcerer has not been recorded as yet'.

The problem of what anthropologists and historians should make of the self-identified witch, or the witch 'confession', is also discussed by Thomas (1970: 64), a specialist in English witchcraft:

> The veracity of such confessions has been the subject of much historical controversy, and anthropologists have found them equally embarrassing, choosing to put them down to 'malnutrition', or 'depression' . . . just as seventeenth-century intellectuals attributed them to 'melancholy'.

Macfarlane, in his comparison of witchcraft studied by anthropologists and witchcraft in Tudor and Stuart England, concluded that individuals who make witchcraft 'confessions' do so from spite, delusion or societal pressure (1970a: 222). Levack (1987: 11–18) also distrusts confessions of witchcraft because, he claims, they were frequently the product of judicial coercion and torture. Those 'confessions' reported to have been unforced were made because the accused wanted to get the execution over and done with, rather than endure the torture they would surely have been subjected to if they remained silent. Some 'confessions', Levack (p. 15) says, were also 'almost certainly the result of senescence'; old women on trial for witchcraft produced fantasies which the interrogators then shaped into diabolical activity.

Historians on the whole have interpreted the study of witchcraft as a history of repression and inhumanity directed against rather pitiful members of communities (Russell 1980: 40). Since they have taken it as given that self-identifying witches never existed, they see 'witches' as victims of labelling by the societies in which they lived. Studies of Salem witchcraft have also typically pursued an understanding of this labelling process (Boyer and Nissenbaum 1974, Demos 1982, Karlsen 1987). They have focused on the social relationships between accuser and accused and on the demographic characteristics of the accused in order to discover what kinds of people were picked out and defined as 'witches', and why these characteristics should have made them vulnerable to accusation.

Karlsen (1987) sees the study of Salem witchcraft as the study of systematic violence against women. She found that accused witches tended to be women who lived alone, especially middle-aged and old women. They were vulnerable because they lacked a male 'protector', and because they had failed to or were no longer fulfilling women's prescribed roles as child-bearers and helpmeets to men. Often they were women who had no brothers or sons, thereby thwarting primogeniture. They were frequently accused of 'discontent' for which, Karlsen says, we might read 'refusal to be submissive'. She concludes that, like their European counterparts, accused witches in Salem were women living outside patriarchal control, at least with respect to their domestic lives, and were therefore seen by their community as posing a serious threat to the social order.

Thus, on the whole, people accused of witchcraft have been interpreted by historians as victims – as scapegoats for community hostilities and tensions, as victims of misogyny and, most importantly, as victims of labelling. People who 'confess' themselves to be witches are likely either not to have been taken seriously by scholars or to have been viewed in an unflattering light as weak or troublesome, sad, impotent and, significantly, female members of their societies. This portrayal of witches as 'almost entirely devoid of intelligence, personality, humour, creativity and power, hapless and helpless victims of relentless and overwhelming structures of power and ideology' was not, says Russell (2001: 122), 'how the great majority of her contemporaries saw her'.

Several writers, however, have challenged this concentration on the persecution of witches and on the function of witch beliefs in societies which have/had them. Carlo Ginzburg is perhaps the strongest critic of the approaches taken by most historians writing in the 1970s and 1980s, charging them with concentrating almost exclusively on the persecution of witches while giving little or no attention to the beliefs and behaviour of the persecuted: 'On witchcraft . . . we possess only hostile testimonies, originating from or filtered by the demonologists, inquisitors and judges. The voices of the accused reach us strangled, altered, distorted; in many cases, they haven't reached us at all' (Ginzburg 1990a: 10).[5]

Ginzburg criticizes historians such as Macfarlane, Trevor-Roper and Thomas for providing interpretations of witchcraft which are reductionist and functionalist. Macfarlane (1970a, 1970b), for instance, influenced by anthropological functionalism, examined the age and sex of accused witches in England, the motives for the accusations and the relationships between witches, neighbours and the community in general, but did not examine what the women and men accused of witchcraft believed or claimed to believe. Trevor-Roper (1969) focused on the problem of how the witch-craze could have happened in Europe at the same time as the so-called scientific revolution: how could a body of popular superstition built on by clerics' fantasies turn into an obsession which gripped Europe for 300 years? He dismissed popular beliefs about witches as absurd fantasies of mountain peasants born of popular credulity and female hysteria. Thomas's (1971) examination of English witchcraft sought psychological, sociological and intellectual explanations for witchcraft accusations but failed, says Ginzburg, to examine what witchcraft meant for the accused.

Ginzburg's alternative approach was to analyse the various elements of beliefs about the witches' Sabbat and their symbolic significance, which he traced back to a core of folkloric beliefs and practices rooted in Eurasian Shamanism. (The origins of the Sabbat are discussed further below.) The *benandanti* of Friuli, for example, were North Italian shamans who claimed before the inquisitors that they were 'good' wizards, and the *calusari* were cathartic dancers and healers of Romania who claimed that their secret society was patronized by the 'Queen of the Fairies', Doamna Zinelor, the Romanian form of the goddess Diana.

Similarly Gustav Henningsen (1990) has examined the records of the Spanish Inquisition in the sixteenth and seventeenth centuries and concluded that in Sicily there was a flourishing fairy cult of women who met in the woods and were healers. In Sicily, fairies and witches were virtually one and the same; the single term used was *donna di fuora* (meaning literally 'the lady from outside'). The women who made 'witch confessions' and those who recorded them, says Henningsen, believed the women's stories about participation in the cult. After examining the financial status of accused witches and finding that in every case the person was poor, however, Henningsen concluded that 'the Sicilian fairy cult was a daydream religion that allowed poor people to experience in dreams and visions all the splendours denied them in real life' (p. 200). The cult was a mainly feminine phenomenon – of the 65 people in Sicily accused of witchcraft between 1579 and 1651, only eight were men. Most of the women who confessed during their trials that they had participated in the fairy cult were practising wise women skilled in various forms of sorcery and magical healing. Many stated under interrogation that they had not known there was anything wrong with the fairy cult until it was explained to them by the inquisitors.

In Sicily there were no notions of wicked witches: fairies/witches were capable of both good and ill, although any harm they caused could usually be repaired by an expiation ritual. Because the Sicilian witch never became diabolized, as happened to witches in most other parts of Europe, Henningsen concludes that the Sicilian form of witch belief is particularly archaic. In Sicilian folklore these fairies/witches survive as 'special gifted individuals serving as intermediaries between the world of the fairies and the human world, with elaborate rituals for curing people and animals' (Henningsen 1990: 207). Henningsen has found parallels between the Sicilian cult and other contemporary cults described by anthropologists in the Mediterranean and eastern Europe – in Greece, northern Morocco, Romania and Tunisia. He claims that because these places are on the European periphery and never experienced witch-hunts, the ancient folk religion survived largely undiabolized.

Fairy cults were not restricted to these areas, however. Fairies also figured in English witch-trials for 200 years. In 1499 three members of the Clerk family from Suffolk were convicted of 'heretical depravity' for consorting with spirits they described as 'gracious fairies' (Oldridge 2002: 9). These fairies cured illnesses, located hidden treasure, and transported Marion Clerk through the air to Canterbury cathedral. Éva Pócs (1999) has examined narratives from Hungarian witch-trials and says that 'fairy merriments' are mentioned in 60 narratives from across Hungary. There are tales of feasting, music and dancing in a beautiful 'heavenly' world – a world of desire realized in dreams and visions. This fairy-world fantasy was characteristic of the fairy beliefs of the central southeastern Europeans, Pócs says, and had close parallels in the Celtic, Italian and Scandinavian regions.

These writers are not the first to raise the possibility of a real pagan cult of witches in Europe which became diabolized by the inquisitors. In 1862 Jules Michelet proposed in *La Sorcière* that those tried for witchcraft in early modern Europe were peasant followers of a pre-Christian religion. In 1893 Sir Lawrence Gomme wrote a highly imaginative work (based on Jacob Grimm's *Teutonic Mythology*, written in 1844) which presented the witch as the medieval and early modern successor of the Druid priestess (Hutton 1999: 32). In 1897 Charles Godfrey Leland published his *Gospel of the Witches* which he claimed was based on information received from a hereditary witch in Tuscany. In 1921 Margaret Murray argued that this witch cult represented the survival of a pagan fertility cult which Christianity was determined to stamp out. Her book, *The Witch-Cult in Western Europe*, was accepted by academics for 50 years, but was later scathingly rejected by historians on the grounds that her witch cult was a 'composite artificially created . . . out of the characteristics of discrete and divergent religions from Asia Minor to Wales' (Russell 1980: 41) and because she drew selectively on witchcraft confessions as her only evidence (Cohn 1975).[6]

Ginzburg and Henningsen suggest that Murray's fault lay in failing to distinguish between the archaic popular belief-complex and the beliefs about witches which were superimposed upon this complex by judges, inquisitors and demonologists. The fault of historians such as Cohn (1975), on the other hand, was to explain the Sabbat as a projection of the fears and obsessions of the demonologists and inquisitors, without giving sufficient recognition to the role played by ancient popular beliefs in the formation of the witches' Sabbat.

For anthropologists, the classic work on witchcraft is Evans-Pritchard's *Witchcraft, Oracles and Magic among the Azande* published in 1937. It was Evans-Pritchard (1976: 1) who first made the distinction between sorcerers, who 'may do ill by performing magic rites with bad medicines' and witches, who 'can injure by virtue of an inherent quality'. As Lewis (1971: 13) said, 'Witchcraft exists only in the mind; it is known by its effects, whereas sorcery (like justice) must be seen to be done'. Thus witches are *believed* to possess powers to harm others, while sorcerers are *seen* to use magic objects and ritual to cause harm. This definition leaves little room for a self-identified witch – a witch is a witch because members of her or his society say so.

Thus, for more than six decades, anthropologists in the wake of Evans-Pritchard, like the majority of historians, have tended to interpret witchcraft beliefs as a social construction which may be projected onto an unfortunate member of that society (or someone outside it) who is perceived as threatening for any of numerous reasons. In some societies, for example the Effutu, the Banyang and the Ashanti of West Africa, this projection on to an individual is powerful enough to induce the suspected 'witch' to confess (Jackson 1989: 93).

While academics have interpreted the witch as 'other' in relation to her own society, as a marginalized or deviant individual, they have themselves also treated the witch as 'other' by choosing to focus on witch-accusers or on social relationships between witches and their accusers, rather than on witches themselves. They have determinedly defined witchcraft in negative terms thereby distorting its meaning from earlier popular meanings. Thomas (1970: 48), for example, notes that in Tudor and Stuart England the term 'witchcraft' was used to apply to virtually every kind of magical activity or ritual operation that worked 'by occult methods':

> Village diviners who foretold the future or who tracked down lost property were often called 'witches'; so were the 'wise women' who healed the sick by charms or prayers. Contemporary scientists whose operations baffled the ignorant were sometimes suspected of witchcraft, while the label was readily attached by Protestant polemicists to the ritual operations of the Catholic Church.

Despite this range of popular meanings, Thomas himself chooses to restrict the term 'witch' to those accused of acting out of malevolence towards others. In doing so he conforms to the authoritative academic definition of witchcraft, but narrows the term from how the people of the day, by his own admission, defined it. Almost 30 years later 'traditional witchcraft' is still being defined in solely negative terms: 'Traditional witchcraft is centred around harm', writes de Blécourt (1999: 151).

Like most historians, anthropologists have tended to concern themselves with understanding the nature of beliefs about witches and with the relationship between accuser and accused (Marwick 1970). They have asked people in non-Western societies about the appearance, character and behaviour of witches; the age, sex, wealth, social status and occupation of witches; and about kinship relationships between accuser and accused. Witchcraft beliefs have been interpreted as providing communities with a means of defining and sanctioning what is acceptable behaviour and what is not. Douglas (1973: 138) says that the witch 'is associated symbolically with the reverse of the way that a normal human lives, with night instead of day. His powers are abnormal, he can fly, be in two places at once, change his shape.' 'These popular stereotypes of witches and witchcraft,' writes Jackson (1989: 91, 96), 'are logically derived through a systematic inversion of what is regarded as ideal social behaviour . . . The stereotype of the witch . . . encapsulates what Monica Wilson so aptly called "the standardized nightmares of the group."'

The culturally learned belief that witches are not 'real' has been (unconsciously) privileged as a given when anthropologists have attempted to make sense of witchcraft in 'other cultures'. Stories about witches eating babies, flying on animals and causing deaths are simply too bizarre and ridiculous to be 'real'. The implicit logic is that if *beliefs* about witches are not real, witches are not real either – this despite the fact that, as Jackson (1989: 96) points out, 'general *beliefs* about witchcraft and particular *experiences* of self-confessed witches are seldom congruent'.

Even where a witch confesses to having been instrumental in causing some misfortune, the anthropological interpretation has tended towards functionalism, focusing on the interpersonal relationships between the confessor and members of her society in order to explain why an individual would make such a claim. For example, Jackson (1989: 98) suggests that among the Kuranko of northern Sierra Leone, where witchcraft confessions are almost always made by women, the resentments that nurture witchcraft stem from a loss of balance between a woman's autonomy as sister or mother and her lack of autonomy as a wife. The loss of balance may come as a result of blatant unfairness on the part of a husband or senior co-wife or neglect on the part of a brother. Jackson's explanation of why it is that men accuse and women confess centres on the inferior status of women in Kuranko society; a woman's witchcraft confession is 'a desperate stratagem for reclaiming autonomy in a hopeless situation' (p. 100). Her confession is not simply a capitulation in the face of men's accusation; she is using the witch stereotype 'to give voice to long-suppressed grievances and to cope with her suffering by declaring herself the author of it' (p. 101).

I began this chapter by pointing to the consistency between the historical and contemporary images of the witch. There is also a fairly strong consistency in witch beliefs across different societies, Western and non-Western, throughout the world.[7] Witches are usually female and elderly; they meet together at night, leaving their bodies or changing shape to fly, naked, to the meeting-place; they suck the blood of their victims and eat children; they ride on brooms; they perform circular dances, possess familiar spirits and indulge in orgies.[8] Some writers (Hughes 1965: 35, Marwick 1970: 14) have favoured a diffusionist explanation for these similarities, saying that the common beliefs had a common origin in Palaeolithic times and were dispersed when groups of people moved to inhabit new areas. Cohn (1970: 11) says that in Europe beliefs about witches belonged to the body of traditional folk-belief, that they were familiar in Graeco-Roman times and to the Germanic and Celtic peoples of pre-Christian times. These ideas continued throughout the Middle Ages; it was the inquisitors who interpreted the ancient beliefs in terms of Satan worship. Cohn states that the inquisitors created the 'fantasy' of the witches' Sabbat, imputing to witches activities that had previously been imputed to heretics – that they met secretly at night to roast and eat babies, have sexual orgies and worship the Devil. The traditional folk-beliefs about witches during pre-Christian times did not include these elements.

Douglas (1973: 148) gives a functionalist explanation for cross-cultural similarities in witchcraft beliefs. She says that they are likely to flourish in small enclosed groups, where movement in and out is restricted, interaction is unavoidably close, and roles are very tightly prescribed or not defined at all. These communities, Douglas concludes, have a 'doctrine of two kinds of humanity, one good, the other bad, and the association of the badness of some humans with cosmic powers of evil is basically similar to some of the so-called dualist religions [which have a God and a Devil] which are discussed by historians' (p. 144). Douglas (1970) classifies witchcraft beliefs into those where the witch is an outsider and those where she or he is the internal enemy. Where the witch is an outsider, she sends 'long-range missiles' to afflict a victim. The witch is often not identified or punished and the social group concentrates instead on curing the victim. Where the witch is an enemy within the community, the group's form of social organization is more complex. The witch may be a member of a rival faction, a dangerous deviant or an internal enemy with outside liaisons. In these cases, the function of the accusation may be to redefine faction boundaries, to realign faction hierarchy or to control deviants in the name of community values.

In her discussion of Yoruba female sexuality, Judith Hoch-Smith traces the widespread consistency of witchcraft beliefs to cultural ideas about feminine reproductive processes. Woman, she says, is attributed universally with both mystical and carnal aspects:

> In her mystical aspect, woman is represented as an active medium or vehicle of creative energy who transforms that energy into life-forms; in her carnal aspect she is represented as being capable of transforming life-forms into malevolent energy directed toward the destruction, rather than creation, of the universe.
>
> (Hoch-Smith 1978: 245)

It is on this carnal image that beliefs about the witch are focused, whether in medieval Europe or in contemporary non-Western societies such as the Yoruba of Nigeria. In what is one of the earliest feminist explanations of witchcraft, Hoch-Smith (p. 246) states:

> The image of the witch depicted in many male-dominated societies [as one who steals male genitals and indulges in cannibalism in order to increase her malevolent power] is a blatant condemnation of female sexuality. Such condemnation is related to the threat to male-dominated society posed by the independence and authority of women.

In Europe this obsession with, and condemnation of, female sexuality is luridly evident throughout the *Malleus Maleficarum* ('The Witches' Hammer'), the witch-hunters' manual written by two German Dominican friars, Heinrich Kramer and James Sprenger, and published in 1486 by the inquisitor Heinrich Institoris after a papal bull issued by Pope Innocent VIII. According to the *Malleus*, woman's evil was rooted in her sexuality. Witchcraft was said to stem from 'carnal lust which is in women insatiable' and which led them to copulate with the Devil from whom they derived their powers. Because of women's 'defect of inordinate affections and passions', Kramer and Sprenger concluded, 'they search for, brood over, and inflict various vengeances' (Bridenthal *et al.* 1987: 213).

Hoch-Smith criticizes writers such as Marvin Harris (1974) and Julio Baroja (1965) who reduce European witchcraft to a 'fantasy' phenomenon experienced solely as the result of using hallucinatory herbal ointments which took women into an imaginary world of night flight, sexual orgies and cannibalism. She points out that while witches may have used hallucinogens, it does not follow that witchcraft was nothing more than fantasy. Rather, hallucinogens may have been used to induce altered states of consciousness in ritual practices as they have been used by shamans, healers and sorcerers throughout the world.

Defending her claim that it was female sexuality which was the real terror of the witch-hunters, Hoch-Smith points to the work of Ehrenreich and English who established that until the Middle Ages healing was in the hands of wise women (or sometimes men) who used herbal remedies and practised dentistry, surgery, bone-setting, hypnosis, massage and midwifery. When, during the Middle Ages, these women were forbidden to heal and medicine was institutionalized as an exclusively male profession, it was claimed that the wise woman's power derived from her sexuality (Ehrenreich and English 1973: 9). It was these women who became the witch-hunters' primary targets.

In Africa, too, says Hoch-Smith, women are accused of 'female sexuality' by men. In Nigeria witches are believed to fly to meetings, practise cannibalism, cause illness and make men impotent and physically weak. In Yoruba plays depicting male–female relationships women are often imputed with powers to bring about men's physical, social and financial ruin. In particular, by failing to produce children women thwart the extension of their husbands' patrilineage, and by becoming successful in business women demonstrate social and economic independence of men. Hoch-Smith (1978: 266) argues that

> the Yoruba witch has much in common with her counterparts in many African societies, and with her sisters in both medieval Europe and contemporary Europe and America, where the image of the 'castrating bitch' is still often applied to women who are seen as threatening men with their aggressive and 'malelike' behaviour.

Hoch-Smith's explanation for witch beliefs in Yoruba society seems convincing, but there is an inconsistency in her comparison of contemporary African and historical European witchcraft. While she seems to believe that there were 'real' witches in Europe (criticizing those who view witchcraft as a fantasy phenomenon), she does not make the same claim in relation to Africa. Among the Yoruba, women may be constructed as witches because of the threat they are considered to pose, but there is no suggestion by Hoch-Smith that these women actually practise the 'craft' as she suggests for Europe. Hoch-Smith apparently believes that male fear of female sexuality and women's independence caused witch-*hating* in Europe while in Africa the same fear leads to the construction of the witch image.

Duerr has explored European 'pagan' beliefs and rituals in order to trace the origins of 'those who flew by night', and found rituals that focused flamboyantly on women's sexuality – practices which incited condemnation by early Christians.

> During women's festivals, as we have seen, men were sometimes handled quite roughly, while the women tore off their caps, a symbol of their submission, danced half-naked, with their hair loose, and the ecstatic dancers of Artemis Corythalia tied on artificial phalli.
>
> (Duerr 1985: 32)

Duerr cites examples of wild women's festivals to honour various forms of Artemis/Diana throughout Europe to Africa. He is not at all surprised that Diana of Ephesus, the most venerated of all the deities of Galatia, was singled out for particularly ferocious attacks by the Christians.

Finally, Russell (1980) offers a structuralist explanation for world-wide similarities in witchcraft beliefs. He says that in folk-tales the witch represents an elemental natural force with huge and mysterious powers against which humans cannot defend themselves. This force is not necessarily evil, but is so alien and remote that it threatens the social, ethical, and even physical order of the cosmos. Russell suggests this portrayal of the witch is very ancient and probably archetypal: 'This witch is neither a simple sorceress, nor a demonolater, nor a pagan. She is a hostile presence from another world' (p. 46).

This view of the witch as 'other', one from 'outside' or one who inhabits the margins of the social world is pursued by Duerr in *Dreamtime: Concerning the Boundary between Wilderness and Civilization* (1985). This work, together with Ginzburg's (1990a) *Ecstasies*, provide perhaps the most detailed investigation so far of the origins of the witch and the witches' Sabbat. Duerr, an anthropologist, and Ginzburg, a historian, produce theories which combine the synchronic and diachronic elements of witchcraft and develop an over-arching explanation relevant to both historical European and Salem witchcraft and contemporary non-Western witchcraft.

Dreamtime begins with a discussion of 'flying ointment' – apparently a salve made from herbs and the fat of various animals which was rubbed on the body and produced hallucinations of flight – claiming that it was popular knowledge during the period of the witch-hunts that there were people who used this salve, and that at least some of those tried for witchcraft were users. Some of the descriptions of the Sabbat given during their 'confessions' were descriptions of hallucinations produced by the ointment. Confessions of night-time meetings with the 'Quene of Elphen' or the goddess Diana were transformed in the court records into meetings with the Devil.

Duerr goes on to ask: 'What kind of being was Diana, in whose retinue these women supposedly roamed through the nocturnal forests?' He traces the origins of the prototype of Artemis/Diana to the last Ice Age, to the well-known, widespread 'Venus figurines' which he says represent a fertile earth goddess or 'Great Mother' (1985: 16). Local variations of this deity are found in numerous past and present societies around the world – there are examples from England, Japan, Siberia, Africa, Austria, Bulgaria and Columbia, as well as from ancient and relatively modern Greece. Duerr argues that the supernatural guides of the night travellers can be traced ultimately to these universal 'earth mother' divinities.

The early Christians, understandably, saw the powerful, ubiquitous Artemis/Diana as a threat to Christianity and eventually, over a number of centuries, her worship declined as Christianity increased its power in Europe. The subjugation of Diana, goddess of the wilderness, is interpreted by Duerr as symbolizing the growth and dominance of the increasingly complex civilization of Renaissance Europe. Since pre-Christian times, there had been those situated metaphorically on the boundary between civilization and the wilderness who had developed their ability to cross the line at times (Duerr 1985: 45). As late as the Middle Ages, the witch was called the *hagazussa*, or a variation of that old High German word,[9] a liminal being who sat on the *hag*, the fence which separated the village from the wilderness. She moved between and participated in both worlds. In Renaissance Europe, with the increasing complexity of society and greater institutionalization of patriarchal control, this state of affairs was no longer acceptable. The proper state of all women was to be 'civilized' and under male control. Hence, argues Duerr, the displacement of 'the ladies from outside' to the inside, or, more specifically, to the outside of the inside, where they were transformed into diabolical witches.

Duerr does not believe, however (unlike Margaret Murray), that the 'witches' of the witch-craze were members of a cult which had survived from pre-Christian times: he thinks accused witches' descriptions of the Sabbat should be taken as evidence of an archaic system of beliefs enlivened by the use of hallucinogenic drugs. He differs from Ginzburg, however, by arguing that these beliefs derive ultimately from actual practices of real women in the period before Christianity established dominance in Europe.

Ginzburg believes that underlying the similarities in witchcraft beliefs across time and space there is a core of common belief, namely in the ecstatic journey of the living into the world of the dead (Ginzburg 1990a: 23). 'To this mythical nucleus,' says Ginzburg, 'are also linked folkloric themes such as night flying and animal metamorphoses'. Éva Pócs's (1999) work on narratives from Hungarian witch-trials leads her to support Ginzburg's thesis. She lists the following phenomena as belonging to the 'predemonologic' European Sabbat: flying, turning into an animal, gathering of the dead and demons, and the Sabbat itself as a trance-like experience. Other variants of these ideas are observed among the Lap and Siberian shamans, the Baltic werewolves, the *armiers* of the Pyrenean Ariège, the *benandanti* of Friuli, the Dalmatian *kersniki*, the Balkan *zduhaci*, the Corsican *mazzeri*, the Romanian *calusari*, the Hungarian *táltos* and the Causcasian *burkudzäutä*. What all have in common is their role as intermediaries between the worlds of the living and the dead.

Ginzburg examines evidence spanning 1,000 years (ending in the period of the witch-craze) from one end of Europe to the other, and identifies the features of a primarily female ecstatic religion, dominated by a nocturnal goddess with many names including the Matron, the Teacher, the Greek Mistress, the Wise Sibilla and the Queen of the Fairies (1990a: 122). In some places she was accompanied by a king or consort. Like Duerr, Ginzburg says that in more ancient times this goddess was a prototype of the 'virgin huntress Artemis, on the border between the city and the formless wilderness, the human and the bestial' (p. 128). She was worshipped as the nurse of children and the protector of young girls and pregnant women. And prior to Artemis, there were the Eurasian divinities of hunting and the forest. According to Ginzburg, the ecstatic experiences of the followers of the goddess recall those of the shamans of Siberia or Lapland. All include the same essential elements: the flight of the soul to the realm of the dead in the shape of an animal, on the back of an animal or on some other magical vehicle.

The 'wicked witch' was a cultural invention gradually formed by the fusion of two main elements: the inquisitors' and demonologists' fantasy of a hostile, heretical sect, projected in turn onto lepers, Jews and then witches, superimposed onto the widespread mythical nucleus of popular belief described above. The dwarves, fairies and trolls of north European folklore were transformed into demons and witches' familiars. The worship of pagan goddesses and gods was redefined as demonolatry. Sorcerers were imagined to be in business with the Devil and were legally regarded as heretics. This fusion of myths created the stereotype of the wicked witch in the second half of the fourteenth century in the Western Alpine arc, and subsequently diffused to other parts of Europe. A century later, fear of the witch had become a craze which obsessed Europeans on the continent, in Scandinavia and in the British Isles for 300 years.

Some 50,000 people[10] were hanged or burnt at the stake (Oldridge 2002: frontispiece) often following an extended period of torture from which neither children nor invalids were exempt (Russell 2001: 128). On the European continent 85 per cent or more of those killed were women (Ben-Yehuda 1989: 233) and in England the figure was 90 per cent (Hester 1992: 108). In 1585, in the bishopric of Trier, Germany, two villages were left with one female inhabitant each (Ehrenreich and English 1973: 5). Girls too young to be executed, according to an edict of 1612, were imprisoned until they were 12 years old. In France, for example, seven-year-old Anne Hauldecoeur was sentenced to five years' imprisonment in 1614 until she could be legally put to death (Muchembled 1990: 143). As well as being vulnerable to accusation themselves, children were used to inform against their mothers and neighbouring women: in 1670 in the parishes around Siljan in Sweden several thousand children informed against 300 accused witches (Ankarloo and Henningsen 1990: 295).

With the end of the witch-killings a little over 200 years ago, belief in the reality of witches and their Sabbat seems also to have dissolved (Ginzburg 1990a: 23). The wicked witch, however, survived as myth and became a powerful and evocative image in folklore, literature and art. The much older myths about 'the ladies from outside', which provided the foundation of the witch stereotype in the first place, were lost from popular belief.

At the beginning of this chapter I suggested that one reason why most historians and anthropologists have approached the study of witchcraft in the ways that they have is that they do not believe 'real' witches exist or have ever existed. One might further suggest that this is because of the ultimate survival of the 'wicked witch' myth over the goddess-following, night-traveller myth. We know that the wicked witch stereotype was a cultural construction and that there were never real women who conformed to the stereotype. Until the relatively recent work of writers like Ginzburg, Duerr, Pócs and Henningsen, however, the older myth, although glimpsed in the distance, has not been the focus of thorough exploration.

The big remaining question is whether the older myth simply belonged to a system of popular belief, or whether there were at one time real women in Europe who met together to perform rituals connected with goddesses, the precise nature of which we cannot now know. The writers above are clear that there was no such sect operating during the centuries of the witch-hunts. But it is much less clear what they believe about the relationship between belief and practice, myth and ritual, in earlier times.

Henningsen implies that it would be pushing credibility too far to accept that members of the Sicilian 'fairy cult' were doing anything more than dreaming about their nocturnal activities. However if one is prepared to go as far as taking seriously the substance of witch 'confessions' and devoting considerable effort to understanding the core of folk-belief underlying them, it does not seem wholly unreasonable to go further and accept that if Sicilian accused 'witches' esteemed as wise women in their communities were prepared to claim, in the face of the inquisitors, that they participated in a 'fairy cult', then that is what they did. Henningsen (1990: 194) says that in Sicily torture 'was applied only to a limited extent, and never at the start of the trial to force a confession from the accused'. Of course the women's interpretations of what actually happened at such gatherings may be open to question in the same way that one might question any religious group's interpretations of the symbolism of its rituals. But to claim that these women were deluded, dreaming or muddled over the difference between belief and practice, in my view, also strains credibility.

It would be far-fetched to suggest a widespread 'women's cult' which became re-interpreted as a witch cult at the time of the witch-hunts. However it is less far-fetched, though perhaps premature, to suggest that there were, at the time of the witch-hunts, pockets of people across Europe who still revered the old local pagan divinities and performed rituals in their honour, continued to believe in a raft of other spirit beings, and still practised sorcery. The work of scholars such as Duerr, Ginzburg and Henningsen, along with that of feminist scholars over the past three decades, has provided a critical challenge to the traditional functionalist interpretations of witchcraft which have emphasized social, economic, political and psychological factors, but have given much less attention to religious factors. The alternative theoretical approaches discussed here point to the need for scholars to consider more seriously the importance of popular religion, sorcery and magical beliefs in attempting to understand the phenomenon of witch beliefs and the witch-hunts. The relationship of popular religion and its magical practices, including sorcery, to earlier shamanistic beliefs and to witchcraft beliefs requires a great deal of further research and disentangling. In Burke's (1990: 441) view:

> The analogy noted by Carlo Ginzburg between shamans and *benandanti* now seems to fit into a much larger pattern. It is as if we are looking at the tip of an iceberg, the shape and size of which is still unknown.
>
> Behind the diabolical witchcraft of the witch-hunters has been discovered a more traditional, neighbourly witchcraft. Behind this in turn we are seeing glimpses of a still more archaic, shamanistic witchcraft.

It has been important to discuss the historical image of the witch and the witch-hunts at some length here because contemporary feminist witches make explicit and important connections with the women accused of and executed for witchcraft between the fifteenth and eighteenth centuries. The fact that modern women have chosen to name themselves 'witches', despite their knowledge that the diabolical witch of the witch-craze was a cultural creation, derives from their perceived connection with these women. They also make important connections with the women of pre-Christian times who, they claim, belonged to groups similar to the 'companies' of the Sicilian fairy cult described above, and who were known in their villages as wise women and healers. I discuss the connections with both groups in more detail in chapter three.

Another reason for my approach in this chapter is that I wanted to show the kinds of approaches scholars in the disciplines of anthropology and history have taken to the study of witchcraft in order to background and situate my own methods. We have seen that academic studies of witchcraft have typically dealt with the witch as 'other' by focusing on how communities think about and act towards witches, rather than on how witches themselves think and act. Only recently has the subjective dimension of witchcraft become the focus of scholarly attention in a relatively small number of ethnographic studies of witchcraft in contemporary Western societies. Given that 'witchcraft' has long been a classic topic for anthropological study and that anthropologists in recent years have been increasingly conducting research 'at home', it is interesting that so few anthropologists have elected to study witchcraft in their own societies. So far, very few have broken with the tradition of studying witchcraft beliefs rather than self-identified witches: it is apparently still more legitimate (and perhaps more comfortable, 'serious' and prestigious) to study the witch as 'other' in an 'other' society, especially when it is believed that 'real' witches do not exist, at home or anywhere else.

Having said that, in the period since I first became interested in feminist witchcraft, there has been a steady trickle of published academic research on modern witchcraft, Goddess spirituality and Paganism in Western societies from anthropologists, sociologists, historians, thealogians (from 'thea' meaning 'goddess') and scholars in religious studies and women's studies. There have been two book-length ethnographies about witches in contemporary England by anthropologists Tanya Luhrmann (1989) and Susan Greenwood (2000a).[11] Luhrmann, who began her fieldwork in London in 1983 by taking magical courses and being initiated into several magical groups, was especially interested in 'the process that allows people to accept outlandish, apparently irrational beliefs' (p. 7). Describing her work as psychological anthropology, she noted that as a result of their involvement with magic witches shifted their perceptions and analyses of events, their emotional and psychological needs, their language and symbolism, and their ways of experiencing. She calls this process 'interpretive drift'.

Luhrmann participated in the rituals of six Gardnerian-inspired covens and there is a great deal more about them in her ethnography than about feminist covens – 'a type of witchcraft relatively rare in England but quite important in the States' (1989: 52). While Luhrmann's ethnography portrays modern witchcraft as gender-mixed and more institutionalized, formal and secretive than the witchcraft I know from New Zealand, this is because her emphasis is on Gardnerian groups. She says that the rituals of English feminist witches emphasize creativity and collectivity and are often quite different from those in Gardnerian groups. The unrehearsed, highly democratic Hallowe'en ritual she describes (pp. 52–3) could easily be a description of a New Zealand feminist witches' ritual.

As well as being focused on modern witchcraft more broadly and being classified by the author as psychological anthropology rather than feminist anthropology, Luhrmann's work differs from mine in that she expressly focused on why people 'practise magic when, according to observers, the magic doesn't work' (p. 4). I was also interested in practitioners' ideas about how magic works and in the worldview that supports their beliefs, but I did not begin from the position of seeing their beliefs as 'irrational' in relation to the 'rationality' of mainstream, science-based, everyday life. In my view witches' beliefs are no more or less rational than those of any other religious belief system; their beliefs, like those of other religions, are rational within the logic of their particular worldview. I wished to understand this worldview, its attractions for witches, and the relationship between women's spiritual and political beliefs.

Greenwood, author of the other ethnography of English witches, has also noted Luhrmann's failure to take modern magicians' ontological reality of the world seriously. For Luhrmann, she says, 'magic must be irrational and necessarily false, because it does not conform to Western scientific criteria; she equates reason with a positivistic view of science' (Greenwood 2000a: 42). The main difference between these two ethnographers' approaches is that Greenwood has engaged reflexively with the magical imagination. Like Luhrmann, Greenwood worked with a variety of magical groups and covens. Her emphasis, however, was not on how magicians overcome scepticism, but on how they learn the language of another mode of reality – 'the otherworld' – through their magical practice. There is not much about feminist witchcraft in Greenwood's ethnography either, although again, the feminist witches' ritual she describes (p. 108) could easily have had a New Zealand setting, and most of what she says about feminist witchcraft is also true in the New Zealand context.

Wicca migrated to the United States in the 1960s and there took on a particularly 'American flavour' incorporating mysticism, ecological concerns, women's rights and anti-authoritarianism, according to sociologist Helen Berger (1999: 12). Berger sees contemporary witchcraft as an outgrowth of globalism, a new religion created from an assemblage of elements borrowed from many different religions, whose growth is assisted by modern technology. Modern magic is a 'technology of the self'; its ritual practices often aim at altering the self, accepting the self, healing or celebrating the self (p. xiii). Berger is especially interested in issues connected with the ageing of this new religion: with the raising of a second generation of witches (one high priestess interviewed was about to start a nursery school for Pagan children) and with the processes of routinization and homogenization within the movement. During 11 years of fieldwork, Berger worked closely with one particular coven for a time and participated in occasional rituals with ten others, two of which were women-only groups. She also conducted a national survey of neo-Pagans and numerous formal and informal interviews with people belonging to a wide range of covens in the northeastern United States. According to Berger, 'the major division within the religion [neo-Paganism] is between all-women's and inclusive groups' (p. 13).

Cynthia Eller's *Living in the Lap of the Goddess: The Feminist Spirituality Movement in America* (1993) deals exclusively with all-women's groups which could be said to constitute the elder sister movement of New Zealand's feminist witchcraft movement. Eller, who is trained in religious studies, bases her study on ten years' familiarity with the movement gained through attending rituals, workshops and retreats; conducting interviews with participants; reading a mass of literature produced by adherents and soliciting information from spiritual feminist organizations. Her goal was to 'get inside the lives of the women who make up the feminist spirituality movement, to identify with their concerns, hopes, and experiences, to listen closely to their voices, and to see how they construct their worlds' (Eller 1993: ix). While the substance of Eller's study is highly pertinent to and directly comparable with the New Zealand feminist witchcraft scene, her research approach is different from mine (and from Greenwood's and Luhrmann's). Eller is very much the 'observer' rather than a participant observer, and as a researcher she makes no attempt at reflexivity.

Loretta Orion's (1995) ethnography of American witches, on the other hand, is presented from an insider's perspective and is based on anthropological fieldwork conducted over a number of years from 1983. Orion attended neo-Pagan festivals, conducted interviews and participated in rituals with two covens, both in New York, one of which she was initiated into in 1986. She also used a questionnaire to collect information for a demographic profile of neo-Pagans. Orion's special interest is in neo-Pagan alternative healing therapies and approaches to maintaining and restoring health.

The focus of Sarah Pike's recent study, also conducted in the US, is neo-Pagan festivals. Pike (2001: xi) wanted 'to learn the ways that Neopagans make sacred spaces, create rituals, tell stories about themselves, and act out their religion through music and dance at festival sites removed from their daily lives'. She was particularly interested in how neo-Pagans work with a number of boundaries: between festival communities and their neighbours, between neo-Paganism and Christianity, between sacred and profane spaces, and between 'self' and 'other'. Pike shows how problematic the project of self-creation is for neo-Pagans, conducted as it is at various boundaries and incorporating a tension between a 'fluid, post-modern self' (which embraces the idea that identity and tradition are not fixed but malleable) and a 'deep, inward, "modern self"', a 'real' self with depths, layers and needs (pp. 220–1).

Another recent work about American witches, written from the perspectives of theology and anthropology, is Jone Salomonsen's (2002) study of

Starhawk's Reclaiming community which was formed 20 years ago to practice and teach witchcraft and now has sister communities throughout North America and Europe. Salomonsen's theoretical interests lean heavily towards the theological: she sees feminist witchcraft as part of a larger new religious movement attempting to overwrite Jewish and Christian religion and culture with neo-Pagan inventions (p. 288). Her method, however, is solidly anthropological and reflexive. The research involved long-term participant observation in which the author became an apprentice, an initiated witch and one of her own informants. Her inside knowledge of Starhawk's spiritual community in San Francisco and her discussion about doing research as an insider are fascinating.

As well as this handful of ethnographies on British and American witchcraft, there is a growing body of scholarly writing on witchcraft and Paganism in the form of edited collections (for example, Hardman and Harvey 1995, Lewis 1996, Griffin 2000a), journal articles, and quite a number of monographs which incorporate a discussion of witchcraft or deal with related topics, such as neo-Shamanism and New Age spirituality. A number of articles particularly relevant to my research because of their reflexive approach and concentration on feminist witchcraft and Goddess spirituality are those by sociologists Lozano and Foltz (1990), Griffin (1995, 2000c), Foltz and Griffin (1996) and Foltz (2001). More than any other authors on this topic, Griffin (formerly Lozano) and Foltz are concerned not only with the subjective dimension of the study of witchcraft, but also with explicitly examining and articulating their own subjective experiences with witches and witchcraft and the self-transformation they underwent in the course of their research. By writing about this they have made a notable contribution to discourse on alternative ethnographic writing and feminist research methodology, as well as to the literature on witchcraft.[12]

Feminist theologians like Mary Daly, Carol Christ, Naomi Goldenberg and Melissa Raphael have made an enormous contribution both to the movement itself and to the scholarly consideration of it. A quarter of a century ago Daly lambasted historians for dealing only with the social function of witch beliefs for the dominant society: for describing, as Midelfort (1972: 195) does, 'the small witch trial' as 'therapeutic' because it 'delineat[ed] the social thresholds of eccentricity tolerable to society, and register[ed] fear of a socially indigestible group, unmarried women'. Daly (1979: 185) points out that no one describes the Jewish pogroms or the lynching of Blacks as 'therapeutic'. The mass murder of women during the witch-craze, she says, was clearly intended 'to break down and destroy strong women, to dis-member and kill the Goddess, the divine spark of be-ing in women' (p. 183).

So far, most academic writing (as well as most popular writing) on contemporary witchcraft in Western countries has dealt with the movement in the UK and the US. Lynne Hume's *Witchcraft and Paganism in Australia* (1997) first brought the attention of scholars in the northern hemisphere to witchcraft in Australia. Hume, an anthropologist, documents a broad spectrum of Pagan activity in Australia, outlines the history and particular character of the movement there, and discusses how and why and what sort of people become Pagans and the issues that preoccupy them. From Hume's account one gathers that feminist witchcraft does not feature prominently on the Australian Pagan scene. Most witches seem to be down-under Gardnerians: in this respect the Australian and New Zealand movements have rather different profiles.

In the review of academic approaches to witchcraft given in this chapter we have seen that until the last 10 to 15 years, with several significant exceptions, witches have typically been treated as 'other' – exotic and dangerous, stupid or weak, ridiculous or mythical, pitiable yet convenient victims. Historians and anthropologists have focused on how societies think and act in relation to witches rather than on how witches themselves think and act. The recent studies reviewed in the last part of this chapter take a different approach by focusing on the subjective dimension of witchcraft and the realities of contemporary self-identified witches' lives. A small sign that such an approach might be gaining legitimacy within the mainstream anthropological study of witchcraft is the inclusion of a chapter titled 'Wicca, a way of working' by Loretta Orion in the new fifth edition of Lehmann and Myers's reader *Magic, Witchcraft and Religion: An Anthropological Study of the Supernatural* (2001). And in the sixth volume of *Witchcraft and Magic in Europe* (1999), which deals with the twentieth century, Ronald Hutton presents a comprehensive and fascinating history of modern Pagan witchcraft covering both Wicca and feminist witchcraft.

In the next chapter we consider the development of the contemporary feminist witchcraft movement and discuss more fully an approach which places the witch at the centre of its focus, not as pathetic victim, but as a symbol of woman's independent knowledge and power.

3

FEMINISTS AND WITCHES

> I think it's wonderful to start reclaiming concepts like 'witch', but in terms of the reclaiming process we have a long, long way to go and I'm quite realistic about that. I'm not on a crusade for the witch. For me it's an inner networking growth thing. Like an underground movement. And I'm very happy for it to be like that, because that's the way it will gather its power.
>
> (Juliet)

When the Sociology Department at the University of Chicago fired a radical feminist professor in 1969, the department was showered with hair-cuttings and nail-clippings by local Chicago witches (Spretnak 1982: 428). On Hallowe'en, the year before, a coven of wand-waving, masked and costumed New York witches converged on Wall Street on the stroke of noon 'to pit their ancient magic against the evil powers of the Financial District – the center of the Imperialist Phallic Society' (Morgan 1978: 75). First they danced to the Federal Reserve Treasury Bank led by a high priestess carrying a papier-mâché pig's head on a golden platter. On the steps of the building they surrounded the statue of George Washington and got told off for defacing the 'Father of our country' with WITCH stickers by Nixon campaigners who did not understand 'that this was a necessary ritual against a symbol of patriarchal, slave-holding power' (ibid.).

They proceeded to the New York Stock Exchange where they told the guards that they had an appointment with the 'Chief Executor of Wall Street himself – the Boss, Satan'. Failing to gain entry (though managing to cause the guards' phone to go unaccountably dead), the witches formed a sacred circle, closed their eyes and, before hundreds of fascinated onlookers, began a chant proclaiming the coming demise of various stocks. The witches then moved on to One Chase Manhattan Plaza and circled the 'glass erection' mumbling a curse containing references to Jericho and a future insurrection involving buglers. And so the day went on. As the witches moved about the city WITCH stickers appeared in subways plastered over Virginia Slim and Diet Jello advertisements.

At dusk, the witches began the evening with a siege at a men-only bar, moved on to exorcise 'two girlie burlesque houses', put a hex on Max Factor at a beauty clinic, and invaded a discotheque where four bouncers rushed and hit the women but were repelled by several of the witches who were trained in judo and karate. Moving on to 'Max's Kansas City', a restaurant patronized by the Beautiful People of the late 1960s, the coven distributed garlic cloves and cards reading: 'We Are Witch We Are Women We Are Liberation We Are We' and chanted 'Nine million women burned as witches'.

The day concluded with a call on the Theatre of Ideas where a group of liberals was discussing the subject of the media. The witches fairly easily took over the meeting and passed around a small cauldron for contributions to the Women's Liberation Legal Defense Fund. Contributors were encouraged by prods with a broom and a toy machine gun. A vigorous discussion on the subjects of theatre, the media, women and 'the revolution' followed. In the conclusion to her article describing these activities, Robin Morgan (1978: 75), a founder of WITCH, warned: 'In the Holiest Names of Hecate, Isis, Astarte, Hester Prinn and Bonnie Parker, *we shall return*!'

Hallowe'en 1968 marked the beginning of WITCH, an acronym for Women's International Terrorist Conspiracy from Hell. Morgan (p. 71) says that WITCH comprised 'women who were self-styled "politicos" – women's liberationists who still strongly affirmed a Marxist analysis and a hip Left style'. WITCH was chosen as the group's name for its symbolic value: it grabbed people's attention and offered theatrical opportunities for protest activities. Morgan says that the women who started WITCH identified with the witches of the European witch-craze, but were not at that time interested in witchcraft for any religious reasons and performed rituals only as public performances. In their rituals, the women did not imagine they were channelling energy in order to bring about change; they enacted such rituals because of the crowd-drawing theatricality they brought to the women's political protests. Morgan writes (p. 72):

> We in WITCH always *meant* to do the real research, to read the anthropological, religious, and mythographic studies on the subject – but we never got around to it. We were too busy doing actions. We also meant to have more consciousness-raising meetings – but we were too busy doing actions. We meant to write some papers of theory and analysis – but we were too busy doing actions.

Writing ten years later about Hallowe'en 1968, Morgan is mortified that the New York coven she belonged to had sought an audience with 'Satan' at the Stock Exchange: 'The members of the Old Religion never worshipped Satan. They were followers of a tripartite Goddess; it was the Christian church who invented Satan and then claimed that witches were Satanists' (Morgan 1978: 72).

Within a few weeks of Hallowe'en 1968, covens had sprung up in Boston, Chicago, San Francisco, North Carolina, Portland (Oregon) and Austin (Texas). The acronym WITCH meant different things to different covens or changed its meaning for a particular political action. It became Women Incensed at Telephone Company Harassment, Women Inspired To Commit Herstory, Women Intent on Toppling Consumer Holidays, and, on Mothers' Day, Women Infuriated at Taking Care of Hoodlums.

The WITCH covens which sprang up in the United States in the late 1960s represent an important strand in the origins of feminist witchcraft. These witches were clearly not given to secret trysts and arcane rituals or to New Age navel-gazing by candlelight as sceptics often claim about contemporary witches. The witch image served the women's political purposes, but little more.

One of the effects of WITCH was to draw women's attention to the atrocities of the European witch-craze and the Church's role in the witch-killings, and to spark discussions about the Goddess and the possibility of pre-Christian matriarchies. The witch came to be seen not purely as a political revolutionary, but as the priestess of a pre-Christian religion centred on a great Goddess (Stein 1990: 247). This appealed to women who were rejecting patriarchal religions along with patriarchal socio-political systems.

At Winter Solstice 1971, Zsuzsanna Budapest, a hereditary witch from Hungary who had been taught the craft by her mother, founded the Susan B. Anthony Coven 1 (named after the famous American suffragist). Budapest had decided to make women's spiritual liberation her focus within the feminist movement. She started the first book and magic shop for feminist witches, the 'Feminist Wicca'. Her *Holy Book of Women's Mysteries*, first published in 1980, became an influential text in the development of feminist witchcraft.

A second important strand of feminist witchcraft is Wicca, which was introduced from Britain to the United States in the 1960s by a student of Gardner named Raymond Buckland (Kelly 1992, Lewis 1999: xxix–xxxii). The essential difference between Wicca and feminist witchcraft is that in Wicca practitioners invoke both the Goddess *and* the God, her son and consort, often referred to as 'The Horned One' after Dionysus, Pan or Cernunnos, whereas most feminist covens invoke only the Goddess. In the United States, however, there are some covens, including Starhawk's, which invoke both Goddess and God and whose members of both sexes call themselves 'feminist witches' (Salomonsen 2002: 12). However, the God has secondary status in relation to the Goddess. These groups are rooted in Wicca, but are often more open about their practices, less hierarchical in their organization, and more creative and spontaneous in their rituals than traditional Wiccan covens.

Starhawk emphasizes that the witches' God is very different from the Christian God and 'is radically different from any other image of masculinity in our culture' (1989: 108). He is the Hunter, the Dying God, the God of Love, Lord of the Dance, the Sun Child, untamed yet sacred sexuality, wild, free, gentle and tender. He is invoked not as 'God the Father Almighty', but sometimes as 'God the father' or, says Starhawk, as 'He Who Changes the Dirty Diapers' or 'He Who Makes Up Silly Games' (p. 233).

I have never heard any mention of the God among feminist witches in New Zealand, and all the covens I know of consist only of women. There are, of course, mixed Gardnerian covens and men-only groups of witches (at least one called a 'God group') as well as Druids in New Zealand, but they are not part of the feminist witchcraft movement and have not been part of my research. As I noted in the introduction, feminist witches have constituted the most prominent community within the New Zealand neo-Pagan scene through the late 1980s and 1990s, and developed quite separately from other neo-Pagan traditions in this country.

Feminist witchcraft began in the United States. When news of it reached Britain, some members of Wiccan covens were horrified. Doreen Valiente, a famous British witch and member of the coven run by the more famous (and infamous) Gerald Gardner, writes (1989: 182–3):

> [I]n spite of the fact that modern witchcraft has priestesses, in fact they started off playing the role that men such as Gerald Gardner designed for them. We were allowed to call ourselves High Priestesses, Witch Queens and similar fancy titles; but we were still in the position of having men running things and women doing as the men directed. As soon as the women started seeking real power, trouble was brewing.
>
> We were told that, 'You may not be a witch alone', in Gardnerian witchcraft at any rate. If you were a woman, you had to find a man to initiate you before you could become a witch; and then you had to find a man to work with before you could practise. So when stories of all women covens started to filter through from the USA, the reaction of male witches in Britain was (and I quote one of them), 'We don't want to have anything to do with them. They're a load of lesbians.'
>
> Of course, the converse was also true. If you were a man, you were told that you had to find a woman of sufficient rank to initiate you and then have a female partner to make 'the perfect couple'. Homosexuality, we were told, was abhorrent to the Goddess, and Her curse would fall upon people of the same sex who tried to work together.

This dismissal of women who conduct their spiritual practices independently of men as a 'load of lesbians' points up the homophobia of Gardnerian witchcraft, at least at that time, and indicates that a fear of women's independent power was as entrenched in this witchcraft tradition as it is in many other religions.

Feminist witchcraft is now established in Britain, but it is very much the late-comer on the scene and is still much less significant than Wicca (Luhrmann 1989, Greenwood 2000a). As we have seen, Gerald Gardner is credited with being the founder of modern witchcraft, although his claim that he was initiated into an ancient coven by one Dorothy Clutterbuck in 1939 has been widely disputed. Valiente's (1989: 39) research showed that 'Old Dorothy' at least existed and that she corresponded to the details given about her by Gardner. Valiente admits, however, that Gardner was given to fabricating facts to support his cause and bolster his own image. For example, he did not, contrary to his claim, have a doctorate and was an unrepentant plagiarist who became indignant when accused. In developing Wicca Gardner borrowed from many sources close to his own experience: he was a Freemason, a Rosicrucian, a spiritualist, a Druid, a probable member of the Ordo Templi Orientis, an active member of the Folk-Lore Society and an admirer of Margaret Murray, who wrote a foreword to his book *Witchcraft Today* (Hutton 1995: 12).

Wicca as a religion was a combination of Murray's ideas and of high ritual magic (Hutton 1994: 29). From Murray's work, Hutton says, 'came the devotion to a Goddess and a Horned God, the use of nudity in rites, the celebration of the four ancient Celtic quarter-days as the year's festivals, and the notion that the main point of the religion was to promote fertility'. High ritual magic 'provided the setting, the sacred circle, and the working tools' (wands, swords and knives). There is reliable evidence that by the end of the 1930s there were a few groups practising Wicca in Britain, some apparently independently of Gardner (Hutton 1995: 12). From the 1950s onward, Wicca spread rapidly. Its central tenets were its equal emphasis on both genders within both the human and divine realms; its celebration of the natural world, the earth's cycle, personal freedom and pleasure; and its system of initiation and training and inclusive participation of all coven members. In the 1950s Solstices and Equinox celebrations were added to the seasonal calendar to create eight Sabbats.

Over time other elements were added to create the broader umbrella religion of Paganism: aspects of Native American religion (totemic animals, vision quests, medicine wheels and sweat lodges) and Hinduism (meditative techniques, *mandalas*, *chakras*, and the Third Eye), along with aspects (myths, deities, rituals) of other ancient and indigenous religions. Jung's ideas about synchronicity, archetypes and the collective unconscious were imported. From feminism came the strong emphasis on the Goddess and ideas about ancient matriarchies (Hutton 1994: 30).

So far, we have seen that the first two strands which contributed to feminist witchcraft were the Wicca tradition and the 'covens' of feminist political activists of the late 1960s. The third main strand is the Goddess movement which began in the United States in the 1970s. It has to be said that many of the women who participated in, and still participate in, rituals designed to explore aspects of the Goddess did not and do not self-identify as 'witches'. Nevertheless the strong emphasis on the Goddess in feminist witchcraft can be attributed in part to the growth of research and literature on the Goddess and to women's experiences of 'Goddess rituals' over the past 25 years or so.

The first woman to teach workshops on the Goddess in New Zealand, beginning in 1984, was Lea Holford, an American psychologist with experience of Goddess ritual groups in San Francisco during the 1970s. She and a number of other women – some local and some American – over the years have run ritual workshops on the Goddess in many parts of the country, and many New Zealand women who belong to ritual groups and feminist covens have attended one or more workshops. Often the workshops themselves spawn on-going ritual groups. Lea described her experience with one of the earliest groups in the United States to me:

> Two of my best friends started a Goddess group. They were amongst the first in the Bay area to do anything like that. It must have been about 1977. I didn't know Starhawk then but I met her within a couple of years.
>
> They basically invited a bunch of friends who were interested in exploring the Goddess and they were just working with very simple archetypes like the Mother and the Sister and the Amazon. They would do the four directions and set up very simple rituals – it was really their idea – and that's what I've copied in my classes – inviting everybody to bring a symbol, to share their stories, and to have a celebration. They had a really hard time finding information . . . I know at that point Esther Harding, Toni Wolfe and some of those Jungian women had talked about some of those archetypes. We would use goddesses' names if we knew some, but it was more like exploring different aspects of the feminine was the basis of our model.
>
> It was extraordinarily powerful! It was just amazing, I suppose because it was so fresh. Most of us had no idea of the power of those symbols! We would come with these symbols and then, after creating the sacred circle, it was amazing what would come out. All of us were absolutely overwhelmed with the power of it.

Lea emphasized that most of the women she knew who joined these early Goddess groups in the US were not motivated by feminist political goals. As a result of their experiences in the rituals, however, many women developed a new view of gender relations, became politically motivated and found a power in themselves which enabled them to become politically active. Lea said:

> As they got exposed to this different way of seeing themselves as women, it helped them access a much deeper power in themselves they didn't know was there. So instead of feeling powerless and angry and fighting back trying to get power somewhere else, they found power inside themselves. They realized the problem isn't 'them' having all the power, the problem is they're actually scared of us, which was a completely different place to come from, and so coming out with, 'Don't be scared of us. We'll share what we have. We want this to work for everybody because that's what the Goddess is all about – the empowering and inter-relatedness of all beings.'
>
> It's a whole different approach to politics than had been taken by the Women's Liberation movement which was very much coming from the place of 'We don't have it and you do, so give it back!' The biggest difference was that women came from a sense of fullness instead of depletion, and found a source to keep drawing on that was actually within them, not somewhere out there. For me that's been the most profound difference.

Thus it was during the 1970s that the political and spiritual strands of feminism came together with traditional Wicca to form feminist witchcraft. Other contemporary preoccupations – the peace and ecology movements, the rising interest in alternative healing and in exploring mystical, ancient and indigenous religions – also influenced the development of the core beliefs of feminist witchcraft.[1]

Another important movement which needs to be considered when discussing the origins of feminist witchcraft is Christian feminism. It was Mary Daly in *Beyond God the Father* (1974) who first concluded 'in a way that received wide attention . . . that feminism and Christianity were never going to be reconcilable' (Hampson 1990: 108). During the past three decades this contention has been debated at length by feminist theologians and among church members, and there is now a sizeable literature which challenges conventional understandings of the Bible and Christian tradition (King 1989: 175).[2] There have been radical re-examinations of the experiences of women in the Church, the gender of God, the relationship between God and nature, the use of male-centred language and symbols, the purpose and message of Christ, issues of race and class as well as sex, the meanings of sin and grace, and the historical accuracy of the Bible. It is no exaggeration to say that the faith has been radically challenged from its foundations upward.

Some feminist theologians have remained within the Church, some have moved out, some seem to be in the process of moving out, and some have embraced Goddess spirituality as well as, or instead of, Christianity. The writings of some who have broken with the Judaeo-Christian tradition, such as Naomi Goldenberg, Mary Daly and Carol Christ, have become widely known and influential in feminist witchcraft. Some of these writers refer to their work as *thealogy*, from the Greek *thea*, meaning Goddess.

Some feminist women have continued to struggle for equality within the Church, and believe they can point to considerable achievements. Others, like Hampson, have decided that Christianity is beyond redemption. She writes (1990: 4):

> While men (and some women) consider whether women can be full insiders within the church, women debate whether or not they want to be. Eleven years ago it was I who wrote the statement in favour of the ordination of women to the priesthood circulated to all members of the General Synod of the Church of England before the vote. Today finds me no longer Christian.

In the course of my fieldwork I met a number of New Zealand women who had left the Church to become witches. I met others who are still active in their churches, engaged in activities such as rewriting liturgies to make them gender-inclusive, but who also participate in witches' rituals. Some women self-identify both as Christian and as witch. I met many, however, who felt Christianity was unsalvageable and who were worn out with the conflict both within themselves and within their churches. These women have opted to embrace Goddess spirituality exclusively for reasons I discuss in chapters six, seven and eight.

Some New Zealand women, especially feminists within the Church, see the term 'women's spirituality' as an umbrella covering both Christian feminists and feminist witches (Benland 1990). Christian feminists read many of the same writers as feminist witches and I have been surprised at how many appear to be very open to the beliefs and ritual practices of feminist witchcraft. Indeed, as one woman told me, they often feel they have more in common with witches than with their fellow church members. Those who have left the Church, however, often after long soul-searching and in painful circumstances, see their old faith as diametrically opposed to their new beliefs. Thus, while Christian feminism cannot be regarded as a strand which has been woven into feminist witchcraft, the two movements have strong connections and, for some women, overlap.

In this discussion of the origins of feminist witchcraft, I must emphasize, echoing Tanya Luhrmann (1989: 81) who worked with English witches, that I never encountered anything remotely resembling Satanism in the feminist witchcraft movement in New Zealand. Satanism, feminist witches claim, is a development in response to Judaeo-Christianity, since Satan was invented by these faiths. Feminist witches and Pagans generally stress that their spirituality, centred on the Goddess, pre-dates patriarchal religions and any notion of Satan by many millennia.

I have been told from time to time by people *outside* the feminist witchcraft movement about groups of people calling themselves 'witches' who lurk in graveyards and perform sacrifices using cats or foetuses and other unsavoury rituals. Feminist witches are as appalled – probably more so given that many are vegetarian and great animal-lovers – as most people in New Zealand society are by these accounts. They are considerably more appalled that anyone should think that feminist witches engage in such practices. If it is not already clear, it will become so in subsequent chapters that the beliefs and practices of feminist witches have nothing whatever in common with those of Satanists.

I return now to the development of the feminist witchcraft/Goddess spirituality movement over the past 30 or so years. During the 1970s and 1980s feminist scholars began doing the work that Robin Morgan and her WITCH co-coveners had not had time to do, and a steady stream of articles and books on feminist witchcraft and ancient goddesses was published.[3] In the last two decades the number of publications on these subjects has grown enormously, ranging from theoretical academic works and glossy encyclopaedic tomes to children's books and D-I-Y spell manuals.

In the introduction to her second annotated bibliography of works on feminist spirituality, Carson (1992) notes that within the movement there has been a growing interest in healing of all kinds, especially in healing the female self, and in archaeological research and Shamanism.[4] She says that the most important theme to emerge out of feminist spirituality during the 1980s was eco-feminism, which has become a political philosophy in its own right and 'contributed significantly to Green Party platforms, uniting feminist principles and women's concerns with activism on behalf of environmental protection, sustainable development, anti-nuclear protest, the promotion of vegetarianism and animal rights' (p. 4).

The vast literature on contemporary witchcraft is avidly read and discussed by participants in the movement. It influences, but does not dictate, the formation of their own beliefs and views. It puts them in touch with new research, lets them see the directions the movement is taking, gives them ideas for rituals, is shared among friends and is referred to when explaining feminist witchcraft to outsiders. On occasion it also sparks violent arguments, as in the case of Cynthia Eller's *The Myth of Matriarchal Prehistory* (1993, discussed in the next chapter). For many women, including myself, first contact with feminist witchcraft comes through reading books on the subject, most of which come from the US. It is a paradox that while they frequently claim that they have no 'sacred book' (like the Bible) which sets out their doctrine and provides a guide for living, feminist witches probably read more on the subject of their spirituality than the members of any other religious group. They are also freer than those in other religions to take or leave anything they read.

Having reviewed the history of feminist witchcraft, I now go on to discuss feminist approaches to the witch-craze. The two are connected because so many of the feminist scholars who have addressed the witch-craze have either adopted the label 'witch' themselves or at least fuelled the modern movement by their writings.[5] Their self-identification as 'witch' has come about for two inter-related reasons. First, they have rejected the designation of the historical witch as 'other' in relation either to themselves or to the witches' own societies. Second, as noted in the previous chapter, they have concluded that the women labelled 'witches' became the targets of the inquisitors and demonologists because they were outside or threatened patriarchal control, particularly with respect to the exclusively male medical profession and to the Church.

In chapter two I reviewed the common academic argument that the women burnt or hanged as witches were not 'real' witches but simply poor, harmless and defenceless old women. This comes close to arguing that the persecution of witches was unjustified because the women were not 'real' witches. The corollary is that if the women *had* been 'real' witches, they might have deserved the treatment they got. While the accused 'witches' did not indulge in the bizarre and diabolical activities the inquisitors accused them of, the activities the women *were* involved in – illicit healing, sorcery, incorporating magical charms in their healing – as well as their possible connection with older pagan beliefs and practices, were at least as distressing to the inquisitors.

From the perspective of many feminist scholars sympathetic to the contemporary witchcraft movement, witches were not the pitiable victims of senescence Levack (1987: 15) describes, nor were they 'wretched women' duped by fantasy or illusion (Duerr 1985: 15). To interpret witches purely as victims, as many historians (including some feminist ones) have done, is to ignore or deny the challenge these women represented to the dominant institutions within their societies. Of course feminist scholars are not the only ones who have taken witches' claims to power and knowledge more seriously on their own terms: we have seen that writers such as Michelet, Murray and Ginzburg did also. In his recent re-evaluation of the targets of the witch-hunts, Russell (2001: 122) points out that the witch's own contemporaries saw her as wielding 'unimaginable power and [having] access to knowledge and experience well beyond their own ken'. Moreover, 'the accused were thought by their judges and accusers, and sometimes even by themselves to have access to forms of knowledge and sources of power which were in competition with those of an emerging and insecure elite' (p. 125). Thus, in the light of such re-evaluations, 'witch' has been redefined by those in the modern movement to mean a woman – a sixteenth-century village wise woman or a modern spiritual feminist – who challenges patriarchal control and claims independent knowledge and power. The WITCH covens formed in the United States in the late 1960s quoted, provocatively and one suspects with a good deal of relish, I Samuel 15: 23: 'Rebellion is as the sin of witchcraft' (Spretnak 1982: 428).

In the last chapter we saw that a number of historians, from Thomas to Henningsen, have made a strong connection between witches and wise women, women who were healers, midwives, counsellors, diviners and sorcerers within their communities. The primary targets of the witch-hunters were these village wise women. A number of writers have explored the roles of wise women and their relationships to the male-dominated institutions of the Church and medical profession. Barbara Walker's *The Crone* (1985) traces the process by which the inquisitors came to focus on wise women and transform them into witches. The Holy Inquisition was founded in the twelfth century to exterminate a great variety of heretics. Because the property of a heretic could be seized, even before the trial, the Inquisition was an extremely profitable institution for the Church. When the numbers of heretics – Albigenses, Bogomils, Manicheans, Waldenses, Jews, Cathari, Knights Templar, Paulicians, Fraticelli, Spiritual Franciscans and others – began to thin, with a consequent diminution of profits for the Church, the Inquisition began to seek another group to target. The new heresy was centred on women who, says Walker (1985: 126), were 'always suspected of a less than total commitment to the patriarchal God who had declared them accursed'.

By the fourteenth century, Walker (p. 127) claims, Christianity had failed to eliminate paganism in peasant communities. Seasonal rituals continued to be performed, many elements of which still persist in the customs of Christmas, Easter, May Day, Midsummer, All Hallows, and many saints' days. Walker proposes that as the pre-Christian religions of Europe centred on Mother Goddesses, versions of Artemis, and it was likely that women had been the priestesses or main followers of this Goddess, there were still those – especially women – in the fourteenth century who practised parts of the 'Old Religion'. Walker cites the women called 'fairies' in medieval Brittany who continued to worship the Mother in sacred groves and the Korrigen, elder priestesses who lived on off-shore islands, especially the 'sacred isle' Sein, or Isle of the Saints, and danced at full moon around holy fountains wearing white woollen robes. Dworkin (1974: 139) says it was 'no wonder that women remained faithful adherents of the older totemic cults of Western Europe which honoured female sexuality, deified the sexual organs and reproductive capacity, and recognized women as embodying the regenerative power of nature'. Christianity, with its singular, jealous, male God, could not tolerate other religions, especially woman-centred ones.

Until the fourteenth century, European villagers with social, psychological or physical problems had typically sought help from female elders or wise women (sometimes men)[6] (Ehrenreich and English 1973, Daly 1979, Walker 1985, Starhawk 1988). The reason medicine was almost exclusively in the hands of old women, Walker suggests (1985: 127), was that these women experienced 'innate communion with the Goddess of life and death, until churchmen began to claim that disease could be cured only by holy water, exorcisms, and prayers to God, and by the laying on of priestly hands'. Kramer and Sprenger declared in the *Malleus Maleficarum* (1971: 66) that 'No one does more harm to the Catholic Faith than midwives'. Midwives were known to use herbal preparations to ease pain during childbirth – pain which had been imposed on women by God as punishment for Eve's original sin. Midwives were believed to possess knowledge about contraception and abortion, the effect of which helped women resist male control of their reproductive functions and thwarted the growth of the Church.

Even the 'good witch' was an anathema to the Church, and in the latter part of the sixteenth century the legal distinction between the 'good' and 'bad' witch was dropped. William Perkins, a Cambridge preacher, declared that the 'good witch [was] a more horrible and detestable monster than the bad [and that] . . . a thousand deaths of right belong to the good witch' (Daly 1979: 193). The Church had decided that the healing 'magic' of the wise woman must come from the Devil, since it did not come from God. Thus wise women, charged with having made a pact with the Devil, were cast among the worst heretics.

During the Middle Ages, the practice of healing was taken away from women and institutionalized as an exclusively male profession. No one was permitted to practise healing who had not studied medicine at a university, and women were not permitted into universities. The Church legitimated male doctors' exclusive right to heal, equating non-professional healing with heresy: 'If a woman dare to cure without having studied, she is a witch and must die' (Ehrenreich and English 1973: 17). In turn, the medical profession legitimated the Church's persecution of witches: the *Malleus* said that if there was any doubt about whether or not an illness had been caused by witchcraft, a doctor's judgement should be called for. Thus, the professional male doctor was placed symbolically on the side of God and the Law, while the wise woman was discredited and placed on the side of evil and heresy. Women healers did, however, hold on to midwifery for several more centuries, until the seventeenth century. Despite the outlawing of the wise women, many villagers, especially the poor, continued to consult them, shunning the new professional doctors because they were expensive and often inaccessible.

Witches were accused of two other crimes in addition to the crime of healing: sexual crimes against men and 'being organized' (Ehrenreich and English 1973: 8). In chapter two I discussed Hoch-Smith's claim that fear of female sexuality is a feature of witchcraft beliefs world-wide. In her chapter on witches in *Woman Hating*, Dworkin (1974: 134) sees males' fear of female sexuality as a projection of their fears about their own sexual prowess: 'We are dealing with an existential terror of women . . . stemming from a primal anxiety about male potency . . . These terrors form the sub-strata of a myth of feminine evil which in turn justified several centuries of gynocide.'

The *Malleus* was quite clear that women's insatiable lust was at the root of witchcraft. Ehrenreich and English write (1973: 9):

> In the eyes of the Church, all the witch's power was ultimately derived from her sexuality. Her career began with sexual intercourse with the devil. Each witch was confirmed at a general meeting (the witches' Sabbath) at which the devil presided, often in the form of a goat, and had intercourse with the neophytes.

The fact that witches were believed to be organized into a secret society, the 'Devil's party', made witches more threatening. The inquisitors spent much of the trials questioning women about what happened at their meetings, pressing for details about orgies, bestiality and baby-eating.

It is clear from examining the crimes witches were accused of that hatred of wise women on the part of the Church and male medical profession stemmed from the fact that wise women threatened these patriarchal institutions' exclusive control of power and knowledge. Wise women possessed healing knowledge and were thought to have access to power independently of God and men; they passed this knowledge on to other women; and, most ominously, they met regularly together to share knowledge, participate in rituals and, feared the inquisitors, plot who knew what. Thus for some contemporary women, beginning with the political activists of the late 1960s and moving through to those involved in feminist witchcraft today, the witch has become a potent symbol of woman as possessor of power and knowledge which is not sourced in nor controlled by patriarchal institutions, and not dependent upon patriarchal legitimation or approval.

According to Starhawk (1989: 11), the witch persecutions of the sixteenth and seventeenth centuries 'can be viewed as a mass brainwashing, a conversion through terror to the idea that women's power, and any power not approved of by the authorities, is dangerous, dirty, and sinful'. Spretnak says (1982: xii–xiv): 'The objective of patriarchy was and is to prevent women from achieving, or even supposing, our potential: that we are powerful in both mind *and* body and that the totality of those powers is a potent force'. She describes some of the ways that this has happened during 3,000 years or so of patriarchal rule, ranging from the slaughter of Goddess-worshipping pagans boasted of in biblical accounts, to the European witch-burnings, to the denial of educational, political and legal rights for women, to the portrayal of women's bodies as pornographic toys. By self-identifying with the women persecuted during the witch-craze, contemporary witches make the point that patriarchal institutions continue to be destructive of women's independent knowledge and power.

Thus the witch is also a symbol of woman as a target of misogyny. In her account of the witch-craze and its origins in *Dreaming the Dark*, Starhawk (1988: 212) says: 'The Witch persecutions were, above all, attacks on women. The propaganda that supported the Witchhunts stressed women's inferiority and defined their nature as inherently evil.' Dworkin (1974: 136) agrees that the *Malleus Maleficarum*, 'with its frenzied and psychotic woman-hating', made it clear that witchcraft was a woman's crime. Daly (1979: 16) believes that the period of the witch-craze should be taken to refer not only to the fifteenth to eighteenth centuries, but to 'the perpetual witchcraze which is the entire period of patriarchal control':

> Feminists who identify their deep centering Selves with the term *witch* are not being merely metaphorical, or cute, or popularizing, or 'trivializing'. I suggest, rather, that the reverse is true: that to limit the term to apply only to those who have esoteric knowledge of and participate formally in 'the Craft' is the real reductionism.
>
> (Daly 1979: 221)

I have explored the symbolic value of the witch in order to explain why the women I worked with choose to self-identify as 'witches'. Those who adopt the label for political reasons perceive their connection with the women labelled 'witches' during the witch-hunts as a symbolic one. Their intention is to challenge historians' conventional interpretations of the witch-craze, to draw attention to a feminist re-evaluation of the women labelled 'witches', and to focus attention on the ways in which institutions in contemporary societies continue to oppress, victimize, devalue or deny opportunities to women. They are quite well aware of the fact that the witch image was constructed by the witch-hunters and that the women killed were victims of labelling and were not self-identified witches (Adler 1982: 129). Nevertheless, in their determination to force a re-evaluation of the historical 'witches' and as a sign of their identification with these women, they re-appropriate the label 'witch' as a potent symbolic gesture.

But for many women the main purpose of becoming a witch is not political but has to do with a perceived spiritual connection with the witches of the fifteenth to eighteenth centuries and with their 'fore-sisters' stretching back into the pre-Christian period and possibly to the Upper Palaeolithic. For these women the term 'witch' is synonymous with 'wise woman' and with 'follower of the Goddess': becoming a witch is an affirmation of a female-centred spirituality. They see the wise women of 500 years ago as practitioners of the pre-Christian religions of Europe for all of whom, they believe, the primary symbol of divinity was some form of fertility goddess. In feminist witchcraft this Goddess is known by many names including 'the Great Mother', 'the Divine Mother', 'the Triple Goddess', 'She of Ten Thousand Names', and simply 'The Goddess'.

This Goddess has appeared and appears throughout the world's cultures and religions in numerous forms and bearing different names. In feminist witchcraft women invoke specific goddesses from the religious traditions of many cultures depending on the appropriateness of a goddess for a particular ritual. Thus, at Winter Solstice, women might invoke the Greek Hecate, the Hindu Kali, and the Maori Hine-nui-te-po because they have to do with darkness and death. The numerous forms of the Goddess are often categorized broadly into what are referred to as 'the three aspects of the Goddess' which correspond to three phases of women's lives: the maiden, the mother and the crone. Hecate, Kali and Hine-nui-te-po, for example, are crone goddesses.

The first two aspects of the Goddess trinity – the sexually attractive maiden and the nurturing mother – appeal to patriarchy and have been incorporated into Christianity in the figure of Mary, the virgin Mother of God. The crone, the old woman past child-bearing who speaks her mind without fear of losing male approval, offers nothing attractive to patriarchy (Walker 1985). 'The wise old woman knows too much. She knows about death, illness, decay, change,' Lea Holford said in a Women's Spirituality workshop I attended. Men's fear of losing sexual potency, which occurs as a 'little death' during intercourse, is exceeded by a fear of physical death. The crone symbolizes death. The witch is Christianity's diabolized crone.

By self-identifying as 'witch', women are reclaiming the crone, reinstating her as the third aspect of the Goddess and, most importantly, identifying themselves as Goddess. In chapters seven and eight I look at the meaning of this for women I worked with in New Zealand.

It needs to be acknowledged, however, that some women in the movement in New Zealand, perhaps a third of those I met while doing fieldwork, choose not to self-identify as 'witch' or are ambivalent about doing so, especially in contexts outside their ritual activities. The reasons they give for not calling themselves witches are that it is not safe to tell people outside the movement for fear of a fundamentalist Christian backlash, or that people outside the movement do not understand and may not be prepared to listen to or accept an explanation of who witches 'really' were and are (and there may be no opportunity to explain anyway). Some women think the term 'witch' is so heavily loaded with negative associations that it is preferable to abandon it and direct energy instead towards reclaiming the Goddess. Other women do not feel personally good enough, sufficiently knowledgeable or ready to take on such an esteemed label as 'witch'.

Over the course of my fieldwork I observed several women whom I came to know well begin to refer to themselves as 'witches' as their involvement in ritual work increased, their self images changed, and they became more familiar and comfortable with the term. Within the movement there is no line drawn between those who do and those who do not self-identify as witches; all participate together in rituals. Any particular ritual group may, and usually does, include women who identify as witches and those who do not. The former refer to their group as a 'coven', while the latter refer to the same group as a 'ritual group'.

While women may change their self-identification over time, at any given point of time there are those who do not, at least openly, call themselves 'witches' because they are frightened of what people will think, and there are those who do self-identify as witches because they are determined to change what people think about witches. Those in the latter group tend to be those with a political motivation for involvement in the movement, although this is not to say that they do not have other, possibly more important, spiritual motivations too. Women's political motivations, even within one ritual group, may be quite different from one another. One may be concerned with reassessing and drawing attention to women's place in history, another may be a midwife, another a Green Party campaigner, a writer, a social worker, or an artist. Each may be politically active to a greater or lesser extent in her own field, and may or may not find it relevant and useful to self-identify publicly as a witch.

For some women, involvement in ritual is a private part of life which gives structure and meaning to their worldview and provides a spiritual base or resource which assists them in their daily lives and individual political activity. This political activity operates in many spheres, from joining a 'Reclaim the night' march, to restructuring the content of a university course, to working in a Rape Crisis centre, to raising one's children to honour the Goddess. The intellectual rejection of the view which designates woman as 'other', and the rejection of a belief system in which divinity is imaged exclusively as an omnipotent, omniscient male 'up there' in favour of a belief system which locates sacredness, knowledge and power within each individual, might themselves be regarded as political acts.

Nevertheless, a very obvious difference between the movement in the United States and the movement in New Zealand is that witches in the US have been much more active in organized, often large-scale, public political work relating to social justice, peace and environmental issues. This activity has not taken the place of private 'inner work'; the two have gone hand-in-hand. There are historical reasons and personal reasons given by New Zealand witches for this difference. The political climate has changed since the early days of feminist witchcraft and so have the types of political activities in which feminists choose to become involved. Large protest marches, demonstrations and sit-ins are much less common tools of protest today both in the United States and in New Zealand. Feminists are working towards their political goals through new channels, often from positions of power within the institutions and career fields from which they were largely excluded 35 years ago. By the time the movement spread to New Zealand in the early 1980s, this shift had begun.

Even so, in her introduction to the second edition of *The Spiral Dance*, Starhawk says that her life 'has become much more politically focused in the past ten years' (1989: 6). She writes:

> So our commitment to the Goddess led me and others in our community to take part in nonviolent direct actions to protest nuclear power, to interfere with the production and testing of nuclear weapons, to counter military interference in Central America, and to

> preserve the environment. It led me down to Nicaragua and into ongoing work to build alliances with people of color and the native peoples whose own earth-based religions and traditional lands are being threatened or destroyed . . .
>
> Over the last ten years, I've worked to build alliances between women of color and white women and have worked in groups with women and men of differing sexual preferences, class backgrounds, and life choices.
>
> (Starhawk 1989: 7)

Starhawk's long history of involvement in political activity continues: in 2001, for instance, she was a protester at Genoa during the G8 summit.

Many women in the movement in New Zealand, especially in the early years, have expressed a reticence to become involved in public political activity saying they felt a need to concentrate most of their efforts on 'inner work' before taking on the responsibility of public, politically-oriented ritual work. For these women, ritual groups provide a secure context in which to address difficult issues in their lives and a place to experience the solidarity of sisterhood. Women in groups provide moral support and sometimes practical assistance for one another.

For almost all the women I have met who identify as 'witch', public self-identification is still context-based. The decision to call oneself a witch is not made once and for always, it is made over and over as a woman judges each social or political context. A choice not to identify publicly as a witch does not necessarily mean that a woman does not think of herself privately as a witch. It may mean that she is aware that the meaning of 'witch' is multiple and contested, and that this has implications for how others will construct and treat her on the basis of her self-identification.

Feminist witches walk a fine line. The historical witch was a hideous image of womanhood invented by misogynists of breathtaking cruelty in order to label, damn and burn women. The point of women today publicly adopting the name 'witch' is to expose the historical witch as an invention, and to explicate the link between the wise woman and the witch and the process by which the former became anathematized – in short, to re-invent the witch. If, however, women claim publicly to be 'witches' but fail to re-invent the witch for the dominant culture, they may turn out to be unwitting participants in a potentially sadomasochistic perpetuation of the most misogynistic fantasy the world has known.

4

FEMINISTS AND THE GODDESS

> There was a time when you were not a slave, remember that. You walked alone, full of laughter, you bathed bare-bellied. You say you have lost all recollection of it, remember . . . You say there are no words to describe this time, you say it does not exist. But remember. Make an effort to remember. Or, failing that, invent.
>
> (Wittig 1972: 95)

> It's a very ancient thing being revived. It doesn't necessarily have to tune in to any sort of truth. That doesn't matter. It's a re-invention of tradition for modern purposes. I reckon that's what most religion damn well is anyway – the Christian religion is obviously that. I see this as part of the postmodern age; it's part of a whole cultural context. It is not an external set of things imposed upon you where you have to have faith to believe it. It's something you are constantly reconstructing for yourself. It would be wonderful to come back on earth in 500 years . . . maybe the feminist church will have replaced Rome. Who knows? Goddess forbid! But who knows what could happen? It's exciting, isn't it? And women love it. They take to it like ducks to water. They really, really love it.
>
> (Joan)

In the last chapter we considered who or what the witch represents for women in the feminist witchcraft or Goddess spirituality movement. In this chapter we explore the question: who or what is the Goddess? Scholars in recent decades have approached the study of the Goddess from a number of disciplines: theology and thealogy, religious studies, psychology, archaeology, anthropology, sociology, the classics, mythology and art history. Others have come to research and write on the Goddess from a variety of backgrounds: some of these include personal experience in feminist ritual work or art-making, a practical training in Wicca, involvement in peace activism and eco-feminism, involvement in Eastern religions, an interest in Shamanism, or through taking undergraduate courses in anthropology.

Starhawk, who has a background in anthropology, political activism and Wicca, emphasizes that women in the Goddess movement today do not imagine they are dusting off and reviving a prehistoric religion which existed in Europe prior to the rise of Judaeo-Christianity. Goddess religion, she says, is 'being recreated rather than revived' and is formed out of a 'rich kaleidoscope of traditions and orientations' (1989: 200, 25). Modern women do not *worship* the Goddess and do not want to convert people to 'One Right True and Only Way' (p. 201). Goddess spirituality is not even primarily a system of religious beliefs and practices centred on a female deity. Rather, the Goddess is a symbol, and as such is given different meanings, including apparently contradictory ones, by different women. All meanings are considered valid and are embraced within the holistic worldview of the movement. Thus, the Goddess symbolizes lover and virgin, female and male, earth and sky, the creative, nurturing Demeter and the destructive, death-dealing Hecate. The Goddess represents the whole of the human and natural world: according to Starhawk, she is manifested equally in a drop of water, menstrual blood or excrement.

> The nature of the Goddess is never single. Wherever She appears, She embodies both poles of duality – life in death, death in life. She has a thousand names, a thousand aspects. She is the milk cow, the weaving spider, the honeybee with its piercing sting. She is the bird of the spirit and the sow that eats its own young. The snake that sheds its skin and is renewed; the cat that sees in the dark; the dog that sings to the moon – all are Her. She is the light and the darkness, the patroness of love and death, who makes manifest *all* possibilities. She brings both comfort and pain.
>
> (Starhawk 1989: 94)

Because women in the movement reject dualistic thinking, paradox is celebrated. Starhawk (p. 95) continues:

> I have spoken of the Goddess as psychological symbol and also as manifest reality. She is both. She exists, *and* we create Her. The symbols and attributes associated with the Goddess . . . engage us emotionally. We know the Goddess is not the moon – but we still thrill to its light glinting through branches. We know the Goddess is not a woman, but we respond with love as if She were, and so connect emotionally with all the abstract qualities behind the symbol.

Feminist witches consciously and deliberately incorporate the poetic and the political in their discourse about the Goddess. Starhawk presents her 'origins' of witchcraft in the first chapter of *The Spiral Dance* as mythology, not history. She says the symbol of the Goddess is 'poemagogic' because 'it induces and symbolizes the ego's creativity'. Writing of women's connection with the moon because of their menstrual cycles, she drifts into the poetic: 'Woman is the earthly moon; the moon is the celestial egg, drifting in the sky womb, whose menstrual blood is the fertilizing rain' (p. 92). A hundred pages later she asserts that the responsibility of feminist witches is to 'engage in the demanding task of recreating culture' and that

> [a] deep and profound change is needed in our attitude toward the world and life on it, toward each other, and in our conceptions of what is human. Somehow, we must win clear of the roles we have been taught, of strictures on mind and self that are learned before speech and are buried so deep that they cannot be seen. Today women are creating new myths, singing a new liturgy, painting our own icons, and drawing strength from the new-old symbols of the Goddess, of the 'legitimacy and beneficence of female power'.
> (p. 199)

This last phrase comes from a well known paper by Carol Christ which was first given as the keynote address at a conference titled 'The Great Goddess Re-emerging' held at the University of California at Santa Cruz in 1978. It was published that year in *Heresies* 5, in *Womanspirit Rising* (Christ and Plaskow 1979) and again in *The Politics of Women's Spirituality* (Spretnak 1982). The paper, titled 'Why women need the Goddess: phenomenological, psychological, and political reflections', discusses the significance of the Goddess as symbol. Drawing on Clifford Geertz, Christ discusses the ways in which religious symbols shape a cultural ethos. Her main point is that 'religious symbol systems focused around exclusively male images of divinity create the impression that female power can never be fully legitimate or wholly beneficent' (Christ 1982: 73). Christ echoes Daly in *Beyond God the Father* in the view that patriarchal religion legitimates male power: the husband who dominates his wife represents God himself.

Summarizing 'Why women need the Goddess', Christ (1992: 248) lists the most important meanings of the symbol of Goddess:

> First, the Goddess is symbol of the legitimacy and beneficence of female power in contrast to the image of female power as anomalous or evil in biblical religion. Second, the Goddess validates women's bodily experiences, including menstruation, birth, lactation, and menopause, and validates the human connection to finitude, which has been denigrated in Western religions. Third, the Goddess symbol in the context of feminist Goddess worship values the female will, which has been viewed as the origin of evil in biblical

> mythology. Fourth, the Goddess points to the valuing of woman-to-woman bonds, including the mother–daughter relation, which is celebrated in the story of Demeter and Persephone but which has scarcely been mentioned in the religion and culture of the past several thousand years. The symbol of Goddess, I argue, legitimates and undergirds the moods and motivations inspired by feminism just as the symbol of God has legitimated patriarchal attitudes for several thousand years.

Christ is quite explicit about the fact that the modern Goddess movement is a recent invention which draws on numerous Goddess images and mythologies including ancient European, Near Eastern, Native American, Mesoamerican, Hindu, African and others. These traditions are tapped eclectically and often partially: some goddesses, such as those who were subordinate to gods, are not considered useful role models and so are ignored. Christ (1982: 76) raises two questions in relation to her thesis regarding the importance of 'Goddess' as symbol: is it necessary to invoke a Great Goddess in order to focus attention on women's power? Do women in the movement believe in a Goddess 'out there' who is not reducible to a human potential? She groups women's responses to these questions into three answers:

1. The Goddess is divine female, a personification who can be invoked in prayer and ritual.
2. The Goddess is symbol of the life, death, and rebirth energy in nature and culture, in personal and communal life.
3. The Goddess is symbol of the affirmation of the legitimacy and beauty of female power.

Some women are adamant that the Goddess is not 'out there' but that the symbol reflects the sacred power or essence within humanity and nature at large. They argue that the concept of a transcendent deity is a legacy of patriarchal, monotheistic religions 'which brings with it the authoritarian, hierarchicalism, and dogmatic rigidity' (Christ 1982: 76). In Goddess spirituality, by contrast, divinity is immanent. When asked 'What does the symbol of Goddess mean?' Starhawk replied:

> It all depends how I feel. When I feel weak, She is someone who can help and protect me. When I feel strong, She is the symbol of my own power. At other times I feel Her as the natural energy in my body and the world.
>
> (ibid.)

As thealogian Melissa Raphael (1999: 58) has said, 'the contemporary Goddess is a shape-shifter'. For some within the movement 'the Goddess is relatively abstract and functions *for them* as an emancipatory metaphor' or as a symbol of a web of dynamic personal, political and cosmic energies – 'the organic relations between all living things within the cosmos'. For others she is 'the divinity of female being'. For others again she is a female deity who may be petitioned and has the power to intervene in human lives. 'The meaning of the Goddess is identical with the meaning of being alive' (pp. 57–8).

In her discussion of the meaning of the Goddess for English witches, Luhrmann (1989: 47) says that while witches generally agree that the Goddess is a metaphor for nature and nature's transformations, they nevertheless 'slip' into referring to her as a personified deity:

> I suspect that for practitioners there is a natural slippage from metaphor to extant being, that it is difficult – particularly in a Judaeo-Christian society – genuinely to treat a deity-figure as only a metaphor, regardless of how the religion is rationalized. The figure becomes a deity, who cares for you.

I agree that women raised in a Judaeo-Christian society are likely to have a strong tendency to conceptualize the Goddess as a personified deity, but I do not think that women 'slip' into conceptualizing the Goddess in this way without realizing it or really meaning to. I think women give themselves licence to think of the Goddess in any way they find useful, at the same time acknowledging that they are personally constructing this 'Goddess' themselves. I have met many who speak of the Goddess as personified deity, but none speaks of her *exclusively* this way, and none claims that the Goddess is limited to this form of conceptualization.

The idea that divinity is immanent liberates women from the legacy of a religious and cultural tradition which invokes a conflict between the spirit and the flesh and tells people, especially women, that their bodies are dirty and sinful. Contemplating Palaeolithic and Neolithic images of what are taken to be 'the Goddess' with their large breasts, bellies and thighs is a powerful antidote to the effects of flipping wretchedly through magazines full of young, slim women judged beautiful and desirable by our society. Because the Goddess is represented as maiden, mother and crone, ageing and death, as well as youth and life, are celebrated as part of the cycle. Griffin (1995) describes a powerful ritual in which a group of ageing and aged postmenopausal American women embraced and celebrated their cronehood and thereby 'symbolically redefined female beauty and worth and so reclaimed their autonomy and power'. A recurring theme in Goddess rituals is reconnecting the material with the spiritual self, liberating female sexuality from its association with sin, and celebrating the erotic feminine in all its forms (ibid.).

A number of psychologists have written about the Goddess as symbol from a Jungian perspective. Whitmont (1983: x) refers to the goddesses as 'archetypal and compelling ideals' which, although not literal objects, are real and powerful. He sees a strong link between religion and socio-political systems: gender relations within a gynolatric society (one which reveres the feminine), Whitmont believes, are quite different from those in an androlatric one (which reveres the masculine). He writes:

> Misogyny and androlatry, then, are indissolubly intertwined with the religious convictions and beliefs that were held during the last two to four thousand years or more . . . Androlatry and misogyny reflect the masculine overthrow of an older order in which the divine was felt to be manifest in feminine forms and values. Divinity then was conceived in the images of the Great Goddess.
>
> (p. 125)

But this kind of Jungian division between masculine and feminine values is not, or is no longer, accepted by other writers including Eisler (1988), Starhawk (1989) and Goodison (1990). Eisler also believes that there was a period in Europe when the pre-eminent deity was a Goddess, but she does not see this as a period in which 'feminine values' prevailed, but as a time when societies organized themselves according to a 'partnership model' instead of a 'dominator model'. In her introduction to the 1989 edition of *The Spiral Dance* Starhawk says that the central change she would make to the first edition would be in the way she discussed maleness and femaleness. She now finds the concept that each woman has within her a 'male self' and each man a 'female self' unhelpful and misleading.

> I don't identify femaleness or maleness with specific sets of qualities or predispositions . . . If we say, for example, 'Male energy is aggressive,' I can easily find five aggressive goddesses without even thinking hard. If we say, 'Female energy is nurturing,' we can also find male gods who nurture.
>
> (Starhawk 1989: 8)

Jean Shinoda Bolen, another psychologist, combines Jungian and feminist perspectives to arrive at her view of the psychology of women. She sees every woman as being acted upon from within by 'goddess archetypes' – powerful inner forces which can be personified by Greek goddesses – and from without by cultural stereotypes – roles which society constructs for women. Bolen (1985: 5) uses 'goddesses' in inverted commas to symbolize 'powerful, invisible forces that shape behaviour and influence emotions'. As a woman becomes familiar with the particular 'goddesses' within herself and at work in her life, she learns about her own priorities and abilities and how to work with them or, if she wishes, how to 'cultivate' a different 'goddess' in her life. The Greek goddess myths become 'insight tools'. Bolen tells the story of when a woman colleague unexpectedly spoke out against the Equal

Rights Amendment Bolen was supporting. In her hurt, angry response to her colleague, Bolen says, she was acting like Artemis, archetypal big sister, protector of women. Her opponent was like Athena, the daughter who sprang fully armed from Zeus's head ready to defend the patriarchy. Bolen's book *Goddesses in Everywoman* (1985) is familiar to many women in the movement in New Zealand and her approach was incorporated into many of the workshops I attended.

The contemporary Goddess movement does not stake its validity or its agenda on proof that Goddess-worshipping societies were the norm for 30,000 years or so before patriarchal religions became dominant 3,000 to 4,000 years ago, although undoubtedly there are still many in the movement who believe this was so. Monique Wittig, in the quotation which heads this chapter, urges women to 'remember' a time long ago when women's lives were free and joyous. If it is too difficult to remember, she says, 'Invent'. Many in the movement are quite comfortable about inventing a religion and a past which serves women's purposes – one which is psychologically and politically useful and empowering to them.

Others, however, are eager to seize upon evidence which demonstrates that once upon a time a Great Goddess, and later pantheons of goddesses, formed the central focus of early European religions. They have particularly embraced the work of archaeologist Marija Gimbutas (1982, 1989, 1991, 1999),[1] who has examined the Neolithic cultures of Europe and concluded that prior to the intrusion of the Indo-Europeans, which heralded the transition to patriarchal and belligerent societies, the societies of Old Europe enjoyed a long period of peaceful living. These Neolithic communities built spacious houses of four or five rooms, towns of considerable size, and temples several storeys high; they were potters, weavers, copper and gold metallurgists; they developed a sacred script; and they developed an extensive trade network circulating obsidian, shells, marble, copper and salt. According to Gimbutas, warfare appears to have been absent. There are no remains of weapons, village sites were not chosen for their defensive potential, and there are no paintings depicting humans fighting. The peaceful nature of these societies, Gimbutas implies, has a great deal to do with their religion. She writes (1991: x):

> The primordial deity for our Paleolithic and Neolithic ancestors was female, reflecting the sovereignty of motherhood. In fact, there are no images that have been found of a Father God throughout the prehistoric record. Paleolithic and Neolithic symbols and images cluster around a self-generating Goddess and her basic functions as Giver-of-Life, Wielder-of-Death, and as Regeneratrix. This symbolic system represents cyclical, nonlinear, mythical time.
>
> The religion of the Goddess reflected a matristic, matrilineal, and endogamic social order for most of early human history. This was

> not necessarily 'matriarchy', which wrongly implies 'rule' by women as a mirror image of androcracy. A matrifocal tradition continued throughout the early agricultural societies of Europe, Anatolia, and the Near East, as well as Minoan Crete. The emphasis in these cultures was on technologies that nourished people's lives, in contrast to the androcratic focus on domination.

Miriam Robbins Dexter, an Indo-European linguist and mythographer, also believes that goddesses were the pre-eminent deities during the Neolithic. From her translation of classical myths concerning Indo-European goddesses from primary sources, Dexter has concluded that the Neolithic peoples of parts of Europe, Asia and the Near East worshipped a goddess who embodied the complete life process of birth, life, and death. She cites, for example, the Indic goddess Devī who is represented as Uma and Parvati in her beneficent aspects and as Durga and Kali in her terrifying aspects (1990: 5). Other death goddesses include the Sumerian Ereshkigal and the Greek Hecate. Persephone both has a maiden aspect and is queen of the underworld.

Dexter's conclusion is very similar to Gimbutas's. As the 'goddess-centred' societies of the Neolithic were conquered by the 'male-centred Indo-Europeans', the image of the divine feminine changed. Some of the goddesses were married off to the conquerors' gods, many lost their autonomous power, and all eventually lost their centrality in the religious systems of patriarchal societies. Some goddesses remained autonomous and powerful, escaping assimilation into Indo-European society. However, Dexter (1990: 182) writes:

> Many autonomous goddesses were transmuted to witches by the Greeks, Romans, and other Indo-Europeans, and they were often removed to far-away islands or stuck underwater, perhaps thus lurking just at the periphery of men's consciousness. Although some male-centred cultures refused to venerate them, they could not eradicate them.

One such 'witch' was the Germanic goddess Rán, old wife of the sea-king, Aegir, who dragged a net under the ocean waiting to catch sailors who fell off ships. The Greek Scylla, a female monster who had 12 feet and six heads and lurked in caves, also lay in wait to grab and devour sailors. Another human–animal hybrid was the Lamia, who stole children from their beds and ate them, foreshadowing the fifteenth-century witch image (p. 179).

In many modern patriarchal societies, Dexter says, there is no worship at all of the personification of the divine feminine. Traces of her survive only in the image of the ugly, evil-doing old witch. This imbalance in the character of the divine in much of modern religion, Dexter believes, 'reflects upon the wellness, in all of its aspects, of our world' (p. 183). She concludes:

> What is missing, particularly in Western culture, is respect for an energy which makes things whole, an energy which honours life. The goddesses provide a clue to how we must restructure our world if it is to survive, a clue both to our past and to our future.
>
> (p. 186)

While women in the feminist spirituality movement eagerly embrace the Goddess, at least as a symbol, and a mythological past in which she was the supreme deity, many other feminists have vehemently criticized the movement on several counts since its inception. In particular, criticisms have come from feminist anthropologists, archaeologists and scholars in religious studies.[2] With respect to their commitment to feminist politics, Goddess feminists have been attacked on two sets of opposing grounds. On one hand they have been criticized as 'romantic, solipsistic and politically lethargic' (Weaver 1989: 62), abandoning politics for mysticism (Evans 1995: 80) and seeking an 'apolitical cop-out from feminist struggles' (Spretnak 1982: xxii).[3] On the other hand, they have been accused of determinedly and self-consciously 'using' the Goddess to pursue a feminist political agenda (Budapest 1982: 536, Meskell 1995, 1998). Thus adherents have been constructed both as self-deluded escapists who have opted for a personal spiritual solution to the problem of patriarchy *and* as exploiting the past, under the guise of a religious agenda, to support contemporary feminist struggles. Either way, the Goddess feminist vision of the pre-Christian past is dismissed as 'simply hopeful and idealistic creations reflecting the contemporary search for a social utopia' (Meskell 1995: 74).

Goddess feminism has also been criticized by some feminists (anthropologists in particular) for embracing a damaging, essentializing connection between woman, nature and nurturance (Ortner 1974),[4] and for fostering passivity, self-absorption and submission in women by substituting a 'tokenized derivative of the Christian God' in the form of a Great Mother Goddess (Daly 1985: xviii). It is obvious to the movement's critics that such essentialist connections rationalize and reinforce the patriarchal agenda which would keep women locked within a narrowly constructed and inferior maternal role. In these opponents' view, a 'Mother Goddess' is the wrong symbol to use and religion is the wrong instrument to advance a feminist cause.

A third related area in which feminist spirituality has been, and is still being, vigorously criticized is in relation to its use or misuse of the past. A number of feminist archaeologists (along with other archaeologists) have argued that the movement misrepresents prehistory and ancient goddesses.[5] As well as being accused of appropriating the past for a contemporary agenda, Goddess feminists are sometimes accused of appropriating the myths, deities, rituals and traditions of living indigenous peoples (as well as ancient peoples), an exercise which may be seen as a form of colonization (Long 1995: 26–7).

Those within the movement have responded to their critics, for instance in the volume *The Politics of Women's Spirituality: Essays on the Rise of Spiritual Power within the Feminist Movement* (Spretnak 1982), but their explanations have often not reached those in the broader feminist community, unlike the writings of their critics. It has to be said that Goddess feminists, who have been situated as defendants in relation to the accusations made against them, have not mounted a persistent defence, preferring usually to state their worldview and spiritual beliefs in literature aimed predominantly at the movement's adherents or those positively disposed towards them and their ideas. What little dialogue there has been between feminists within the movement and those outside appears to have had no effect in terms of altering the nature of the accusations put by the movement's opponents, while the perspectives of those in the movement appear to have shifted to accommodate, for example, new archaeological perspectives on the Neolithic and the on-going feminist discourse on essentialism. Despite these shifts within the movement, and because the movement has not been particularly successful at getting its voice heard by outsiders, opponents of the Goddess movement have been able to misrepresent the beliefs of those in the movement to outsiders. I will deal here firstly with the criticism about Goddess feminists' involvement in feminist politics.

First it should be said that Goddess feminists abhor the polarization of the political and the spiritual, especially as part of the movement's roots in the US, as we saw in the last chapter, lay in the feminist political activism of the 1960s and 1970s. Most of the women I have come to know within the movement in New Zealand have broadly the same political goals as other feminists, working in their personal and professional lives for the transformation of gender relations and all relations of unequal power. Within the coven I joined during fieldwork, for example, there were women who worked voluntarily for Greenpeace, the AIDS Foundation, a People with Disabilities network, Rape Crisis, and as a Lifeline counsellor. Their spirituality seemed to underpin rather than undermine their political activity, and was far from an 'apolitical cop-out'.

Having said that, while feminist witches in New Zealand have and do become involved in various types of feminist and other political activity, they do so as individuals rather than as a community of witches, and they do not identify openly as witches when they do.[6] The movement as a whole in New Zealand has not had the overtly political profile that the movement in the US has had, where witches have been much more active in organized, often large-scale, public political work relating to social justice, peace and environmental issues (Starhawk 1988, 1989, 1990).

Some women talked to me about the 'anti-spirituality' stigma attached to involvement in feminist spirituality. They had heard derogatory remarks about it, and claimed that *Broadsheet*, New Zealand's best known feminist magazine (until it ceased publication in 1997), had a tradition of being averse to publishing pieces about spirituality. One woman told me:

> Radical feminists working politically always feared that anything spiritual was going to mean that women would get self-indulgent and forget about political change. I think the challenge for the women's spirituality movement is to keep its feet on the ground, and to be aware that we do need change at that level too – that we should be embracing all levels. We don't have to split off and build castles in the air.

Some witches I met came to witchcraft through feminism; for other women it was the other way around. Kez, one of the members of the ritual group I joined, explained how her discovery of feminist spirituality gave a fresh boost to her political consciousness:

> When I first came into women's politics, we didn't talk about spirituality or witches or goddesses at all. We talked about women being strong, burning their bras, and having a voice and having a women's community. We were not talking in terms of the spiritual side of things, but in terms of having a sense of our own material worth, and being able to own homes together, and being able to have skills that men had, and have information-sharing on those lines.
>
> Whenever a group arose that was 'spiritual', the so-called 'political' women didn't really take that group seriously as a feminist group. We didn't look upon our spiritual side as being important in those days. We were more interested in getting knowledge that men had, and having the right to have abortions, and the right not to be raped, and the right to walk the streets safely.
>
> Really it's only in the last ten years of my women's politics that spirituality has become a political issue. I came across Anne Cameron's *Daughters of Copper Woman* – that was the first political/spiritual book I ever read. I thought, 'Gee, this is a different way of looking at stuff'. Now I see my spirituality as strengthening my womanhood. It's grown into a spirituality that is much bigger than I had ever thought possible, and it's made me excited again to look at feminism. I think that's happened for a lot of women. And I think it's allowing other women to come in and be part of the politics.

Of course women's reasons for being part of the movement and their modes and levels of involvement vary considerably. There *are* witches who have tucked themselves away in isolated parts of the country, alone or with children or like-minded others, to grow herbs and commune with nature in relative seclusion. These women might claim that feminist politics are not very important to them compared with living spiritually connected to nature, or they might claim that they are not opting out of political work but are opting out of a patriarchally dominated rat-race. Or they might have a strongly eco-feminist political consciousness and be in the habit of joining with other ecologically minded groups to protest against, for example, renewed gold-mining on the Coromandel Peninsula.[7] Most of the witches I worked with, however, were urban feminists who seemed no more or less politically committed or active than other urban feminists, and certainly no more likely seriously to propose religious, separatist or utopian solutions to the problem of patriarchy.

I turn now to discuss the criticism that feminist witches have dreamed up an ancient utopian past wherein communities were matriarchal and worshipped a deity usually referred to as a 'Mother Goddess' or 'fertility goddess'. In this mythic ideal world the worship of the Goddess went hand-in-hand with a universal reverence for women's natural procreative and nurturing qualities. The Goddess was also seen as the 'Earth Mother' and 'Mother Nature', and because of the connection between her and nurturing human mothers, a symbolic connection was made and celebrated between women and nature. This dream about the past becomes a mirage for a desperately wished-for utopian feminist future. At least this is how critics of feminist spirituality have represented the movement's beliefs for 30 years or so. Given this exaggerated scenario, it is easy to see why those who deplore essentialism throw up their hands in despair when faced with feminist spirituality.

In May 1979 Sally Binford, a feminist anthropologist, attacked 'the Mother Goddess/Matriarchy madness' in an article in *Human Behaviour*, arguing that matriarchy did not precede patriarchy, that matrilineal inheritance and kinship systems are not evidence of former matriarchal societies, and that prehistoric art in the form of Venus figurines and cave art does not attest to a period of Goddess worship. Addressing Goddess feminists directly in an appendix to *The Politics of Women's Spirituality* (where her article was reprinted), Binford (1982: 558) dealt specifically with what she perceived were the essentialist connections made by Goddess feminists: that 'women are by nature sensitive, loving, and nurturing, while men are aggressive, brutal, and violent'. Such clichés, she argued, oppress all women and rationalize the status quo: they encourage the powerless to 'dream of and long for a mythic past and waste precious time attempting to document its reality' (p. 559).

A stream of feminist anthropologists and other feminist scholars have criticized the Goddess movement in similar terms (for example, Ortner, Bamberger, Rosaldo, di Leonardo and, most recently, Eller). In her benchmark paper 'Is female to male as nature is to culture?', Ortner explained the universal devaluation of women in terms of their symbolic association with nature – 'something that every culture devalues, something that every culture defines as being of a lower order of existence than itself' – while men occupy the high ground of culture (Ortner 1974: 72). The answer to this dilemma, according to the anti-essentialists, is to sever woman's connection with nature. They have complained long and loud about the Goddess movement's thwarting of this project. 'The dichotomizing, essentializing threads in 1970s feminist evolutionary models today weigh, to paraphrase Marx, like a nightmare on the brains of living feminists,' laments di Leonardo (1991: 26).

Hackett, a specialist in the study of the ancient Near East, has complained that ancient Near Eastern goddesses are 'often admired not because of their many sources of power and their multifaceted personalities, but rather because they are said to be "fertility goddesses"' (Hackett 1989: 67). They are thus reduced to functions to do with love, sex and fertility. Hackett thinks that Goddess feminists choose to place these goddesses 'into the category of fertility or mothering' because these are the aspects of womanhood most familiar and least threatening to modern Westerners, and in this way the 'fullness and breadth of power these goddesses represented in the ancient world' need not be confronted (p. 75). Woman's alignment with nature is thus left unchallenged.

This is a small sampling of the accusations levelled at feminist spirituality. How have women within the movement responded to them, and are the claims fair? It is true that in the early days of the Goddess movement, women inspired by books such as Elizabeth Gould Davis's *The First Sex* (1972) used to fantasize about glorious matriarchies in the past and future. They were not the only feminists who did so at the time. In her history of the Goddess movement in Britain, Asphodel Long describes the Matriarchy Study Group which was founded in London in 1975 as an offshoot of the London Women's Liberation Movement. The group claimed in its first publication *Goddess Shrew* that patriarchal religion had played a part in demeaning and exploiting women, but that 'there was a time when society was organized on the basis of a woman-led culture' which worshipped a fertility Goddess, and that 'a total re-appraisal of patriarchy in politics' was now necessary (Long 1995: 14). Eller (1993, 2000) makes it clear that stories of ancient matriarchies also circulate widely in the US movement. During my fieldwork among Goddess feminists in New Zealand, I have certainly heard women refer to a period of matriarchy prior to the arrival in southern Europe of the patriarchal Indo-Europeans, although such references were much more common ten years ago. It seems that wherever the movement has taken root, some women have latched on to a belief in a utopian matriarchal era 'in ancient times'.

But not all Goddess feminists believe that there were ever widespread matriarchies, and as time goes on belief in them has dwindled or been modified, a fact which the movement's opponents have failed to acknowledge. Carol Christ (1997: 58) writes that the 'term *matriarchy* is not used by Goddess scholars who are aware of its controversial history'. Rather, Palaeolithic and Neolithic societies are viewed as 'prepatriarchal, matrifocal, probably matrilineal'. As long ago as 1982 Spretnak replied to Binford that a belief in a 'Golden Age of Matriarchy' exasperates most Goddess-researchers as much as it does feminists like Binford, though she pointed out that just as proof of Goddess worship is not proof of matriarchies, neither does the absence of matriarchies mean an absence of Goddess worship, for which Spretnak (1982: 553), along with many other scholars, considers the evidence irrefutable.

Lucy Goodison, a classicist and Goddess feminist, has re-examined the evidence from prehistoric Crete (often upheld as an example of a matriarchal society) and concluded that 'none of it proves that we are looking at a society which is matriarchal in the sense of a society run by women' (1990: 118). While women apparently figured prominently in the religion as deities or as priestesses, it is unknown whether this pre-eminence translated into other kinds of social or political power, Goodison says. She believes that the matriarchy fantasy has more to do with 'our needs and struggles today than with life in Crete in the third millennium BC' (p. 120).

The fantasy of matriarchy – as myth not history – provides some Goddess feminists with a way to imagine a society which is not patriarchal where the values and meanings attached to 'woman' were different. To them it no longer matters particularly whether matriarchies existed historically or not. As Goldenberg says:

> Although witches do often speak of the times of the matriarchies, most are more concerned with the concept as a psychological and poetic formula than as historical verity. A popular aphorism among modern witches is Monique Wittig's statement that 'There was a time when you were not a slave, remember . . . Or failing that, invent.' Witches consider any thought or fantasy real to the degree that it influences actions in the present. In this sense a remembered fact and an invented fantasy have identical psychological value.
>
> (quoted by Eilberg-Schwartz 1989: 90)

The psychological value of inventing a past when women were more powerful is that women can more easily envisage and create a future in which power relations are constituted differently. This, they claim, does not lull them into passivity as their critics propose, but motivates them to work towards feminist goals. The goddesses function as role models, as metaphors, as a reminder that the qualities of, for example, hunter (Artemis) and warrior (Athena) as well as mother (Demeter) were once and can still be associated with the feminine and revered. In the course of fieldwork I met many women who began to take small and large steps towards liberation, usually at the level of the self, but sometimes at a broader social level. For example, a woman might leave or change a problematic relationship, undertake a task she previously did not feel confident to do, deal with an eating disorder, confront someone who previously seemed intimidating, help set up a women's health collective, lobby a school to change the way it teaches about women in history, or raise her children to have a feminist consciousness.

It could be argued that it is not Goddess feminists who are locked into understanding women's roles in patriarchal terms, but their accusers. The debate about essentialism has been structured within the dominant binary logic of Western societies, so that accepting a maternal role has to mean accepting a patriarchal construction of maternity with its inferior status and rejecting any number of other roles women might wish to have. Like Irigaray, Goddess feminists want to confound this binary logic and move beyond it, to reconceptualize woman and femininity '*otherwise* than in phallocentric terms' (Grosz 1989: 110). Their solution to the low value attached to the maternal role is not to reject this role, but to assign it new value and affirm it as one of any number of roles a woman may choose for herself.

Contrary to what the movement's opponents claim, I would be surprised if the Goddess for most women adherents today predominantly symbolizes a nurturing fertility goddess, and neither is the Goddess seen as the female counterpart or reversal of the Judaeo-Christian God. Starhawk (1989: 249) sees as false ideology the idea that 'men are inherently violent and prone to domination, while women are inherently nurturing and cooperative'. Long, in her insider's discussion of the British Goddess movement, declares: 'I should say formally that there is total disagreement with the conventional view that the goddesses signify fertility only' (Long 1995: 20). In her article on the Indian Goddess tradition, Johnsen (1996: 30) goes to pains to show that the belief that the focus of the tradition is fertility or sexuality is an 'insidious misconception'. Margot Adler (1989: 97–8) says that, as a Pagan polytheist, she has problems with the notion of a single Great Mother Goddess. To her, this idea is suspiciously monotheistic; she thinks it more reasonable to assume that different cultures created different deities out of different needs. On the question of matriarchy, Adler says, 'it is unlikely there was ever a universal matriarchy, for the same reasons there was probably not a single Goddess religion'. Hume (1997: 87) says that most Australian witches 'do not want to revert to the fantasy of an ancient matriarchy. Rather they are searching for symbols that will not compromise their ideals and the goals of feminism.' Only once in 13 years of attending feminist witches' rituals (around 170 rituals) have I been invited to one specifically to celebrate women's procreative fertility, and that was organized by two lesbian women who were in the process of organizing IVF, and in any case saw fertility more broadly than in terms of women's biology.

The fact of the matter is, at least in New Zealand, that because of the high proportion of professional and lesbian women in the movement, a Goddess associated predominantly with procreation and nurturance would not hold a great deal of appeal for many adherents. Of course some of these women are mothers who undoubtedly dote on their children, but their maternal role is only one of a number of roles they regard as important. There are also women in the movement whose days are occupied with taking care of their children, some of whom value this role highly while others have ambivalent feelings about it. The point is that all of women's roles, choices, experiences and individual priorities are valued whatever they happen to be.

Just as feminist spirituality rejects the patriarchal representation of maternity, it challenges a representation of nature that situates it in inferior opposition to culture, and rejects the idea that identification with nature should be gender-based. When women in the movement say that they want to 're-connect with nature', they do not mean that men cannot do this too, and they do not think that re-connecting with nature means they are shunning or estranging themselves from culture. Indeed they would say that for humanity to survive and flourish, men as well as women need to re-connect with nature, and they explicitly see themselves as having a role in re-creating culture.

The notion that nature and the body need to be transcended and dominated is seen by Goddess feminists as a legacy of Judaeo-Christian ideology. They are intent on confronting somataphobia and reclaiming the female body. In my view this does not justify putting them in the essentialists' camp. Their ideas about the body fit more comfortably with those feminist theorists – Irigaray (1985), Grosz (1989), Kirby (1992), Schor (1994), Frye (1996) and others – who have been rethinking essentialism, difference, feminine specificity and the body. In *Addressing Essentialism Differently*, Kirby (1992: 6) writes of feminism's anxiety about 'returning to the body', of the 'fear of being discovered unwittingly behind enemy lines'. In her view this somataphobia 'underpins the legacy of phallocentrism's mind/body split' and needs to be exorcized. Embracing and assigning positive meanings and value to the female body, female sexuality in whatever form it takes, and female biological functions (for example, menstruation) are an important preoccupation of Goddess feminists not simply to reverse the patriarchal devaluation, but because they are important to women, give women pleasure and pain, preoccupy women from time to time, and are essential (yes, essential) to women's being.

Constructing a positive category of women (to which Irigaray is committed) is not to define or essentialize 'woman'. In Frye's (1996: 997) view, 'Until a positive category of women is historically constructed, the man/woman distinction *will be* the *A/not-A* universal and exclusive dichotomy it has historically been in many of its deployments', where man is subject and woman is not-man, non-subject, absolute Other. Only by constructing 'a concrete and historically real positive category of women' which deliberately elaborates and articulates differences among women can a positive category *B* with its own subjectivity be created on the other side of *A* (to replace the indifferent *not-A*), says Frye (p. 1,002).

Rooney (1994: 152) has described the body as 'essentialism's great text'. For Goddess feminists the body is a personal sacred text to be read not as 'the essence of woman' thereby endorsing one of phallocentrism's strategies, but as a valued site of knowing for each individual. In this way of thinking the body is not being set in opposition to the mind, and it is not being constructed particularly or necessarily as a gendered entity, or only in so far as women perceive themselves as assigning new positive meanings and values to their female bodies. Embracing the corporeal means attempting 'to reclaim our intellects as well as spiritual and physical needs from intervention by patriarchal concepts', and perceiving physicality 'as part of the divine, our bodies no longer "dirty", our menstrual cycle no longer a "curse"' (Long 1995: 20). As well as being a personal spiritual exercise, this is also a feminist political act.

Just as it is unsatisfactory to position woman in relation to man as not-subject, not-self, absolute Other (*not-A* in relation to *A*), in feminist spirituality Goddess is not God's Other, God's feminine substitute, reversal or counterpart. Just as it is necessary to construct a positive category of woman which is not constituted in relation to man, it is necessary to create a Goddess who is beyond God. For feminist witches 'Goddess' is a political and psychological tool for women seeking liberation and empowerment, but 'she' is a great deal more. 'Goddess' is a metaphor for the entire web of life, incorporating masculine and feminine and all apparent dualisms, contradictions and paradoxes.

Next I address the claims made by those who have criticized the Goddess movement for appropriating archaeology and history for what Wood (1996: 13) calls 'millenarian reconstruction'. Most of the attention has concentrated on the work of archaeologist Marija Gimbutas whose books, as we saw earlier, have been immensely influential within the Goddess movement because of their portrayal of 'Old Europe' as peopled by matrifocal, peaceful, egalitarian societies who worshipped a female deity. Gimbutas has assumed iconic status for both adherents and critics of the Goddess movement: critics point to the many faults in the scholarliness of her work and blame her for encouraging Golden Age theories, while many adherents, but by no means all, treasure and ardently defend her works.[8]

Feminist archaeologists, in particular, have criticized Gimbutas, stating that

> she illustrates material that validates her assertions, rather than presenting reasoned arguments; she uncritically selects objects from scattered sources, regardless of era, geography, or context, eliminating those that do not 'fit'; and she ignores alternative explanations for the images she cites, including ones not at all clearly associated with a Great Goddess.
>
> (Brown 1993: 255)

They are usually unsympathetic to visions of a past pansocietal matristic culture (p. 261) and accuse Goddess feminists of hijacking what are assumed to be goddess figurines for purposes other than academic archaeological study (Hamilton 1996: 284). Indeed, Hamilton (ibid.) believes, 'goddesses have little place in current figurine theory, and are seen as millstones round the necks of feminist archaeologists', who fear being tarred with the same brush as Gimbutas in a discipline which has been slow to admit feminist perspectives.

Lynne Meskell (1995: 74) sees the Goddess movement as another 'fad and fiction' to exploit archaeology, intent on 're-weaving a fictional past with claims of scientific proofs' without aiming for a complete understanding of ancient societies. She deplores the harnessing of a re-created, idealized past to serve a contemporary socio-political agenda, even if it is a feminist one. It is not the goal of the agenda to which Meskell objects, but the Goddess movement's means of achieving it. Meskell implies that it is misguided, or downright dishonest, to claim that archaeological evidence proves that a Goddess was the primordial deity throughout Southern Europe, when in her and many other archaeologists' opinion, the evidence confirms no such thing. She emphasizes that the ancient Mediterranean was not a single cultural unit, that Old European societies may not have been as peaceful and egalitarian as they have been portrayed, and that even if female deities were worshipped, ethnographic evidence shows that in such societies, women may still occupy a low-status position.[9]

I have outlined earlier in this chapter where Goddess feminists sit in relation to these claims. Some, as we have seen, firmly believe that past societies were 'matrifocal' ('matristic' and 'matricentric' are also used) and Goddess-worshipping, however a belief in matriarchal societies is much less prevalent in the movement today than it was ten and more years ago. Despite what many of her critics claim, even Gimbutas (1991: x) herself says that the social order during the Neolithic 'was not necessarily [a] "matriarchy"'. There are others in the movement who have offered a critique of a Gimbutas-style re-creation of the past (Adler 1982, 1989, Spretnak 1982, Goodison 1990, Lunn 1993, Long 1997). A number of the New Zealand witches I interviewed thought matriarchy was a nice, but naïve idea, and emphasized that alongside the positive aspects of ancient societies, there were also negative ones. One woman who has run numerous Goddess workshops in New Zealand told me: 'The goddess cultures in Europe were not "Golden Ages" – this is narrow-minded thinking. We don't want to bring them back again.'

As we saw earlier in this chapter, for quite a number of Goddess feminists it no longer matters whether matriarchies or matrifocal societies existed historically or not: the existence of goddess-worship and societies organized along different lines from those of patriarchy are sufficient to provide inspiration and an originary myth. While the use of the past as a form of mythopoetics by the Goddess movement may be understood by some archaeologists, it is lamented nonetheless because of the loss or transformation of the original contextual meanings which result from such appropriation (Long 1997: 16). This points up the stark difference between the agendas of science (archaeology) and religion (Goddess feminism). Even so, Goddess feminists do not disregard the 'facts' about the past to the extent they are accused of: when a particular scenario is shown to be false, it is reconstructed, for example, in the way that 'matriarchal' has been exchanged in much Goddess discourse for the term 'matrifocal' (although that term is still going too far in most archaeologists' view).

While objecting to Gimbutas's 'monolithic account of "Goddess-oriented Old Europe"', critics unfairly present the movement as a monolithic entity which has produced a single story of the past 'following the authority of Gimbutas' (Conkey and Tringham 1995: 223, 228). Thus a sense of the many differing and dissenting voices within the movement is missing. Reviewing feminist archaeologists' criticisms of Gimbutas, I have to agree with Long that 'interesting and useful though their work is on its own terms, it has been caught up in a sort of contra-Gimbutas fever' (Long 1997: 25–6). Gimbutas has been set up as a straw woman. By dismissing her – and, because she over-stretches some of the evidence and has a high profile in the Goddess movement, she is an easy target – many of her critics seem to believe that they have convincingly and legitimately dismissed the whole idea of belief systems centred on female deities in European Neolithic communities. Others concede that Gimbutas's interpretation can be considered plausible as one possibility within the constraints of the material evidence (Conkey and Tringham 1995: 223).

The familiar criticisms of the Goddess movement – that it fosters essentialism and clings to an erroneous belief in ancient matriarchies – have been recapitulated by Cynthia Eller in *The Myth of Matriarchal Prehistory* (2000). While Eller's argument is not new, it has caused a much greater stir than any created by previous critics, perhaps because Eller has written for a popular audience rather than a strictly academic one, because she has devoted a whole book to her topic, and because she is seen by some as having betrayed a movement which received her earlier book, *Living in the Lap of the Goddess* (1993), well.[10] They probably find the critique in the recent book all the more galling because of the book's tone: Eller frequently seems to be ridiculing the ideas of those she calls 'feminist matriarchalists'. For example, on page 119 we read: 'This proliferation of purported goddess symbols makes it possible to find evidence of goddess worship in virtually every scrap of prehistoric art. Even the simplest of signs can shout "goddess"', and on page 123 we read, 'Feminist matriarchalists have enthusiastically embraced the interpretive scheme that sees the walls of Paleolithic caves plastered with disembodied vulvas'. The book has etched more deeply the division between spiritual feminists and their critics (especially other feminists); it must be hoped that it will also provide a further impetus to anthropological and archaeological research in this area.

The first half of the book details the nature of 'the myth', while the second half presents a case against it, first by looking at ethnographic evidence from contemporary and historical societies and then by considering prehistoric art and architecture. Eller (2000: 104) makes the important point that women's status in living religions with goddesses is not necessarily high or equal to men's, and that 'goddesses are often known to support patriarchal social customs'. Christ (1997: 62) has shown, however, that this happens when the culture of a religion with goddesses becomes patriarchal: goddesses are subordinated (or vilified, demonized or slain) in the society's myths and forced to serve and legitimate the new social order. It may be that when goddesses are observed 'to support patriarchal social customs', they have been made to do so as part of such a historical process (although this would need to be demonstrated on a case-by-case basis).

Eller also makes the point, echoing others' criticisms of Gimbutas, that those who believe that there were matrifocal societies in the past assume 'that a relatively stable set of cross-cultural meanings are attached to femaleness, and in turn to the symbols thought to represent it' which leads them to 'speak as though there were no relevant differences between the essential focus of religion in Siberia in 27,000 BCE and Crete in 1500 BCE' (Eller 2000: 118). Critics of the book have been quick to point out gaps in the evidence presented, material which would lend weight to the counter-claim that there have indeed been societies in which gender arrangements were different from those we are familiar with in patriarchal societies (Dashu 2000, Coleman 2001).[11]

My own disappointment with the book was that the sub-title, 'Why an invented past won't give women a future', which seemed to promise a highly relevant discussion, was dealt with in just a few pages in the book's conclusion. Here Eller argues that nostalgia for a lost past, even if it is a mythical past, 'is rarely functional: or rather, its function is usually escapist' (2000: 183). This is the familiar Marxist argument about the role of religion, and in my research I have not found it to be generally true, as I indicated earlier when discussing feminist witches' political commitment.

I have more sympathy with Eller's next point: that it is faulty reasoning to think that ancient societies' life-styles reveal 'the natural', instinctual way for humans to live or that observing contemporary foraging peoples gives us a window into our own past or lessons for our future. All human cultures are complex constructions (rather than 'natural states') no matter how old or technologically simple they are. But I think that most Goddess feminists now know there was no 'Golden Age', no 'natural', stable, perfect world uncontaminated by inequity, conflict, hardship or any other ill. Nonetheless some find the idea of a matrifocal past an attractive and powerful originary myth (at the very least). It is not ignorant, mistaken faith on their part, but an active, knowing acknowledgement of the power of myth and a deliberate employment of it. And in any case, there is still a great deal to learn about gender arrangements in Neolithic societies. Many Goddess feminists and scholars think that the hypothesis of Goddess-worshipping societies where women held important and revered roles offers the most convincing interpretation of the archaeological evidence as it presently stands. Even Eller

(2000: 14) herself says, 'there is simply no evidence that can *definitively* prove the matriarchal hypothesis wrong' however implausible it is 'to those not already ardently hoping it is true'.

In my view Eller overstates and mislabels the position of those who look to past societies for alternative gender arrangements which position women much more positively. 'Feminist matriarchalist' is an unfortunate and inaccurate term to use, especially when Eller (2000: 12) admits calling women by that term who have explicitly objected to it because of its literal meaning – 'rule by women' – the inversion of patriarchy. She lists substitute terms offered by 'partisans of the myth', including 'matrifocal', 'matricentric', 'partnership' and 'prepatriarchal', but says they haven't gained currency or are, in the case of 'prepatriarchal', too vague. It is incomprehensible how 'partnership' and 'prepatriarchal' could be regarded by Eller as equivalent terms for 'matriarchy'. If 'prepatriarchal' is vague, it is precisely because women in feminist spirituality acknowledge that we do not know all the details of gendered life in past societies, a fact Eller herself acknowledges several times. And 'partnership' is obviously not 'matriarchy'. It is true that terms like 'matrifocal', 'gylany' and 'matricentric' emphasize the importance of women's roles in these societies, but this is still not 'matriarchy'. When taken to task by Coleman (2001: 249) for inappropriately using the term 'feminist matriarchalists', Eller's (2001: 266) extraordinary reply was, 'Coleman may not like the term I chose, but I had to call these individuals something'. It is as if Eller will not allow Goddess feminists to abandon the extreme term 'matriarchy' for more moderate terms like 'partnership', 'matrifocal' or 'prepatriarchal'.

Eller claims, rightly, that feminists do not need a matriarchal myth to tell us that sexism is bad or to right the wrongs of patriarchy. 'Indeed, there is a respected tradition among liberal social reformers to call for redressing the wrongs of ages, without any concomitant attempt – or any felt necessity – to say that things were ever different' she writes (Eller 2000: 186). True, but we are not only talking about 'liberal social reformers' here. Partisans of this 'myth' are social reformers who belong to a particular religion, and religions have originary myths. The arrival of the Indo-Europeans into southern Europe with their belligerent, god-worshipping patriarchy is Goddess feminism's story of 'the Fall'. It seems likely that the story is part-historical, part-metaphor, part-myth, which is what many, if not most, Goddess feminists would today claim.

'What the movement provides is not a "belief system"', says Coleman (2001: 248), 'so much as a system of valuation that has broken through the male-constructed metaphysic on which Westerners have been raised'. Feminist witches have always acknowledged that their religion is made up, a 're-creation' (Starhawk 1989: 200). Feminist witchcraft is unique as a religion not only because it is being self-consciously created, but also because this fact is openly articulated, heartily celebrated and, at the appropriate moments, deliberately forgotten.

5

RESEARCHING WITCHES

Becoming enchanted

> Feminist participant observation . . . means openness to complete transformation.
>
> (Reinharz 1992: 68)

I had a charmed entry to the world of witches. My early fears about the difficulties of finding and gaining access to groups of witches, about what might happen if they decided part way through that they did not approve of my research, or worse, that they did not approve of me, quickly proved to be unfounded. For about the first year, however, I worried about my position as a feminist researcher in relation to the women among whom I was conducting research, about the intrusion that I was making into their lives, and the inevitability of transforming them into research 'objects' about and from whom 'data' would be collected.[1] I was uncomfortable about constructing myself as subject/writer/knower and the witches as objects/written/known. Indeed Judith Stacey has said that even the most well-meaning feminist research 'places research participants at grave risk of manipulation and betrayal by the ethnographer' (Mascia-Lees *et al.* 1989: 21).

I was concerned about the differential rewards which would come as a result of the research enterprise. I stood, I hoped, to gain sufficient material to write a doctoral dissertation and ultimately a meal ticket; I could not see what the witches had to gain. Later I came to see that it was not my responsibility to decide what or how much the witches might gain from the research. They could work that out for themselves. Later again I began to see that the research act itself had the potential to contribute to the witches' consciousness-raising objectives, one of the basic epistemological principles of feminist research (Cook and Fonow 1986: 5). Given this level of what probably seems like neurotic self-consciousness on my part at the beginning of the research, one that I did not conceal in academic contexts let alone among witches, it perhaps seems a wonder that I continued.

Lewis (1986: 4) has described anthropologists as 'true transcultural transvestites, professional aliens, cross-cultural voyeurs'. Schechner (1982: 80) describes the fieldworker as one who is not at home either in their own or in another culture – an 'in-betweener'. According to these definitions, the role of participant-observer means becoming a mutant or hybrid, belonging wholly to neither society, having to endure the discomfort of belonging nowhere. During a seminar I gave in my university department a few months into the research, I became acutely aware of the awkwardness of the researcher's position. I was asked: 'How do you identify yourself, as a social scientist or as a witch?' I felt I was being prodded to jump off the fence on to the side of social scientists, or on to the side of witches. To land in either camp meant damnation: it seemed better to be an 'in-betweener'.

Later I read that as late as the Middle Ages, the witch was still the *hagazussa*, a being who sat on the *hag*, the fence – yet a being who participated in both worlds (Duerr 1985: 46). Traditionally, then, witches were attributed with the power to be in two places at once. I saw the hag as a useful symbol in relation to my dilemma of belonging nowhere: I could claim to 'sit on the fence' between the two worlds of academia and witchcraft, and at the same time inhabit and participate in both worlds.

This business of drawing boundaries, of where to locate the 'other' and where the ethnographer, has been central to an important debate among anthropologists since the mid-1980s. It is now widely accepted that anthropologists need to present their own actions and reactions in the field context as part of the data to be analysed. The ethnographer is no longer privileged with the special status of an omniscient, invisible spectator who reports on the 'natives' to those at home. Of course the visible presence of the researcher in the text along with those being researched does not mean their identities merge. The sense of otherness is retained and is reciprocal. 'Ethnography encounters others in relation to itself while seeing itself as other' (Clifford and Marcus 1986: 23).

The ethnographer's job, according to Strathern (1987: 288), is to 'translate another's experience through his or her own and then render experience in the written word'. The anthropologist's experiences 'are the lens through which others of his or her own society may achieve a like understanding'. Paradoxically, however, the self can be consciously used as a vehicle for representing the 'other' only if the self breaks with its own past (p. 289). Ruby (1982: 30) also refers to this dilemma: 'In one sense the success of ethnographers is measured by how well they can become not themselves, while at the same time retaining the original identity'.

This paradox invokes the classic dilemma – or classic conceit – of the participant-observer. Traditionally anthropologists have gone to extreme and sometimes painful lengths to make themselves as thoroughly 'native' as they can, believing this will help them understand a society 'from the inside'. At the same time, they have believed that a full and proper understanding of the other society requires an objective analysis using the paradigms of social science, and so have retained the privilege of stepping outside the other society when it suited them.

Coming to terms with this movement to and from the research context, along with the issue of personal identity, is often a tricky business for researchers studying contemporary witchcraft. More than many – perhaps most – other researchers, it seems, those who study witches feel obliged, and are required, to publicly nominate their own identity, to position themselves as belonging or not belonging to the modern witchcraft movement. On one hand, like other ethnographers, they must claim that their text reveals what it is like to be an 'insider', a knowledge which comes from long-term, intimate involvement with the community being studied. This claim justifies the legitimacy and strength of their work as anthropologists. On the other hand, they must claim that they are not *really* insiders, that they have not 'gone native', that they are not themselves witches. To fail to make this claim is likely to mean that they will not be taken seriously as scholars, to invite, at the very least, light-hearted ridicule and sideways glances. As Griffin (2000c: 14) has said:

> research in this area has been actively discouraged. One colleague was advised not to put an article she had published on Goddess spirituality into her tenure review file because the topic was 'questionable'. Fundamentalist Christians picketed a presentation she gave on her research. Another was told to take the word 'Goddess' out of the title of a book she was working on, as 'the Goddess was passé.' Funding for doing research into religious and spiritual groups in general is typically hard to come by, unless, of course, these groups are suspected of being dangerous cults threatening to kidnap children or kill themselves and others. Funding for research into Goddess spirituality is especially difficult to obtain.

Given these difficulties, it has been interesting to look at the ways other researchers of modern witchcraft have dealt with the dilemma of how to position themselves in relation to those they have studied. Luhrmann (1989), who wrote the first ethnography about contemporary witches, became immersed in the culture of witchcraft during her fieldwork in England, was initiated into four magical groups, and joined many others in their rituals. Yet she tells us near the beginning of her ethnography, 'I am no witch, no wizard, though I have been initiated as though I were' (p. 18). She interrupts the story of how she became 'hooked' when reading a teach-yourself guide to witchcraft, declaring, 'I never have and do not now "believe" in magic'.

Berger, a sociologist who spent 11 years researching witches in the north-eastern United States, is also quite unequivocal in stating that she did not become a witch in the course of her study. She joined a coven and participated in its rituals for two years, participated in occasional rituals with many other covens, and joined an organization called EarthSpirit Community. Yet Berger asserts in her preface that she did not 'join the religion' herself. 'I tried to make clear to every group I joined and each person I interviewed that I was a researcher, not a Witch,' she writes (1999: xvii). Berger wants to clear up any confusion about her self-identification: 'To some people that I met informally, I did not get a chance to explain that I was a researcher; these may think that I am a Witch, because they have seen me at a number of gatherings and rituals'. Had Berger or Luhrmann been studying witchcraft in an exotic context rather than in their own societies, the kind of context in which academic studies of witchcraft were traditionally conducted, I doubt that either would have felt the same necessity to explicitly distance herself personally from magic and witchcraft by such statements.

Unlike Luhrmann and Berger, Hume, in her book about Australian witches and Pagans, does not shy away from embracing or admitting full 'insider' status – although this 'self' does not permanently eclipse her other selves, including her academic one. Echoing Ruby, Hume (1997: 8) acknowledges the paradox that '*unless* one is willing to forgo one's "original" identity it is not possible to fully acquire, and therefore understand, an identity that is not one's own'. She felt it was necessary to 'let go' her self-identification as teacher, mother, anthropologist and so on in order to fully 'become' a witch, and then, at the appropriate times, step back into her prior roles. She likens these role changes to the daily role-juggling in which we all engage as we move between, for example, our professional and domestic lives.

Occupying the role of 'witch', however, meant for Hume engaging 'in a continual mind battle', an inner monologue of self-examination. While being drawn further into the Pagan world over a five-year period, and gradually modifying her own behaviour and discourse, she nonetheless was able to step outside herself and observe these changes (and register the alarm or incredulity in others as they also noticed changes in her). Among witches Hume sometimes felt she presented herself as 'overly rational, hopelessly academic' (p. 10), while among her academic colleagues she was seen as someone who had 'gone native' and become caught up in New Age nonsense. 'Becoming a witch' was complicated by her constant oscillation between the realities of her informants' world and those of academia (p. 11). This is the condition of the in-betweener.

In her study of English witches, Greenwood (2000a) also discusses the perennial anthropological dilemma of being simultaneously an 'insider' and 'outsider', and needing to marry the objective and the subjective perspectives. Sometimes she felt she occupied two worlds at once, an experience which produced feelings of schizophrenia. Yet in Greenwood's view, an anthropologist wanting to understand magic must open his or her subjective self to experience 'the otherworld' (pp. 12–14). Unlike Hume, however, who was also highly reflexive in her engagement with witches, Greenwood felt she could 'never totally become a magician' (p. 15) because it was impossible to switch off the constant academic questioning in her mind when she was in the field. Hume's and Greenwood's field experiences were similar in this respect, however Hume seems to have felt that her role as academic researcher did not preclude her from also assuming a role as a witch.

Two sociologists who have written extensively about their position as researchers among witches are Wendy Griffin and Tanice Foltz, who undertook a joint study of American Dianic witches. As feminist researchers interested in the experimental movement in ethnography they have mapped their 15-month research journey in order to reveal the transformation they underwent as they learnt to accept, and were in turn accepted by, the witches. At the beginning of the study Foltz and Griffin took 'peripheral membership researcher roles' in the coven, which enabled them to maintain a certain distance from the witches. As time went on and trust and comfort developed, the witches effectively redefined the researchers' roles to make them much more active. Although they never officially joined the coven, Griffin and Foltz were treated 'like coven sisters' (Foltz 2001: 91). The transformation they experienced was not limited to the field context or the timespan of the research: 'It is clear to us that, as researchers participating in feminist rituals, we created the women we became. As our inner landscapes changed, they colored the way we view ourselves, our research, and the world' (Foltz and Griffin 1996: 325).

A witchcraft researcher whose entry into fieldwork was similar, in some respects (but not in others), to my own is Jone Salomonsen, who studied Starhawk's Reclaiming community in San Francisco. Salomonsen took classes with Reclaiming, became a member of a new coven which grew out of one of the classes, and became increasingly drawn into the Reclaiming community. Salomonsen, however, was from a different culture (Norwegian) from that of the community she was studying, and this contributed to the 'rather reserved attitude' of the witches towards her in the beginning. Some also thought she asked too many questions and a few got tired of 'being around a person who was *also* a continuous observer' (Salomonsen 2002: 23).

Finally she was accepted and the reservations of most people faded. She went through initiation to become a witch in 1994 'primarily for hermeneutical and experiential reasons', an action taken after much soul-searching because she thought it would help her to understand 'the other' more deeply. However, she 'could not do it only for curiosity or for empirical insight', the act had to be consistent with a minimum of her own beliefs and values while not violating her integrity as a theologian (p. 19). There is a good deal of ambivalence in Salomonsen's attitude towards her 'witch' status. She is fully convinced of the importance of becoming an insider and did so for the purposes of research, but is adamant that it did not and should not compromise her status as a scholar. While functioning as a coven member, Salomonsen was always 'on duty' as a researcher; yet, she says, she was always also 'herself', 'an opinionated and compassionate woman, feminist, mother and Norwegian scholar, having no trouble with any of [her] roles' (p. 23). Thus, unlike Hume, Salomonsen claims that she held a number of roles simultaneously, rather than juggling them according to context. Her claim that she had no trouble with any of them, however, is not entirely convincing. She is clearly at least a little concerned that her insider status could have some negative impact on her status as an academic.

Given the way witchcraft is regarded in Western societies, it is scarcely surprising that many researchers studying modern witches have felt it necessary to explicitly deny that they were themselves witches, despite, in some cases, over a decade of intimate involvement in the world of witchcraft. (I acknowledge, however, that these researchers may have genuinely not thought of themselves as witches.) To fail to declare oneself *not* a witch leaves the possibility for suspicion that one *is* a witch, and this is to invite a range of negative responses. I have already noted how academia views the witchcraft researcher. But there is a more worrying response, one which indicates that the 'witch' stereotype of the evil, dangerous woman still lingers in the minds of some, especially some fundamentalist Christians.

In early 2001 I was telephoned by the producer of a current affairs programme and asked to participate in a piece they wanted to do on witchcraft in New Zealand. News of my research had reached him through an American tele-evangelist who was touring New Zealand and alerting churches, among other things, to an insidious danger in their midst – a revival of witchcraft. A video of one such meeting was couriered to me and, to my horror, I saw an enormous picture of myself on a screen – evidence of this creeping evil – with the evangelist standing in front warning his audience about this 'leading New Zealand witch' and 'avowed feminist'. The photograph was one which had appeared shortly before in a small article in the local newspaper about a lecture I was giving on witches at my university's open day. While I was a little amused at being called an 'avowed feminist', I was appalled at being named a 'leading witch' and reeled at the knowledge that slanderous accusations about me were circulating in the country's fundamentalist congregations. (The newspaper had certainly not described me this way, but had referred to me as an academic researcher.) My horror at being called a 'witch' was related to the context in which the 'accusation' was being made and the damnation it intended. The experience made it very clear that the witch (and even the witchcraft researcher) still provoked fear and hatred, was still seen as a threat to the Church and to Christian society, and was still apparently defined in the same terms as she was 500 years ago – at least in this portion of the community. Unwilling to participate in, and thereby escalate, the evangelist's witch-hunt, I turned down the invitation to appear on the programme with my accuser and the programme was not made.

I was and am happy, however, to accept the label of 'avowed feminist'. Feminist research, Harding (1987) states, places women, their experiences, needs, demands and interpretations at the centre of the research's focus, while, at the same time, locating the researcher as a subject in the research field. It is concerned quite explicitly 'with feminism's political goal of changing the power relationships which underlie women's oppression' (Mascia-Lees *et al.* 1989: 32). For the feminist researcher, the political goals of her research are essentially aligned with the political goals of her research participants. Research on women, Dorothy Smith argues, must start 'with women as they experience the world, . . . with the world seen through their eyes and not with how the observer sees the world of women, as if they were laboratory objects' (Farganis 1986: 57). The ideal is not to achieve an objective and impartial stance. The feminist researcher abandons the oppositional stance of *looking at* women and takes up a position alongside women *looking with* them at their world. The emphasis is shifted away from describing them in their world to describing the world as they see it. 'Feminist methodology,' state Cook and Fonow (1986: 9), 'rejects the assumption that maintaining a strict separation between researcher and research subject produces a more valid account'.

In order to be able to represent the world as witches see it, I have tried consciously to see the world this way myself. This has been surprisingly easy. I found that I already shared many of witches' beliefs and values: their broadly liberal politics, their feminist perspective, their concern for the environment and their interest in spirituality. Rather than exchanging one worldview for another, it felt as if I was extending my repertoire of ways of looking at the world. While there were aspects of their beliefs and practices that did not interest me personally or about which I felt sceptical (for example, the use of tarot cards, a belief in the power of crystals, constant reference to 'the energy'), on the whole, I found the witches' worldview attractive. The fact that I shared the same cultural, class and educational background as many of my research participants made it easier to find a vantage point close to my participants from which to try to view the world as they saw it. I would not have proceeded with the research had I seen their beliefs and ritual activities as nonsense.

Like other researchers of modern witchcraft, I have wrestled with the question of how to position myself in relation to the movement. I did not find moving between my everyday world and the world of witchcraft particularly difficult, although at first the latter seemed a great deal more fascinating and exciting than my 'ordinary' life. I doubt that my constant travelling between the world of witchcraft and my everyday life was any more difficult than the to-ing and fro-ing which other women in my ritual group experienced. They all had multiple roles, engrossing jobs and busy lives just as I did. Indeed, in some ways, I had to make fewer mental shifts than they did because I was, at least during the years of doctoral study, thinking and reading about little except witchcraft.

Like Greenwood, Hume and Salomonsen I was always aware of the inner academic voice commenting and questioning during rituals and, like Greenwood (2000a: 15), I occasionally felt 'predatory' as a researcher, especially when I had no opportunity to tell people that I was conducting research (for example, at large Sabbat festivals open to members of many groups). In the early days I sometimes worried about seeming like a fraud or a user among witches, while among academics I was concerned about seeming to have abandoned the 'proper' role of the anthropologist and to have succumbed to an irrational and ridiculous cult.

Over the course of my research I became very familiar with the ways witches see the world, and became conscious of these modes of thinking filtering into my own thinking and influencing my worldview, particularly with respect to their ideas on holism and the sacralization of all life and, of course, women's healing and empowerment. I learnt to think and act like a witch: I became familiar with the moon's cycling and developed a greater sense of connection with nature, I created an altar at home and tried – not very successfully – to meditate. I helped plan and lead rituals and, towards the end of my doctoral studies, began (reluctantly at first) to teach workshops on feminist witchcraft and the Goddess at the invitation of my university's continuing education department.[2] The transformation I experienced was similar to that described by Foltz and Griffin (1996).

I go on now to outline the practical process of my fieldwork. As I stated in chapter one, my first field experience took place when I participated in a continuing education weekend workshop called 'Rites of Passage for Women' in April 1990. This was a perfect beginning. Each of the nine participants on the course was asked to nominate a rite of passage, an important transition or 'gateway' in her life: mine was initiation into fieldwork. Other women's gateways included: success in business (she was a textile artist); freedom from family, financial or health problems; new motherhood; deepening spirituality; and freedom to give up a teaching job to become a full-time artist.

The course was held in a pleasant staff tearoom with windows opening on to bush in the beautiful old stone Clock Tower building at the University of Auckland. The facilitator was a warm, wise, quietly-spoken woman who had a degree in psychology and some shamanic training, and worked as a therapist and group catalyst. Over the weekend we used psychodrama and ritual to work with our rites of passage. The aim was to empower each woman to achieve the goal she had nominated, to make the psychological shifts necessary to see that it was achievable, to identify blocks which needed to be removed and resources required for the goal's achievement.

At the beginning of the workshop we were each invited to tell the group our reasons for wanting to participate. When it was my turn, I explained that I had chosen to write my doctoral thesis on feminist witchcraft/Goddess spirituality and that I also had a personal interest in this form of spirituality. This was accepted and greeted with interest and encouragement. At the end of the workshop, two of the women invited me to join a ritual group they were starting. Delighted, I met for several rituals with these women along with some of the others who had participated in the workshop, but the group folded when one of the initial pair moved overseas and no one else took the initiative to organize another ritual.

Shortly afterwards I attended a series of workshops on feminist ritual-making which ran for six Thursday evenings from the home of the facilitator (a different woman). I wrote to the facilitator prior to the beginning of these workshops telling her of both my academic and personal interests in the course and seeking permission to attend. She replied warmly welcoming my interest and participation. While it was wonderful to be accepted so readily by the facilitator, I did have qualms about turning up at the workshop and announcing to the other participants that I was a researcher, albeit one with a personal interest in feminist spirituality as well. I knew they would not be counting on a researcher being present, and it seemed unfair to present them with the fact once they were already paid-up members on the course. With these misgivings and somewhat nervous, I decided to explain my situation to the group on the first night, and also assure them of my intention to participate fully in all rituals. If there was the slightest hint of an objection from anyone, I would willingly leave.

I explained my situation to the group and there was no problem.[3] At the conclusion of this series of workshops, the group had bonded strongly and enjoyed the ritual work together. Most women were keen to continue meeting. It was decided that those who wanted to form an on-going ritual group should put their names and telephone numbers on a list. I added my name to the list, wondering if I would be welcome in the on-going group given my additional researcher role. At this stage, however, no one wanted to take on the responsibility of organizing the new group's first meeting, so the plans to form a group were put on hold. I was disappointed and would have been willing to organize a gathering myself, but my researcher status held me back from offering.

At an open Winter Solstice ritual organized by another coven a month after the conclusion of the course, several of us met up again and someone suggested holding a meeting to launch the ritual group. It was clear that I was just as welcome to participate as every other member of the original workshop group. The meeting took place and the fledgling group, with much trepidation and excitement, held its first ritual at new moon on 22 July 1990. I was unable to attend the meeting because of another commitment, but was present at the first ritual.

The group, based in Auckland, has continued to meet for Sabbat rituals, social gatherings and meetings for 13 years. Membership has ranged from ten to 13 women; over the years members have joined and left; three of the original women remain. As well as celebrating all the Sabbats, the group has held rituals to celebrate full and new moons, to bless houses, for members' birthdays, to celebrate the group's birthday and choose a group name, to celebrate a marriage and to mark the death of a flat-mate of two group members. In its early days the group held evenings for wand-making, spell-making, circle-dancing, tarot reading, and shared meals. Each year an AGM is held to plan the year ahead, reflect on the group's direction, renew commitment and provide a context for members to communicate and discuss any concerns. Most of my experience of feminist witches' rituals has been within this group. Throughout the period of my doctoral research I discussed my work with coven members and benefited hugely from their input and unstinting support. I am indebted to all of them for many years of wise and loving advice about both academic and personal matters.

I have also participated in rituals in numerous workshops (as a participant and later as a facilitator) and in large rituals organized by one or other ritual group and open to any women who wished to attend. For two years I belonged to a witches' group in Hamilton, and after finishing my doctorate and moving to Wellington I became involved in many feminist spirituality activities and several ritual groups there. The more involved I became in the movement, the more difficult it became to draw a line between 'doing research' and my everyday life.

During rituals I participated fully, making field-notes only after I arrived home late at night or the following day. I could not have come to understand witches' experiences without participating fully, and, in any case, it would have been improper – in fact, impossible – for me to have made notes during rituals. Spectators are not admitted. As Salomonsen (2002: 17) found, 'in Witches' rituals, covens and classes, there is no outside where an observer can literally put herself . . . You are either in, or you are not there at all.' The only time I made notes in the field was during some workshops when other participants were also taking notes. I was concerned that my behaviour during rituals should not set me apart from other participants or disrupt rituals in any way, even though the other participants knew that I was an anthropologist and occasionally made comments about my 'going home to write all this up'. (My field-notes have contributed importantly to the institutional memory of the ritual group I joined in 1990.)[4]

I wanted to supplement my field descriptions with women's own accounts of their beliefs, feelings and experiences as participants in the movement. To achieve this I interviewed a very small sample of 12 women. Their ages ranged from 21 to early sixties. Half were lesbian and half were heterosexual. Half belonged to the ritual group I joined; the others lived in other parts of the country or had been influential in the movement's development. All were Pakeha,[5] middle-class, well-educated and articulate. I wanted the interviews to be informal, relaxed discussions and so only interviewed women I had come to know reasonably well over a period of time. Finch (1984) discusses how identification between interviewer and interviewee makes for a more relaxed and fruitful interview. Women are more forthcoming when they can 'place' the interviewer. The fact that I self-identified as belonging to the movement and that women knew me undoubtedly contributed to the relaxed nature of interviews. In fact, I think a would-be interviewer who did not belong to the movement would have had a difficult time finding witches willing to be interviewed.[6]

I constructed the following list of themes and questions for discussion in interviews:

- How did you become involved in feminist witchcraft? What attracted you to it?
- Could you talk about the place and value of ritual in your life?
- What is the purpose of ritual? How does magic work? What actually happens?
- How do you get ideas for rituals? Do you do rituals alone as well as in groups?
- Could you talk about your beliefs and worldview?
- Who is the Goddess? What does she mean to you?
- What is the relationship between politics and spirituality for you?
- How do you identify yourself (e.g. ritual-maker, witch, Pagan, something else)?
- What are your feelings about Christianity and other religions? What has been your involvement in other religions, now or in the past?
- What are the attitudes of other people towards your involvement in the movement (e.g. family, friends, colleagues, others)?
- Where do you think/hope the Goddess spirituality movement will lead? Do you think it will grow?
- Do you think this kind of research is worthwhile?
- Is there anything else you regard important that we haven't covered?

I gave each woman the list of questions before the interview to give her time to collect her thoughts and to allow her to take the lead in the interview if she wished. I told women that the questions were intended as starting points for discussion and could be dealt with in any order. Mostly the woman being interviewed held the sheet of questions, talked freely in response to each, and then moved to the next question when she wanted to. I did not interrupt except to clarify or to ask for clarification or elaboration. Some women preferred me to take a more conventional interviewer's role, posing questions for them to answer. Towards the end, interviews became discussions during which we shared ideas and experiences. Sometimes women asked me specific questions and sometimes they pointed out where their beliefs or interpretations differed from mine. At the end of interviews we usually gossiped about shared experiences in workshops and rituals and about our personal lives. Women were later given the opportunity to check, change or censor any part of their transcribed interview.[7] I asked them each to choose a name by which they wished to be known in my writing. These names are: Juliet, Noreen, Megwyn, Sybil, Scarlett, Bonney, Kez, Galadriel, Lea, Joan, Joy and Alex.

I also conducted a group interview with the witches in the coven I joined. They decided how this would work. Before the interview we shared a meal and some social time at the home of two members. Then we sat in a circle in the living room and began the interview in the same way we would begin a ritual. We lit candles, performed a purification, cast the circle, invoked the elements (these aspects of ritual are explained in chapter nine), then passed out the question sheets and turned on the tape recorder. The women decided that they wanted to take the questions one at a time and give each person in the circle an opportunity to respond. This general pattern was used, followed by free discussion in which they commented on one another's responses. The women reported that they found the group interview very interesting and stimulating and suggested getting together again for a similar session.

When I have written and talked about my research findings over the years I have, like any ethnographer, been selective in what I have chosen to discuss. My choices have been determined by my particular interests, a sense of academic responsibility to represent the movement as fully and accurately as I can (while acknowledging that my perspective is necessarily partial in both senses of the word), and a sense of responsibility to the women in the movement to write about what they deem important. There are also aspects of my research that I have not written about because I considered it would be inappropriate to do so. Some things could not be meaningfully translated from the experience of a highly-charged ritual atmosphere to a sheet of paper – an attempt to do so would have misrepresented and reduced the experience. Some things which were said or occurred during rituals were too intimate to be taken outside the ritual context. The ritual space is designated a 'safe space' where women are 'free to be fully themselves' and can trust the confidentiality of other women present. I used my judgement about what was appropriate to record and what I should omit, and checked back with women where I was unsure.

During some rituals and workshops, women exposed highly vulnerable parts of themselves, experienced intense pain, and expressed deeply-felt emotion. I decided it was inappropriate to record these experiences and subject them to analysis in an academic arena and to the scrutiny of an audience outside not only the particular ritual context but also the world of feminist witchcraft. I considered that presenting close-ups of women's pain and expressions of deep emotion would have been voyeuristic and parasitic, and would have dishonoured the 'safe space' of the ritual.

In the process of becoming an ethnographer of feminist witches I also became a native. Moreover, I became a native in much the same way and at the same time as the women with whom I worked most closely over the research period – we took a course on feminist ritual-making together, read a lot about witchcraft, and then started a witches' ritual group. As a member of this new group, I was in the position of helping to construct the phenomenon I wanted to study. This posed a dilemma. I could not set myself apart from other members by becoming a passive observer because feminist covens in New Zealand work through the active, committed participation of all members. On the other hand, if I became very active in decision-making and leading rituals I would be in the unusual – if not farcical – position of fabricating the phenomenon I wished to understand.

I tried very hard to occupy the middle ground between these positions. When I was responsible for planning a ritual with one or two other women, I was always conscious of trying not to be too active or too passive. I suggested ideas and helped to implement others' ideas. I took my turn in doing practical organization. During administrative meetings I contributed ideas but avoided pushing them forcefully. Rituals involve a lot of turn-taking – talking about personal symbols, sharing experiences after guided meditations, performing symbolic acts and so on. Sometimes I waited to go last, occasionally I went first, most often I took my turn somewhere in the middle. Because of my intimate involvement with this close-knit, newly-formed group, it was impossible for me to avoid manipulating the research setting.

This made me feel awkward, especially in the light of exhortations to researchers to avoid such manipulation (for example, Patton 1990: 39). I quote from my field notebook, written nearly two years into the research, my response to thinking about this problem:

> The ritual group's beginning and my joining it were simultaneous – they had no established norms, ways of being together, or ways of doing rituals when I arrived on the scene (although what we learnt in the workshop formed the basic pattern). These were worked out in my presence and with my full participation. I gave them things I had written to read – conference papers and seminars – which must have influenced their thinking about their beliefs and ritual activity, and raised their consciousness about what they were doing. Given this, I cannot claim (not that I do) that this group is 'typical', but it would certainly have been *atypical* had I made my presence felt at the beginning any more than I did by asking a lot of questions. This would have been like hijacking (or kidnapping?) the group in its infancy. At first I had less involvement – a quieter role. I became more and more drawn in, gradually doing more to the point where, after a year, I helped plan and facilitate a ritual to initiate new members.

There were several reasons for the increase of my involvement over time (although I never became more active than other group members). Firstly, I felt the ritual group was sufficiently well established after about a year for it not to be significantly affected by my more active involvement. Secondly, in relation to feminist methodology, I came to see my fuller involvement as sound so long as I shared the women's goals and commitment to the movement. Thirdly, I came to personally value ritual more and *wanted* to become more active. There were times during the research when I was impressed with the irony of my 'native' status – in particular, on occasions when new witches were initiated or when the group said farewell to a member who was leaving. In these instances my 'native' or 'insider' status in the group either pre-dated or was more enduring than that of some of my research participants.

The overall structure of my fieldwork experience in some ways resembles the structure of ritual as van Gennep (1960) and Turner (1974a) have famously described it. First there was the initial 'separation' phase when I was intensely self-conscious about issues of self-identification and belonging both within and outside the research context: I had begun the research process but was not yet 'at home' with witches. Next I entered the liminal phase of the research; I was an 'in-betweener' learning the special knowledge of 'insiders' and how to think and act like a native. Finally I completed the research and shed my researcher role.

Other anthropologists have also drawn a comparison between the process of doing fieldwork and the ritual process. Lewis (1986: 5) writes:

> As a number of anthropologists have noticed, and none more perceptively than Rosemary Firth, we see here the familiar tripartite structure common to most transition rituals. In the first phase, the neophyte prepares to surrender his old status and to shed ethnocentric assumptions. In the second 'liminal' phase, he retires to learn the new culture of his hosts. In the third phase, he re-emerges to be readopted within his own academic culture in a new role as professional anthropologist.

As for other neophytes who emerge from a rite of passage, my point of exit from the research is different from my point of entry: I have formed many new friendships, my ways of understanding and dealing with difficult situations have altered, my feminist political stance is stronger and my 'green' consciousness has been raised. The 'field' is now part of the landscape of my life. I have learnt new ways of seeing the world.

6

FEMINIST WITCHCRAFT IN NEW ZEALAND

Origins and development

> I once dreamt of a world, other than the one I know . . . a place where I would be welcomed, accepted and respected, where my experience would be heard and valued, where I would share freely with women all that is woman-in-me . . . a place where, after a long journey, I would be welcomed with a kiss, a warm embrace and a gift of wild jasmine, symbol of my belonging and of our deep connection with each other.
>
> (*Women's Spirituality Newsletter*, no. 16, 1989)[1]

In the introduction to this book I noted that throughout the 1980s and 1990s feminist witches were more visible and numerous in New Zealand than other kinds of witches or Pagans. This situation has changed in the last five years or so, and there is now evidence – through publications,[2] festivals, gatherings and web-sites – that the wide range of forms of Paganism that one sees in, for example, Britain, America and Australia is now also present, or at least more visible, in New Zealand. Because of the specific focus of my research and this book, I confine my attention here to the origins and development of feminist witchcraft/Goddess spirituality in New Zealand and give a general profile of the movement and its adherents.

When I began seeking the origins of feminist witchcraft in New Zealand, I assumed that the North American movement, following its own dramatic birth at the end of the 1960s and rapid growth in the decades since, was the New Zealand movement's natural parent. Famous American witches are quoted frequently by New Zealand witches and most of the sizeable literature on the subject available in New Zealand comes from the US. The format for rituals set out in American books is followed by many New Zealand witches; invocations, chants and spells are sometimes borrowed from them; and the important beliefs, values and few rules[3] of the craft are noted.

While it is true that this literature and the American movement's influence have played a major part in the growth of the movement in New Zealand, the latter's beginnings cannot be attributed quite so simply to a straightforward diffusion from the United States. Even more clear is that the early development of feminist witchcraft in New Zealand was separate from the development of Gardnerian Wicca and other forms of neo-Paganism in the country. Quite a number of women I talked with said that they began working alone with ritual, experimenting with spells and exploring the Goddess before or about the same time that books such as Christ and Plaskow's *Womanspirit Rising* (1979), Starhawk's *The Spiral Dance* (1979) and Budapest's *The Holy Book of Women's Mysteries* (1980, first published as *The Feminist Book of Lights and Shadows* in 1975) were published. Women's points of entry into the movement varied considerably – from exploring feminist art-making, to discovering lesbianism, to sensing a strong affinity with nature, to a childhood fascination with witchcraft, to Christian feminism.

Among women's stories of how they came to be involved in feminist witchcraft, there were no tales of blinding revelation or instant conversion.[4] For many women the path to Goddess spirituality had been a long personal quest for a satisfactory religion or spirituality or a desire for meaningful rituals unframed by a patriarchal religious context. Not only were some of these women unaware of the newly flourishing movement in the United States at the time they were beginning to explore ritual-making, but they were also unaware that other New Zealand women were involved in similar activities and quests. The origins of feminist witchcraft in New Zealand lie in the diverse, uncoordinated and often solitary ritual activity of women during the late 1970s, making it difficult to gain a clear or coherent picture of the movement's beginnings. One woman I interviewed, Joan, explained the reasons for this:

> It's part of our oral tradition. We don't have the Bible. We don't have the institutions. We don't have the rules. We don't have any of the trappings of other religions. It's not a sect, let alone a religion. It's a will-o'-the-wisp.

When I asked them how they had got the idea of doing their solitary rituals if not through literature or contact with other women, they spoke of a strong inner need and personal enjoyment and fulfilment. Several invoked Rupert Sheldrake's theory of morphic resonance to help explain how apparently isolated women seemed to be spontaneously 'picking up on what was out there'. Sheldrake, a controversial biochemist, visited New Zealand in 1990 and gave lectures in various centres including a weekend retreat at Tauhara Centre in Taupo. According to Sheldrake, ideas and practices acquired by people in one place can facilitate the acquisition of the same ideas and practices by other people distant in time and/or place without any obvious means of connection or communication (Sheldrake 1988: 181). 'Through repetition,' Sheldrake says (p. 198), 'the nature of things becomes increasingly habitual'. Structures of thought and experience contribute to the building up of morphic fields which link a person to the surroundings in which she or he acts. People in other places can tune in to these morphic fields, 'picking up on' distant structures of thought and behaviour. In his books (1988, 1991) Sheldrake quotes numerous experiments carried out by himself and others with plants, animals and humans in support of his theory.[5] In *The Rebirth of Nature: The Greening of Science and God* (1991), Sheldrake espouses a worldview which extends Lovelock's 'Gaia hypothesis',[6] a view which is extremely attractive to Pagans. It is easy to understand why Sheldrake's work, with its emphasis on the influence of unseen forces and energy fields, appeals to women who describe their rituals as 'working with energy', and who frequently talk about 'tuning into', 'tapping', 'channelling', 're-setting' and 'grounding' energy.

For women who find Sheldrake's work convincing, the theory of morphic resonance provides part of the explanation for why isolated women in New Zealand began to work spontaneously with ritual about the same time as each other and, apparently, about the same time as women in the US and elsewhere. It also provides a theoretical base for women's belief that in performing rituals they are connecting with women – including the wise women/healers of 500 years ago and the priestesses of the Goddess of 5,000 years ago – who performed similar rituals long ago. One woman I interviewed, Bonney, said:

> I think that ritual can lay the conditions for the Goddess to be with us and for the wisdom of the ages to be with us. I believe very strongly in this morphic resonance thing. I heard the lecture by Rupert Sheldrake at Waikato University last year. He said that when Buddhist monks today enact the same rituals that Buddhist monks have used for thousands of years, they can bring into their presence the knowledge and the wisdom and the life experiences of the monks who did it back then. They are drawn by the incense, by the smells, by the incantations and by the receptivity. There's a base there that you can establish to resonate with the past, with the ancestral wisdom that you're drawing on.

She went on to say that, like contemporary Buddhist monks, contemporary witches may be able to connect with women's ancient wisdom and power through ritual.

None of the women I spoke to attributed the development of the movement in New Zealand wholly to morphic resonance: its spread is also seen as a natural evolution within the women's movement, and as a result of diffusion through literature and through women talking together informally. Whatever the role of morphic resonance in the movement's origins, it is clear that New Zealand was not virgin territory into which the movement was imported from the United States. Since the late 1970s at least some women had been working on their own and in small groups, and by the early 1980s, when news and literature about the movement began to flow into New Zealand from the US, the stage was well set for the development of a New Zealand movement.

As well as the embryonic witches, there were other women in New Zealand towards the end of the 1970s who were exploring new ways of imaging the divine and devising new religious rituals. These were Christian feminists. Many of them are still Christian feminists, but some have left their churches to join covens or feminist ritual groups. In her chapter in *Religions of New Zealanders* (1990), Benland includes under the 'Women's Spirituality' umbrella both Christian and neo-Pagan women. In doing so, she is emphasizing the antipathy both groups of women feel towards male-dominated religions and their determination to embrace a spirituality which affirms their womanhood. Despite their identification as 'Christian', Benland says, Christian feminists often feel they have more in common with neo-Pagan feminists than with fellow members of their own churches.

However, I think that portraying Christian feminism and neo-Paganism as two branches of the one movement suggests a closer relationship between the two than actually exists. Christian feminists and neo-Pagans share many of the same beliefs and values and may share comfortably in the same rituals, but they have ultimately different preoccupations. Christian feminists' chief concern seems to be women's status and roles within the Church and with transforming the oppressive patriarchal structure of the Church. They often see themselves as a rebellious, marginalized, even unwelcome minority in their individual churches, yet essentially as still belonging within the Christian community. It may well be that the Christian feminist, perceiving an oppositional relationship between her views (and perhaps herself) and those of the male-dominated Church hierarchy (and perhaps most Church members), feels closer to neo-Pagan women because she knows they, too, are in this position. However, the relationship between the Christian feminist and unsympathetic Church members is still *contained within* the Christian community, however marginalized within that community she may feel. Witches, on the other hand, see no point in wasting more effort on an institution which, in their view, has already exacted two millennia of misery from women.

There are some women who straddle both camps as committed members of both covens and churches, but they are few and they tend to be more publicly open about their Christian identity than their witch identity. One member of a neo-Pagan ritual group was not prepared to talk about her ritual activities because of the difficulties she feared this might cause for her marriage and church life – her husband was a Presbyterian minister. Her fears are probably justified. Another woman, ordained within the Church and a member of a neo-Pagan ritual group, has been the victim of witch-hunting which has exposed the fear and hatred the Church still feels for witches and has caused an upheaval in her professional life.

It has to be said that many feminist witches still feel considerable antipathy towards Christianity, although this is certainly not directed at individual Christians, and least of all at feminists in the Church. My impression is that, more than anything else, witches are astonished at the patience, determination and fortitude of Christian feminists who manage to follow their own spiritual path while struggling to transform the Church from the inside. One of the neo-Pagan women I interviewed spoke of her great respect for Christian women's outspokenness on ethnic and environmental issues and felt that neo-Pagan women could do more in this respect. Witches' antipathy is directed at the Church as an institution which, they believe, has historically devalued, silenced, punished and, during the witch-craze, murdered women.

Interestingly, Christian feminists seem more open to neo-Paganism and feminist witchcraft than witches are to Christianity. They are almost as likely as witches to own a wand, wear a 'Crone' badge, invoke the Goddess, know some circle dances, and have read Mary Daly and Starhawk. They may attend open rituals organized by neo-Pagan groups to celebrate the Solstices and meet together to create their own rituals. One of these, which occurred during the third National Ecumenical Feminist Women's Conference held in Christchurch in September 1988, is described by Benland and in the Resource Book which was published after the conference.[7] The women, Christian and neo-Pagan together, formed a circle on a lawn around a large fishbowl filled with red wine symbolizing menstrual blood and, for the Christian women, communion blood. The priestesses were the oldest and youngest women present – a crone in her eighties and a 19-year-old maiden. Women talked about their feelings about the symbolic wine/blood in small groups and then, one at a time, went up and dipped small rags in the 'blood' and pinned the rags to their clothing. After this they danced a spiral dance chanting, 'We are the flow, we are the ebb. We are the weavers. We are the web of life!' This chant is commonly used in feminist witches' rituals.

Since the early 1980s the small amount of media coverage modern witchcraft in New Zealand has attracted has almost all been remarkably free of sensationalism and has gone to pains to point out that modern witches do not conform to the familiar negative witch stereotype. Back in 1985, for example, a lead article in the *Listener* (8–14 June) by Bruce Ansley titled 'Witchcraft: women's rites' presented interviews with two Christchurch witches and went on to give a reasonably sound introduction to feminist witchcraft. More recently the *Sunday Star-Times* (7 May 2000) sympathetically reported the difficulties a witch in Hamilton experienced when she tried to rent premises owned by Environment Waikato for her New Age shop Forever Now. The local council was concerned that some ratepayers could be offended by the shop and suggested that the witch was not a 'respectable' tenant, whereupon the witch filed a complaint with the Human Rights Commission claiming her character had been defamed and that she had suffered discrimination on account of her religion. The article went on to explain what modern witchcraft was really about.

When Zsuzsanna Budapest visited New Zealand in 1996 to run workshops on witchcraft, the *Sunday Star-Times* (11 February 1996) gave her a substantial write-up, attempting to illuminate readers about the craft and including a spell from Z's book *The Goddess in the Office*. Similarly, when New York lawyer and high priestess Phyllis Curott visited New Zealand to promote her *Book of Shadows*, the *Star-Times* (4 July 1999) gave her almost a full page, and when Titania Hardie visited from Britain to promote *Hocus Pocus*, her book of spells, *The Dominion* (23 June 2000) did an excellent job of explaining modern witchcraft. The only negative media coverage of witchcraft I have come across was in a Sunday tabloid, *New Truth*, whose lead article on 29 May 1992 warned readers about 'a frightening move being orchestrated from a house in Helensville', which turned out to be the home of someone who had advertised in the *Green Dollar Exchange* newsletter for members to join the Auckland Pagan Fellowship.

A handful of books on feminist spirituality and ritual-making have been published by New Zealand authors, and a number of unpublished MA theses in various disciplines from several universities have been completed.[8] Juliet Batten's books *Power from Within: A Feminist Guide to Ritual-Making* (1988) and *Celebrating the Southern Seasons: Rituals for Aotearoa*[9] (1995) are extremely popular books among witches and non-witches interested in creating rituals attuned to the New Zealand landscape and seasons. *Power from Within* was written especially for New Zealand women and provides an introduction to the meaning and importance of ritual. It sets out a process for creating rituals in seven stages (along the lines of those set out in Starhawk's *The Spiral Dance*), includes sections on trance, chanting, music, dance, magic, invocations, goddesses, symbols and ritual equipment, gives suggestions for how to form a ritual group, and sets out 'The Wheel of the Southern Year' charting the eight Pagan seasonal celebrations as they fall in the southern hemisphere (discussed further in chapter nine). (The numerous books from the UK and US which set out 'The Wheel of the Year' all gear their dates to the northern hemisphere.) Many New Zealand witches and followers of Goddess spirituality own a well-thumbed copy of *Power from Within* and refer to it constantly when preparing rituals.

Celebrating the Southern Seasons, which was intended for a wider audience than a strictly Pagan one, brings together Celtic and Wiccan myths and traditions with Maori traditions and rituals in relation to the seasonal calendar.[10] While wanting to acknowledge and honour indigenous Maori rituals that, prior to colonization, connected people intimately to their landscape, Batten is also sensitive to the dislocation felt by Pakeha who have been cut off from the seasonal rituals of their European roots. Batten herself became involved in making rituals at the end of the 1970s through her work as an artist. In an interview with me she explained that in the late 1970s she became very interested in working with process – partly as a reaction against Judy Chicago's preoccupation with the art product.[11] Her first rituals were spontaneously created in the context of this work with process, initially performed alone on the beach at Te Henga (Bethell's Beach on Auckland's west coast), and later in collaborative art projects with groups of women. She introduced ritual because 'the works seemed to be calling for it'. Notably Batten had not at this stage read *The Spiral Dance* or any of the other early books on feminist ritual-making from the US. She describes her response when, later, she did read these books:

> Like so many feminist ritual-makers in this country, I have been inspired by the writings of modern North American witches, Starhawk and Z Budapest in particular. But theirs is a very different land from ours; the seasons are reversed and even the sun goes round the sky in another direction. Their stars are not our stars. I longed for something relevant to my experience as a Pakeha woman of Aotearoa. In the end, I realised I would have to write it myself.
>
> (Batten 1988: 1)

She emphasizes that her aim is not to be prescriptive or limiting in her suggestions for what to do during rituals:

> Because I would like everyone to be able to take that power from within and to create their own rituals, the book takes a very practical line. My aim was to share what I have learned about process, to toss out ideas, to stimulate, but not to inhibit anyone from providing their own content. Too much delineation of what any one ritual should look like can dampen the creative spirit.
>
> (ibid.)

Batten's encouragement to women to be creative when devising rituals, and the fact that she has, since 1984, taught ritual classes to many hundreds of women around the country, have contributed to a trend whereby women's ritual groups in New Zealand seem less likely to follow strict Wiccan forms, including set invocations and actions, than those in other countries (although it needs to be acknowledged that feminist witches' rituals everywhere tend to be more creative and less formal than traditional Wiccan rituals). Most groups in New Zealand do, however, use the basic structure suggested by Batten and North American writers; beyond this they create their own words and actions or mix their own ideas with ideas borrowed and adapted from books (discussed further in chapter nine). In more recent years Batten has become interested in creating rituals which include men and children, saying: 'For years we concentrated on doing it just for women because we needed to build our spiritual power and reclaim it. Now it's so strong it doesn't matter who we do the rituals with, because we are holding our power' (Kearney 1997: 124).

Another book which many women have told me they have found moving and inspirational is Céline Kearney's *Faces of the Goddess: New Zealand Women Talk about their Spirituality*. In this book Kearney presents the stories of her own and 13 other women's spiritual journeys based on a series of interviews she conducted. The book includes Maori and Pakeha women, only some of whom would self-identify as 'witch' but all of whom are located outside 'mainstream religious institutions'. One of the women is Noreen Penny, who has been active for more than 20 years in the development of feminist ritual groups in the Canterbury region, and who in 1994 published a book titled *Women's Rites: An Alternative to Patriarchal Religion*. The book tells the stories of women who have been involved in a Goddess spirituality group which Penny helped start in 1981 and from which other groups have since developed. Another privately published book is Helen Heliotrope's *God and Goddess in Conflict* (1999), which gives a detailed exposition of the scientific ideas, such as those of quantum physics, which underlie the neo-Pagan worldview and contrasts this perspective with that of 'God religion'.

The best printed source of information about Goddess spirituality in New Zealand is the *Women's Spirituality Newsletter*. The *Newsletter* was begun early in 1985 by Lea Holford and the ritual group of 11 women to which she belonged. It has come out four times a year (on the Solstices and Equinoxes) since then. The *Newsletter* has, in recent years, been edited and distributed by a woman from another ritual group, is available only on subscription, and has 110 subscribers spread throughout the country. The *Newsletter* is designed to help women network, offer ideas for rituals, provide a forum for women to discuss spirituality and share their personal experiences with ritual, give notice of upcoming ritual events and workshops, and offer space for book reviews, articles, poetry, artwork and advertisements.

A vast variety of rituals has been described in the *Newsletter* over the years: for blessing a baby and for letting go a child leaving home; for honouring menstruation and for emerging through menopause; for blessing a new home and for saying farewell to a home; for peace during the Gulf War and to honour the Treaty of Waitangi,[12] for birthdays and funerals and of course Sabbat celebrations. The *Newsletter* contains notices and advertisements about all manner of Pagan and feminist activities, products, books, exhibitions, workshops, festivals and retreats. It has had an important role in the development of a sense of community among neo-Pagan women, initially by making them visible to each other (although not to New Zealand society in general). Various other magazines and newsletters have emerged at various times, but none has survived as long as the *Newsletter*.[13]

While New Zealand seems full of witches when you know where to look, the phenomenon of feminist witchcraft is less well established and probably less visible in New Zealand than it is in the United States. Such comparisons are hard to make, however, because of the enormous differences in population sizes. New Zealand witches hold gatherings, open rituals, festivals and retreats, but they are usually relatively small (fewer than 100 women), and regionally based. There have not been the large-scale, media-drawing, political protests, nor the large, regular conferences and festivals that have taken place in the US, Britain and Australia (although these tend to be mostly for Pagans and witches generally, rather than for feminist witches specifically).[14]

Occasionally larger festivals for women have taken place in New Zealand. Benland (1990: 244) describes a 'Wise Woman Within' festival held at Tauhara, Taupo, in 1988:

> Well over a hundred attended including some workshop leaders from overseas. The festival was to 'explore, nurture and celebrate the many aspects of our "wise woman", sharing through circles, sacred dance, song, play, workshops, good food, magic, miracles, and celebration; to explore together our journeys, the Goddess within, herstories and histories, spirituality, feminine theology, Papatuanuku Earth Mother links and nature knowledge, mysticism and witchcraft, creativity and expression, abundance, wisdom, visions, dreams and challenges'.

On the whole, in New Zealand there is still relatively limited physical contact between ritual groups, especially between groups geographically distant from one another (Auckland and Christchurch, for example). Apart from at open rituals – mostly held for Winter and Summer Solstices – members of different groups have few opportunities to meet each other in a ritual context. They may meet at workshops – 'Divinely Dangerous Dance' or 'Celebrating Woman Spirit', for example – but many of the women who attend these workshops do not belong to existing groups; some attend because they are looking for a group to join. Workshops, especially those explicitly about ritual-making, are seen as providing a structured, informative introduction to Goddess spirituality where there is no pressure for commitment or further involvement. One woman told me she took a ritual course because she wanted to 'dip her toe in the water'.

Often, as in the case of the group I joined, women who have attended a workshop together want to continue to meet once the course is over, and decide to form a new group. Workshops are led by a growing number of New Zealand women and, occasionally, by an overseas facilitator.[15] None of those who have taught Goddess classes has achieved, or sought, the status of those prominent in the movement in the US, although Juliet Batten and Lea Holford are very well known and respected, particularly in Auckland, because they have introduced so many women to feminist ritual-making through their classes held in the 1980s and 1990s.

Unlike other religious groups and organizations in New Zealand, the feminist witchcraft movement, and the neo-Pagan movement generally, have no national leaders, spokespeople, gurus, or centralized organization. The movement is explicitly against the creation of gurus, higher authorities and 'power over' structures, instead emphasizing the importance of each woman – or person – discovering the divine in herself and 'power from within'. The movement is not neatly bounded – as I have noted, there are women who identify both as witch and Christian, and others who are atheist and detest any form of Christianity. There are those who have sampled and abandoned eastern religions and those who are still very involved in Buddhism, Sufism and various forms of meditation. Some women do not belong to a coven but define themselves as feminist witches, hold similar beliefs to those in groups, and mostly perform their rituals alone. Women who are 'solitaries' may be so because they prefer this, because they cannot find a group to join, or because they do not want to give the time and commitment group membership requires.

In so far as the neo-Pagan movement in New Zealand is an amorphous, loosely-connected group of people, it reflects the movement in England of which Luhrmann (1989: 32) writes: 'It is a floating, ill-defined collection of people, practices and organizations'. In New Zealand I would guess that there are several thousand women who are on the fringe of the Goddess movement. They may occasionally attend an open ritual or a ritual organized by a friend for a special event (like a birthday), and they may have attended a workshop or two. They are sympathetic to witches' beliefs and values, but they do not self-identify as 'witches' or even as belonging to the movement.

It is very difficult to estimate the number of women who self-identify as belonging to the feminist witchcraft or Goddess spirituality movement in New Zealand. In Auckland alone Lea Holford and Juliet Batten have each had several hundred women pass through their classes, and of course workshops have also been run by a number of other women in Auckland and in many other parts of the country for nearly 20 years. Not all women who have attended workshops, of course, would now identify as being part of the movement, and many who do say they belong have not attended a workshop. Only 110 women subscribe to the *Women's Spirituality Newsletter*, but many witches do not subscribe, including almost all the women in the ritual group with whom I have kept contact for 13 years.

It is almost impossible to estimate the number of women's ritual groups or covens in New Zealand. At the time of completing my doctoral thesis in 1993 I figured that there were perhaps 30 to 35 groups throughout the country. Some of these have since folded and other new groups have begun. In the 2001 New Zealand census 5,862 people identified as Pagan, of which 2,196 said they were Wiccan. These numbers might be expected to be conservative given many people's probable reluctance to identify as Pagan or witch on an official form. Taking all this into account, my rough estimate of the number of women who identify as belonging to the Goddess movement in New Zealand is about 5,000. I would think considerably fewer than this number would also self-identify as feminist witch, and there are probably fewer than a thousand women who currently belong to a feminist ritual group or coven. (I am not counting explicitly Christian feminist groups or Wiccan covens.)

Women involved in the Goddess movement are overwhelmingly Pakeha, middle-class, well-educated and urban-dwelling. These tend to be the women who can afford the time and money to attend workshops and buy books about their religion.[16] Many of the workshops during the 1980s and 1990s were run through continuing education departments in universities, so women attending them needed to be comfortable in a university environment, and many already held a university degree.[17] With respect to its socio-economic profile, the New Zealand Goddess movement is similar to the neo-Pagan movement generally in the United States and England (Adler 1986; Luhrmann 1989; Orion 1995; Berger 1999).

Luhrmann (1989: 29) regards the fact that most covens in England are city-based as predictable given that there are many more opportunities in, for example, London to become involved in Pagan activities. The denser population means there are more groups which create more ritual activity and a larger sympathetic audience. Living in a city gives Pagans access to bookshops which sell books on various forms of Pagan religion. In New Zealand, too, Auckland has many more witches than anywhere else and this can be attributed to the fact that Auckland has by far the greatest population density in New Zealand, and that this is where interested women have the greatest access to workshops, open rituals, and bookshops selling books about magical practice.

Christchurch also has a relatively large number of women involved in feminist spirituality, and this relates to the fact that an early ritual group was established there in 1981 after a women's spirituality conference was held in Christchurch. The woman who was largely instrumental in launching this group, Noreen Penny, the author of *Women's Rites: An Alternative to Patriarchal Religion*, has been very active in helping women network over many years.

Luhrmann (1989: 29) also makes the point that in England 'many practitioners . . . became interested in magic and paganism and moved to the country as a result'. This is also true in New Zealand – in the groups I have worked with a number of women have moved to the country over the years, either commuting or exchanging high-powered professional jobs in the city for jobs which enable them to live more in tune with nature (but which are also very busy and challenging).

The occupations of women involved in Goddess spirituality reflect the movement's middle-class bias; there are many highly-qualified professional women and, as one might expect, many work in those fields traditionally assigned to women: health and education. While doing my doctoral fieldwork in the early 1990s, I collected a small sample of 100 occupations of women who attended Goddess workshops; just over half worked in the broad areas of health and education as nurses, doctors, counsellors, therapists, herbalists, homeopaths, naturopaths, health administrators, pharmacists, childbirth educators, university lecturers, students and schoolteachers. Among the rest, artists, art students and art teachers featured most significantly. Only seven women were full-time mothers.

This profile differs in one significant respect from the occupational profiles offered by Adler and Luhrmann for neo-Pagans in the United States and England. Adler (1986: 446) reports in the United States

> an amazingly high percentage in computer, scientific, and technical fields . . . Out of 195 answers, 28 people or roughly 16 percent were either programmers, technical writers, or scientists – and I'm not even counting the lab technicians or the students who said they were studying computer programming.

Luhrmann found similarly that in England a high proportion of witches worked in computers. She says (1989: 99) 'if any profession predominates, it is the computer industry' with perhaps one or two out of every ten witches she met working in this field. She suggests that the most important reason for this may be that

> both magic and computer science involve creating a world defined by chosen rules, and playing within their limits. Both in magic and in computer science words and symbols have a power which most secular, modern endeavours deny them. Those drawn to the symbol-rich, rule-governed world of computer science may be attracted to magic.
>
> (p. 106)

Only one of the 100 women's occupations I recorded was in the computer industry. However both Adler's and Luhrmann's research included male and female witches, and they were not dealing specifically with Goddess or feminist groups. Women in these groups are much less likely to be drawn to the movement by a symbol-rich 'world defined by chosen rules'. I found, in contrast with Adler's and Luhrmann's findings, that an unusually high proportion of New Zealand participants in the Goddess movement are artists. This is probably because many have attended classes run by Lea Holford and Juliet Batten, both of whom encourage women to be extremely creative in their ritual-making: to work intuitively, choose their own symbols, give their own meanings to symbols, create their own altars or centre-pieces for rituals, write their own invocations, make up their own methods of initiating new group members, and so on. Hume (1997: 161) also notes that many Australian

Pagans are 'creative and artistic' and Orion's study of American neo-Pagans' occupations found a high proportion of artists; it formed the second largest category after 'helping and healing' (Orion 1995: 66). Computer-related occupations ranked third in her study (10 per cent compared with 16 per cent in Adler's American study).

Like the feminist spirituality movement in America described by Eller (1993: 18), the movement in New Zealand has a high proportion of lesbian members. The ritual group I joined in Auckland has always had a majority of lesbian women, and I know of other groups with similarly high proportions (including the group I was a member of in Hamilton for two years). There are, however, also groups comprising only or mainly heterosexual women – this was the case with the group I worked with in Wellington. I would estimate that perhaps a third of feminist witches in New Zealand identify as lesbian or bisexual. Benland (1990: 242) mentions the high proportion of lesbians in the movement and notes that 'lesbians are usually unwelcome in patriarchal religions'. The lesbian witches I spoke to said they left the Church not so much because they felt personally rejected or unwelcome but because they found a male-identified religion in which one is required to worship an omnipotent male God alien to their sense of their own spirituality. It is the same reason that many non-lesbian witches give for leaving the Church.

Feminist witchcraft attracts women of all ages, and in any one group there is often a wide spread of ages. Ritual groups greatly value having members in different age groups: younger women are said to bring playful maiden energy while older women bring crone energy and are valued for their wisdom. Occasionally ritual groups hold a 'croning' ceremony to honour a woman who feels she is moving into this phase of her life – 'crone' is a highly esteemed title which women embrace with pride. There have also been croning workshops, where whole groups of women create and enact a special ritual together.[18] While women of all ages participate in the movement, I would estimate, based on my attendance at open rituals and workshops, that it attracts rather more women in their thirties, forties and fifties, thus the age distribution within the movement in New Zealand resembles that in the US (Eller 1993: 18). Many of the women now in their fifties were young women in the early days of the women's movement and have been involved in feminism for over 30 years.

When one sees the high proportion of middle-aged women at open rituals – Winter Solstice at Te Henga, for instance – it is tempting to think that, like feminism itself, feminist spirituality is no longer attracting as many younger women as it was during the 1980s and 1990s. As I was contemplating this in October 2002 I received an e-mail from a young woman student at the University of Auckland asking if she could interview me for a range of projects she was working on in relation to raising public awareness about Goddess religion. She told me she currently runs the Auckland Young Witches Group (which has 47 members, male and female, aged 13 to 24 years) and is very active in her students' association with respect to women's rights.[19] During the university's 'Women's-fest' in 2002 she helped organize an 'Inner Goddess' day. She wants to create a Dianic/feminist witchcraft web-site for young women world-wide and is working on a number of awareness-raising articles on women's spirituality to place in various publications: her student newspaper, two teen magazines and a Pagan magazine.

Only a small proportion of the Auckland Young Witches Group, however, follows a Goddess or Dianic-based practice. My correspondent writes:

> A lot [of young witches] start on the books by Silver Ravenwolf who has done a lot to raise awareness of Wicca among young people . . . Feminist spirituality is harder, I think, for young women to find because it is not often aimed at them, and the 'post-feminism' and anti-feminism attitudes that have become prevalent and acceptable in our society often scare young women off what may be the most wonderful and empowering thing in their lives. Of course that is part of the reason I am so determined to get the Goddess out there in a form that young women can touch.
>
> (e-mail, 27 October 2002)

This e-mail indicates what may be a very interesting turn in the contemporary witchcraft movement in New Zealand. Whereas in the 1980s and 1990s the phenomenon of feminist witchcraft seemed quite separate from Wicca and other Pagan paths and attracted feminist women of all ages, now, in this group at least, followers of a variety of Pagan traditions, including Dianic witches, are coming together for mutual support, but are distinguishing themselves from other witches and Pagans using a different criterion: age. It may well be that if feminism continues to seem stale, unnecessary and alienating to many young educated women, as time goes on feminist witchcraft may transform itself: the role played by feminist politics in the movement may become less important than the religious aspects of witchcraft. Whatever the case, 'second generation' witches will undoubtedly contribute a new dimension to the movement in New Zealand.

The organizer of the Auckland Young Witches Group tells me that most of those who join are young spiritual seekers who have encountered witchcraft in the course of their personal spiritual searches.[20] I noted earlier that many women come to Goddess spirituality as the result of a long spiritual quest. Only two of the 12 women I interviewed had not been deeply involved in at least one other religion or spiritual path during their adulthoods. Most undertook their spiritual quests quite independently: they were not raised by devout parents – in most cases their parents were either nominal Christians or atheists. The range of religions and spiritual paths explored by the women I interviewed includes Methodism, Presbyterianism, Anglicanism, Catholicism, Pentecostalism, Quakerism, Jehovah's Witnesses,

Unification Church, Siddha meditation, Buddhism, Krishna consciousness, Hinduism, Sufism and Taoism.

In her study of Christchurch neo-Pagans Yolanda Wisewitch (1987: 24) found that all of the women surveyed had had some significant involvement in other religions before their participation in women's spirituality. Her list of women's religious backgrounds includes a number of those I have listed and adds others: the Baptist church, Spiritualism, and Christian Science. She interviewed an ex-nun, an ex-missionary and several ex-fundamentalist Christians. According to Wisewitch (p. 16), women left the Church because they could not accept the domination of men within the Church hierarchy; they had difficulty believing the Christian doctrine; and they disliked the Church's hypocrisy, arrogance, rigidity and attitude towards 'pleasures of the flesh'. Above all, they left because they found they no longer wanted to worship a male God. The ex-nun said, 'Overnight I lost my faith. I just couldn't pray any more to a male god. The more I read literature written by women I found it difficult to relate to this male god image presented in the Mass.'

From Wisewitch's research and from my own it is clear that women's disenchantment with patriarchal religion grew as their commitment to feminism and to honouring their own knowledge, experience and power as women grew. Women's accounts of their dissatisfaction with Christianity and the attraction of Goddess spirituality reinforce Carol Christ's point that 'religious symbol systems focused around exclusively male images of divinity create the impression that female power can never be fully legitimate or wholly beneficent' (Christ 1982: 73). In Goddess spirituality, women's knowledge and power are legitimated and vigorously celebrated.

But the implications of Goddess spirituality go further than women permitting themselves to image the divine as feminine and to see themselves as sacred. In *Laughter of Aphrodite*, Christ, writing eight years after her famous paper 'Why women need the Goddess' was published, and in the wake of the Chernobyl disaster, states:

> For me Goddess has always been more than a symbol of female power. Goddess symbolizes my profound conviction that this earth, our source and ground, is holy. I have always known this. I will never know anything with stronger conviction.
>
> (Christ 1987: 209)

It is interesting to reflect on the descriptors applied by historians (see chapter two) to the 'witches' targeted during the European witch-hunts in the light of the contemporary witches I have been profiling in this chapter. I would not describe any of the women I have met as a weak, pitiful or impotent member of society; as spiteful or melancholic; as suffering from hysteria or senescence; as 'dangerous deviants' or as 'enemies within the community'.[21] On the whole, witches in New Zealand are friendly, well-educated, successful in their careers, creative, concerned about peace and social justice, and concerned about the environment.

Yet, in so far as a high proportion is lesbian and all are feminist, there is a sense in which witches in New Zealand today are, like those targeted in the witch-hunts, on 'the outside of the inside' and inhabit 'the margins of the social world' (Duerr 1985). Undoubtedly there are those in mainstream society who, like the tele-evangelist I referred to in the last chapter, would see them as a threat to the community. Like the historical witches who were frequently accused of 'suffering from discontent', feminist witches also feel considerable discontent when faced with, for example, social injustice and environmental destruction. In the same way that witches were intolerable to the Church 500 years ago, feminist witches are probably still an anathema to many sections of the Church. As New Zealand society has become more secularized, however, and as feminist witches have now been around in New Zealand for a generation, the antipathy, ridicule or fear many people traditionally felt towards witches has started to ease and a re-evaluation of the witch figure is beginning, at least in some quarters.

7

THE ATTRACTION OF WITCHCRAFT

> What attracted me to witchcraft? I think a sense of magic. And a feeling of being able to creatively visualize how my life could be . . . having the right to decide.
>
> (Galadriel)

> As I started to delve into women's spirituality, I had a sense that I was remembering. It felt very comfortable. Just as becoming a lesbian felt like coming home, finding women's spirituality felt like coming home. It felt like every cell in my body was remembering sensations, feelings that must go back centuries and centuries for women.
>
> (Sybil)

When I began this research, I was intrigued to learn what attracted women to witchcraft and how they came to self-identify in this way. It seemed paradoxical that women, especially feminist women committed to challenging gender stereotypes and ending women's oppression, should choose to adopt a category name which evokes, arguably more than any other could, the misogyny of patriarchal societies. I outlined in chapter three how 'the witch' has been deconstructed by feminist scholars and discussed the symbolic value of the witch for contemporary women who choose to adopt the label for political (as well as spiritual) purposes. We saw in chapter two that the 'subjective dimension' has been omitted from historians' studies of European witchcraft because it has been too difficult to document or has been considered irrelevant, with the result that the voices of those tried have reached us 'strangled, altered, distorted' in testimonies filtered by the demonologists, inquisitors and judges (Ginzburg 1990a: 10). In contrast with that approach to the study of witchcraft, and in consideration of what first intrigued me about this topic, this chapter is preoccupied with the subjective dimension of contemporary witchcraft, particularly as it is revealed in New Zealand witches' accounts of how and why they were attracted to witchcraft and came to think of themselves as 'witches'.

The first questions I asked the women I interviewed were: how did you become involved in feminist witchcraft? What attracted you to it? Unsurprisingly, the women's stories contained no examples of antisocial malevolence or diabolism. Essentially women described how feminist witchcraft affirmed their sense of their own sacredness and their connections to the earth and to one another, and how the impulse to make rituals enabled them to celebrate these connections and mark important transitions in their lives. But they also talked about their disaffection with Christianity and their desire to create a spirituality outside patriarchal religions and churches, about the satisfaction of being able to choose their own beliefs and create their own rituals, about personal empowerment and 'dabbling in alternative medicines'. Feminist scholars have argued (see chapter three) that in fact these were the real 'crimes' of the historical witches, and, as Sybil pointed out in an interview, 'Any one of us would have been burnt then'.

Women in New Zealand who choose to self-identify as feminist witches make a strong connection between themselves and the historical witches. During our discussion about her self-identification as a 'witch', Joan said:

> It was tragic how many people got tortured. It was like a mass hysteria, sexually perverse . . . People talk about how wonderful the Renaissance was, but alongside that, in conjunction with that, women were being tortured and raped and burnt in a terrifying holocaust. I really believe that the witch ripples are still very much there in our psyche. They're in our cultural knowledge. They're in our literature, in our fairy tales. They're everywhere.
>
> I see the witch-craze very politically. I see it as the final attempt to suppress Pagan religions and to suppress the power and healing of women. And also as a way for the Church to gain a lot of property. Somebody only had to point the finger and you were gone. It was an incredibly powerful form of social control. I see it as the medieval equivalent of the KGB where people were spying on each other and telling on each other.
>
> I cannot read that *Malleus Maleficarum* [the witch-hunters' manual]. It brings up something so frightening to me. This is where I find this reclamation work so healing. It's a retrieval of tradition. I think it had to happen. I think it's giving us an understanding of why the witch-craze happened and it's getting rid of the fear of it.

The stories presented in this chapter show that there is no typical path to involvement in feminist witchcraft. Some women had a religious upbringing but more had parents who were lapsed church-goers or atheists. The women who were not brought up in religious homes expressed just as strong an antipathy towards Christianity and patriarchal religions as those who had consciously turned against them.

The spiritual odyssey is a recurring feature in women's stories: most women consciously set out to find a spiritual path with intellectual, moral, political and spiritual appeal. Just as Eller (1993: 25) found that American spiritual feminists had most often been girls who had 'experienced a deep spiritual sense in themselves', many of the New Zealand feminist witches I met traced their spiritual quest back to their childhood or teens. Only one of those interviewed, Joan, had never been interested in spirituality before discovering feminist witchcraft in her late forties. Bonney's quest began when she left her parents' Anglican church and took her via the Unification Church ('the Moonies'), the Hare Krishnas and Buddhism. Sybil experimented with Christianity and eastern religions before 'coming home' to feminist witchcraft. Kez tried out Catholicism and Pentecostalism. Alex spent some time with the Jehovah's Witnesses and then began researching traditional witchcraft and trying out spells in secret. Noreen and Megwyn spent many years of their adult lives intensely involved in Christian churches, then became interested in Christian feminism, and eventually left the Church. After leaving her parents' church at 21, Galadriel decided she needed to find an alternative religion, shopped around, and chose witchcraft.

It is not clear why these women should have felt the urge to embark on a spiritual search in the first place. It could be argued that those who had become disenchanted with Christianity needed to find a substitute religion. But most did not come from religious backgrounds: they spontaneously became aware of personal spiritual needs and set out to find a spiritual path which satisfied these needs and fitted their worldview. Once they had embraced feminism, the spiritual tradition which best suited their political perspective and worldview was feminist witchcraft/Goddess spirituality.

But what inclined them to embark on a spiritual quest? Feminism in itself does not propel women to seek a woman-identified spirituality. Indeed, as became clear in chapter four, many feminists think that women who take up religion are shirking the political work of feminism. All the women I interviewed had a strong sense of connection with the earth and a desire to protect the environment, but there are plenty of nature-lovers and Green activists who are not interested in religion, let alone witchcraft.

Many sociological studies of new religious movements try to figure out whether members of these groups share particular psychological or socio-economic characteristics which predispose them to want or need a spiritual dimension to their lives. Luhrmann (1989: 99) found that although most sociological accounts suggest that 'people join marginal groups out of socio-economic frustration', this claim is 'patently false' in regard to contemporary English witches. It is also false in relation to New Zealand witches. As I showed in the last chapter, women involved in feminist witchcraft/Goddess spirituality in New Zealand tend to have successful, satisfying, and often lucrative careers.

Luhrmann goes on to say that the witches she met (whom she frequently calls 'magicians') tended to have certain personality traits in common: they were often

> imaginative, self-absorbed, reasonably intellectual, spiritually inclined, and emotionally intense. [S]he also may be rebellious and interested in power, possibly dreamy or socially ill at ease. [S]he may be concerned on some level with issues of control – controlling [her]self, or the world, or the two in tandem. This is a descriptive, not a causal, account. The basic point is that magicians are middle-class people of a particular, and not uncommon, temperamental cast – not people with similar socio-economic profiles.
>
> (Luhrmann 1989: 100)

With qualifications, Luhrmann's description fits many of the women I met. The relatively large number of artists, writers and musicians (16 per cent of my sample of 100 women) suggests that women in the movement tend to be imaginative, creative, inclined to value intuition and perhaps 'emotionally intense'. I would not say that they are overly concerned with controlling themselves or the world, but they are concerned with finding their own 'power from within' and achieving personal goals. In the political sphere, they are very concerned with the issue of patriarchal control in society. Nor would I say that the witches I met are 'socially ill at ease' – I found them friendly and socially confident. The kinds of careers they have indicate that they work well with people. They have strong connections with and commitment to community. The communities they mix with socially and sometimes professionally, however, may be viewed as marginal in relation to New Zealand society generally, given that a high proportion is lesbian and all are feminist. Quite a number of witches are involved in alternative healing as professional practitioners or as consumers: while this community is growing in New Zealand, it is still marginal.

Luhrmann describes English witches as 'self-absorbed'. All people are self-absorbed, but it is true that women involved in feminist witchcraft/Goddess spirituality devote considerable time and energy to understanding their own psychological processes and working with them during rituals.[1] However, to call feminist witches 'self-absorbed' suggests that they are preoccupied with themselves to the extent that community concerns and goals are unacknowledged or unimportant to them. This is not the case. Apart from the fact that many work in the 'helping professions' (as women have traditionally done), New Zealand feminist witches frequently devote their spare time to a wide range of voluntary community activities ranging from supporting people with AIDS and counselling troubled youth to campaigning for the Green Party and working in cooperatively-run organic gardens. In this respect they are like the American feminist witches Griffin (1995) describes, who are involved in activities like working in Rape Crisis centres, family planning centres and women's resource centres. During interviews I was told that ritual is 'a very good way of building community' and that it has 'a much wider application which spills over into the community I meet and work with'.

Luhrmann says that a characteristic of English witches is that they are 'spiritually inclined'. While it is obvious that this should be so, 'spiritual inclination' seems to be the singular, common characteristic shared by those who become involved in witchcraft. The majority of people who are imaginative, self-absorbed, intellectual, emotionally intense, rebellious and interested in power obviously do *not* become witches. What all witches have in common is a sense that spirituality is fundamentally important in their daily lives. What causes some people to be spiritually inclined, especially in an increasingly secular society, remains unclear. As Luhrmann says, her account of the typical witch is descriptive not causal.

Women who become witches share similar worldviews, politics, socio-economic backgrounds and perhaps personality traits, but they are only a small proportion – the 'spiritually inclined' proportion – of women who share these characteristics. And, indeed, they are not the whole of the 'spiritually inclined' proportion of these women – some opt for Christian feminism or for Eastern or New Age religions instead. I can be no more definitive than Luhrmann about what causes people to embark on a spiritual quest which ends with them becoming witches. What induced Kez (see below) to begin hugging a tree and thinking of it as her God/Goddess when she was eight years old, long before it became fashionable to hug trees? Why did Juliet intuitively begin to make art works on the beach at Te Henga and offer them to the sea? What induced Sybil, from the age of 12, to begin avidly reading books on Christianity and eastern religions? While it may be true that, as she suggests, puberty is often a time of spiritual awakening and experimentation, it seems most people leave this behind when they emerge into adulthood. The causes of 'spiritual inclination' are elusive. One can only observe that some people do, and others do not, see spirituality as important to their lives.

While women's paths to feminist witchcraft are diverse and tend to begin as solitary quests, there are several common immediate causes for becoming involved. Women come across books or web-sites on the subject, they meet other women who are involved in the movement, they attend a workshop, they are invited to an open ritual by a friend, or they read a magazine or newspaper article. These avenues to participation in witchcraft are the same as those noted by Berger (1999: 9) for US witches and Hume (1997: 80) for Australian witches. Some New Zealand women become involved by beginning to create their own rituals which they perform alone, usually in natural settings, either spontaneously or in conjunction with their reading. While women arrive at witchcraft via diverse routes, there are recurring elements in their stories – elements which could be taken as the reasons why women are attracted to witchcraft. These include:

- the desire for a woman-identified spirituality and to belong to a women's spiritual community
- the desire for a spirituality which celebrates connection with the earth and the natural world
- feeling a need to bring a spiritual dimension to feminism
- disenchantment with Christianity
- wanting to affirm or to create one's own spirituality independently of institutionalized patriarchal religions
- feeling a need to consciously mark life transitions using ritual
- the intellectual appeal of feminist theology/thealogy
- desiring a religion which offers the elements of magic, excitement, fun and play.

Some of these elements, such as the desire for a spirituality which celebrates connection with the earth and for a woman-identified spirituality, are common to all women. Sometimes all eight elements above are important to a particular woman, and sometimes only one or two.

The attraction of feminist witchcraft for New Zealand women seems to be similar to its attraction for their English counterparts. Greenwood (2000a: 109) says that for the latter 'healing the wounds of patriarchy' is a priority, and that the 'practice cannot be separated from politics – a politics of reclamation and re-invention of lost tradition'. I would not agree, however, that this is a politics of nostalgia focused solely on the retrieval of a Golden Age. Certainly there is much talk of a time long ago when women were highly valued and a Goddess or goddesses were worshipped, but a contemporary feminist project involving working towards social equity for all oppressed groups is of greater importance.

The attraction of feminist witchcraft for women has much in common with the attraction of Paganism more broadly, especially with respect to its love and concern for the environment. Indeed, feminist witches' extreme sense of affinity with, and action on behalf of, the environment puts them closer to Pagans generally than to Gardnerian witches, among whom Greenwood (2000a: 113) witnessed little active interest in the environment, beyond using it as a beautiful 'backdrop' for their rituals.

But in other respects the appeal of feminist witchcraft overlaps with that of Wicca. Greenwood (p. 121) talks about English witches' rituals having an important role in 'healing the individual from the effects of a fragmented rationalist and materialist world – it is a re-enchantment of the self'. In Australia, too, witchcraft 'can be seen as a creative response to the problems of alienation in a world of high technology and fast-paced modernity' (Hume 1997: 2). I have no doubt that these statements would resonate strongly with New Zealand feminist witches (and probably with witches generally in this country). Many would also agree with Hume's statement (p. 7) that 'the spirit of Paganism, its quintessence' is play, a time out of time where anything may happen, and that 'the excitement of *becoming* amid a highly charged atmosphere' has strong appeal for witches and Pagans.

Hume (p. 88) emphasizes that people do not become witches through the processes that most people join religions: through socialization and enculturation within a family or community, or through pressure to convert. Rather, she found, as I did, that many of those who embraced Paganism often did so because of their dissatisfaction with mainstream Christianity, and after exploring other religions as part of a spiritual quest, often begun early in their lives.

Whatever the process by which a woman comes to self-identify as a witch, it is a process which in every case she initiates and controls herself. No one is 'converted' to witchcraft in the way that people may be converted to, for instance, Christianity. They do not decide to swap one worldview for another as the result of reading a convincing book, listening to a convincing speaker, meeting charismatic individuals or having a 'conversion experience'. Witches do not proselytize – a person's spiritual path is regarded as her own business and responsibility. Witches' priority is not to build up a large spiritual community: they are much more concerned about effecting broad attitudinal changes in society with respect to social justice and environmental issues. Women may invite friends whom they judge to be sympathetic to, or interested in, witchcraft to an open ritual, but pressure is never placed on anyone to adopt particular beliefs or to join a ritual group. On the contrary, I have met many women who spent years actively searching for a ritual group or coven to join before they found one. Over the years I have had numerous approaches from women seeking information about joining a group.

Women's autonomy in the process of their embracing witchcraft is very important. Because there is no pressure or even encouragement to join a ritual group, and because personal choice, responsibility and empowerment are central beliefs within the movement, women's autonomy is assured. When a woman decides to leave a ritual group, as has happened on quite a number of occasions over the 13 years in the group with whom I have worked most closely, the decision is respected. A farewell ritual is held, the woman's decision to leave is acknowledged as being 'right for her', her time spent in the group is celebrated, the group's blessing is given to the woman's future path, and gifts are sometimes exchanged.[2]

For spiritually inclined feminists, witchcraft is a means of sacralizing feminism. For many women, discovering witchcraft simply means discovering a name for what they already believe and value, and for what some of them have already been practising spontaneously. Many times I have heard women say that finding feminist witchcraft or Goddess spirituality felt like 'coming home'. This phenomenon is reported over and over by researchers of modern witchcraft. Eller (1993: 24) says, 'If the metaphors for fundamentalist Christians are "being saved" and "being filled with the love of the Lord," the metaphors for spiritual feminists are "coming home" and "finding myself"'. Berger (1999: 9) says, 'Adherents frequently assert that when they first encounter information about Neo-Paganism or Witchcraft they have a sense of "returning home"'. Lewis (1996: 3) writes that many neo-Pagans claim they didn't convert to the religion, they were 'born' pagans: 'they felt at home from the very beginning of their involvement'. Harrow (1996: 12) says that 'you don't *become* Pagan, you discover that you always were'. And Griffin, writing about her own experience of conducting sociological research among feminist witches in the US, writes: 'My encounter with feminist Witches and the larger Goddess Movement was like coming home' (Foltz and Griffin 1996).

Let us see, then, how several New Zealand women found their way, or their way back, to feminist witchcraft. The following (necessarily abbreviated)[3] stories emerged in the course of women answering my question: how did you become involved in feminist witchcraft? What attracted you to it? The accounts illustrate the importance of a number of recurring features in the processes by which women become involved in feminist witchcraft/ Goddess spirituality: feminism, lesbianism, Christian feminism, a strong ecological awareness, reading books on the subject, taking workshops and meeting women already involved in the movement.

Sybil

Sybil's spiritual quest began when she 'hit puberty', a time, she says, when 'a lot of kids start to go through an emotional and spiritual awakening'. Her family was not religious – her father was 'a very lapsed Catholic' and her mother was a lapsed Anglican. As a child she was sent to Christian Youth Camp in Ngaruawahia during the school holidays where she was 'saved' and returned home singing Christian songs – the conversion lasted two weeks.

At puberty Sybil began seriously searching for a religion which answered her emerging questions and 'felt right'.

> I'm not quite sure what I was looking for. I shopped around for a religion. I was reading books avidly on Buddhism and Hinduism and Sufism and Taoism and everything else. My family used to make smart comments like: What's the religion this week? What are you allowed to eat this week? All these weird practices I got into virtually did change weekly.

After sampling many religions, she began experimenting with psychedelic drugs, and temporarily thought she'd found God – but later changed her mind. Her eventual discovery of feminist spirituality was closely linked to her emerging identity as a lesbian.

> Many years later I started to challenge my life style in terms of my whole way of being in the world. My spirituality wasn't awakened again until I became a lesbian in fact, and that brought about for me another period of questioning and an awakening. I felt I'd been literally dead for years, not feeling, numb. As I started to delve into women's spirituality, I had a sense that I was remembering. It felt very comfortable. Just as becoming a lesbian felt like coming home, finding women's spirituality felt like coming home. It felt like every cell in my body was remembering sensations, feelings that must go back centuries and centuries for women.

Sybil was living in Australia at the time and, although she met individual women who were involved in the movement, she was not able to find a ritual group to join.

> I did a lot of private practice on my own, went to a few healing centres, used to do some meditation or work with friends. It wasn't until I came back to New Zealand that I heard about a workshop of Juliet Batten's and got immediately extremely excited. I'd looked everywhere in Australia for a ritual group. I knew they were out there. I wanted to join one but it felt like a secret society, a well-guarded secret. I got a sense that now the time is right. Things do come to you when the time is right.
>
> What attracted me basically was that thing of remembering – it was home – something that was very familiar, very affirming, very empowering and very exciting.

Kez

Kez was attracted to feminist spirituality because of the ritual. Ever since she was a small child, she sought to build ritual into her life, whether it was saying grace before dinner or making sure her room was 'just right' before she went to bed. When she was eight years old, she 'used to go and hug this tree all the time' and thought of it as a kind of deity. As a child she used to visit and sit in Catholic churches alone and wished she could have one of the white candles. She resented the fact that her parents were not Catholic because Catholicism seemed to incorporate a lot more ritual. 'My parents were boring old Baptists and we didn't go to church very often, just on Christmas day'.

> When I was 12 or 13, I discovered the Pentecostal church. That was pretty way out stuff! I was quite intrigued by all the speaking in tongues and singing out praise to the Lord. I stayed with that church about six months because of all the ritual, singing and dance. But

> I got very freaked out too, because of my father's reaction – he thought Pentecostalism was really about witchcraft. There was a woman pastor who ran the group, which I always thought was quite significant. I got put off the church because I got very close to being abused by one of the guys who took me there. I left, and left myself high and dry for a long time.

For some years Kez lived in the Bay of Islands, making her own rituals, often on the beach, but she missed being part of a spiritual community. Back in Auckland, she began searching for a ritual group to belong to: 'I knew it had to be with women because of my lesbianism'. She took a course on feminist ritual-making with Juliet Batten and finally found a ritual group as a result of moving into Sybil's house.

> I knew women's ritual groups existed but I never thought that I would be able to be part of one. I thought they were for women who'd known each other for *ages*. You got passed this secret word in the hall and you could join. In a way, that happened when I moved into Sybil's house. I mentioned my interest, and she said, 'Well, we have this ritual group', and it was like getting the secret word. I was so excited!
>
> So that's what it was for me. I knew it was out there somewhere. I was like Alice in the Looking Glass really. I just had to find it. I'm very pleased to be part of it now. I came to my first real ritual at Candlemas. I felt it was very, very powerful . . . it was like all of a sudden what I'd been searching for in ritual had just come to be. It was just amazing! That's what brought me to feminist ritual-making – it was the ritual and that unity of women.

Joan

Joan had never been interested in spirituality before becoming a witch. She was, however, an ardent feminist who read widely among feminist literature. When some of her feminist friends became interested in feminist spirituality, Joan became curious and began to research it herself. She attended a weekend continuing education workshop run at a university along with 35 other women – 'an immense diversity' – and was impressed with 'the very, very good things that happened' among the participants and the way in which they began 'to tune in to the landscape and to the earth more'.

> It was so exciting! It struck me that women really liked it, that it was tapping into something really – I hate this word – *elemental*, something that women could create for themselves outside the patriarchal religions and churches. That to me has been the driving force – the

fact that it's an alternative thing, it's a fun thing, it's something that you can create yourself. It's highly individualistic, but it's also a very good way of building community.

I saw this as a very exciting development in the feminist community. But I didn't see it as a personal need. I still don't. I see it basically as a fun thing and very useful.

Joy

Joy came to feminist spirituality just before her sixtieth birthday, after many years of observing Juliet Batten's work with women in collaborative art-making and ritual-making. Joy was about to retire from a demanding 13-year job in a large bureaucracy and wanted to use ritual to help her manage the transition meaningfully. She saw Juliet as a 'superb teacher' who would be able to help her do this, so enrolled in a feminist ritual-making workshop and later joined the ritual group which grew out of the workshop.

> I suppose I was more and more thinking that I wanted to deepen my own spiritual experience. That was something I'd done through my gardening and through the influences from my childhood. I had been brought up in the country in a place which was very remote, very high up, a place where it was very windy, very wild, where I was very conscious of the elements.
>
> My mother encouraged me to be open to experiencing the elements. We were encouraged to play with fires, to light fires, to mould clay, to run wild, naked in the rain, and if there was ever flooding – which there frequently was – we were always very conscious of those elements, conscious of the seasons. So that was instilled in my childhood as being really, really important.

Thus feminist spirituality's embracing of the natural world and elements, along with the therapeutic ritual work it offered, were important attractions for Joy. Her commitment to community and the environment are core threads in her life.

> Ritual has a very immediate, personal application where I feel enriched in that small group, and a much wider application which spills over into the wider community I meet and work with.

Megwyn

Megwyn's mother was an atheist and her father a lapsed Anglican. She was sent to Sunday School as a child, which she hated, and to Christian youth holiday camps, which she loved because 'that was one wonderful way to get a holiday'. While at secondary school she became involved in a very active Presbyterian youth movement in Southland, and at teachers' college in the mid-1950s she joined the Student Christian Movement, a group considered very radical by mainstream churches because 'it was based on social action and socialism'. The group produced some significant leaders in the anti-racism movement in New Zealand.

> At that stage I was still kicking – I was still a bit of a rebel in the Church. I hadn't any awareness about sexism – looking back I can see that all those people were incredibly sexist. There was still a very male-based structure in the Church.

Megwyn switched to the Methodist church which she found much less constricting, began to do some self-esteem work and to read feminist literature. She moved to Auckland in 1981, the year of the highly contentious South African rugby tour to New Zealand, and joined 'lots of radical groups': anti-apartheid groups, conservation groups and a Christian feminist group. Along with many thousands of New Zealanders Megwyn demonstrated against the Springbok tour; it was 'a time when lots of people had their whole insides shaken up, their whole value system, everything'. She became 'more and more angry with how the Church was not taking part in what was going on in the world'.

One of the groups she belonged to was an alternative worship community comprising 'a lot of fringe church people' that met on Friday nights. The group 'did lots of things like lighting candles and meditating and creative visualization'. One woman had been to a course on Goddess spirituality run through a university continuing education programme. Megwyn, who had already been reading Mary Daly, *Changing of the Gods* by Naomi Goldenberg and other Christian feminist literature, was introduced to Starhawk.

> Without really realizing it, I shifted from Church-based ritual into feminist ritual-making, and found that absolutely wonderful. It was the freshness of the symbols and how they could mean something personally. After that I really couldn't go back to the Church. It had actually been a struggle all along – the feeling that I wasn't good enough because I wasn't fitting into what was expected of me by the Church authorities.
>
> I went to Lea Holford's Goddess course where straight away we were into a whole variety of symbols and different things that seemed so alive and so vital and touched me immediately. I would go exhausted at the end of a teaching day to one of her courses, wonder how on earth I was going to get involved, but every time there was a feeding. I'd go home feeling really integrated.

Galadriel

Galadriel grew up in a strict fundamentalist Christian home.

> One of the results of this upbringing was that I lost a sense of magic and beauty and wonder of life. And so I loved science fiction and fantasy books. Magic had always fascinated me, but I didn't attach any importance to it because of my upbringing.
>
> When I was 16 I started getting a really strong sense of despair, and I thought I needed to break away from Christianity. But at church people said you couldn't leave and go to a void – if you didn't have God in your life, you had a void. And I knew that. I'd seen lots of people who'd left the church and didn't make it for that reason.
>
> When I was 21 I disliked myself and my life so badly that I made a suicide attempt. Once I came to that point, I realized I needed to make some real changes, and one of them was finding an alternative religion.

She went to Pathfinder bookshop in Auckland, a store which specializes in books on a vast range of spiritual traditions, and began searching for her alternative. There she came across a book about 'women making it their own way' spiritually.

> And that's basically what I did – I started developing my own way. I thought about it for a long, long time. There were a lot of risks involved for me. I really had been trained to believe from childhood that getting involved in witchcraft was like saying: 'I'm quite willing to go to hell'. It's an amazing shift in your thinking to pursue your own path in the face of that. And so I decided on my witch name and I began my career as a witch.

A year later Galadriel attended an open Sabbat ritual, and then a course on feminist ritual-making out of which developed the ritual group that she joined.

> What attracted me to it? I think a sense of magic. And a feeling of being able to creatively visualize how my life could be . . . having the right to decide.

More than anything else, witchcraft is attractive to these and other women in the movement because it provides a theory and experience of connection. This connection works on three levels. First, it gives women an experience of inner connectedness. In witchcraft there is no spirit/body split whereby spirituality and carnality are conceptualized as being in conflict with one another.

Witchcraft permits women (and men) to embrace and celebrate their bodies and their sexuality in whatever forms they take.

Secondly, witchcraft provides a theory and an experience of connection with other people, both within and outside the witch community. Witches say that every person is an expression of the Goddess and all are equal irrespective of cultural, ethnicity, class, gender, age, ability or any other distinctions. Five of the six women above talked about the importance of belonging to a community of like-minded women. While their primary sense of connection is with other women, feminist witches are not antagonistic towards men (although they are antagonistic towards patriarchal institutions).

Thirdly, feminist witchcraft gives women a strong sense of connection with the earth. Witches believe that all of nature, as well as every person, is an expression of the Goddess. Starhawk (1989: 22–3) writes:

> She *is* reality, the manifest deity, omnipresent in all of life, in each of us. The Goddess is not separate from the world – She *is* the world, and all things in it: moon, sun, earth, star, stone, seed, flowing river, wind, wave, leaf and branch, bud and blossom, fang and claw, woman and man. In Witchcraft, flesh and spirit are one . . .
>
> Religion is a matter of relinking, with the divine within and with her outer manifestations in all of the human and natural world.

This belief in the interconnectedness of the whole natural and human worlds is the source of witches' extreme concern with environmental issues. The sacralization of nature means that witches tend to anthropomorphize nature. Admiring a full moon or a rounded hill, they might say: 'Isn't she beautiful!' Women in feminist witchcraft place a great deal of emphasis on becoming aware of the earth's seasonal cycle and the moon's lunar cycle. The eight Sabbat festivals mark points in the annual seasonal round. In every ritual the four elements – air, fire, water and earth – are invoked, and women associate the symbolic meanings of the elements with aspects of their own personalities. Air is symbolically linked with the intellect and will, water with the emotions, fire with passion and energy, and earth with the body. A woman who is said to be 'all air' is highly intellectual and pays little attention to the intuitive, emotional aspects of herself. One who is an 'earth woman' is self-sufficient, 'grounded' and intuitive. The constant use of natural metaphors enhances women's sense of connection with the earth and its/her natural processes and cycles.

My findings about what attracts women to witchcraft echo those of Yolanda Wisewitch (1987) in her study of Christchurch women involved in women's spirituality. Wisewitch found that, firstly, women were attracted by a religion which connected them with other women and which was 'totally woman-identified'; secondly, they enjoyed the spiritual freedom and autonomy it offered after the rigidity of their past religions; thirdly, women's spirituality appealed because it affirms women's power and beauty; and, finally, it provides a connection with the earth and the seasonal cycles. Concluding her discussion of the reasons for women's involvement in the movement, Wisewitch (p. 37) writes: 'The word that comes up again and again in what they say is *connection*'.

In the remainder of this chapter I discuss some issues surrounding women's self-identification as 'witch'. In chapter three I said that women's intention in adopting the label 'witch' today is to challenge conventional interpretations of the European witch-craze and to draw attention to a feminist re-evaluation of the women labelled 'witches'. I noted that feminist witches are well aware that the women killed were victims of labelling and *not* self-identified witches. For contemporary women who choose to use the label, I stated, the witch has become a potent symbol of woman as possessor of power and knowledge which is not sourced in, nor controlled by, patriarchal institutions and not dependent on patriarchal legitimation or approval.

The women I met who self-identify as 'witch' do so according to these terms. Their image of the witch clearly differs from the conventional popular image. As one can see in the quotations below, the definitions which emerged in the interviews I conducted represented the witch as woman of wisdom, healing and power:

> I like the title 'witch'. A witch to me means 'woman in control' and 'woman directing her destiny'. Part of venerating the Goddess within me is being a witch and claiming that.
>
> (Galadriel)

> For me 'witch' means the person who can be fiery. The 'witch' part of me is the part that will be me regardless of other people's expectations.
>
> (Scarlett)

> I'm very proud about identifying as a witch in the fullest sense of the word. I am a healer, a storyteller.
>
> (Sybil)

> I'm a feminist witch. I like that term. A 'witch' to me is just a woman who makes rituals. We're not somebody against Christians who's having sex with Satan – all that Christian-invented crap. A witch is a healer and a wicca and a woman who has a herb garden.
>
> (Joan)

> I certainly wouldn't deny it if anyone called me a 'feminist witch'. I would see myself more in that category than in any other. Sometimes when I'm cooking up a cough remedy I see myself as a witch.

> At those moments I really do identify with the women who've done that for thousands of years. And it's really quite wonderful.
>
> (Bonney)

> It took me a long time to put that sticker – 'My other car is a broom' – on my car. I didn't want to have to justify myself to anyone and I didn't want to start to feel vulnerable. Women throughout the centuries have been made vulnerable because of what they know.
>
> (Kez)

> Yes, I am a witch. A witch is a wise woman who is gaining the wisdom of centuries, of passed-on intuitive and healing ideas, values for the earth. A witch is a woman who is free to be herself. The Church couldn't cope with women being wise, so they had to squash them.
>
> (Megwyn)

In a group discussion women contrasted their own images of the witch with mainstream society's image:

> I think I've always been fascinated with witches. Even as a child I was aware that the witch was thought of in totally different terms – you know, the image of the old witch down the road. I was always fascinated with them, never, never horrified. I don't have any memories of fear attached to them.
>
> (Sybil)

> I've got this lovely image of the witch . . . the Queen of Wands. She's got lots of energy; she's bright, cheery, gets things going. She's the person I'd like to be.
>
> (Galadriel)

> Sometimes I see the witch as Kali. The name 'witch' is very much a part of woman's culture for me.
>
> (Scarlett)

> I always associated the witch with magic. I was always very curious about how the gingerbread castle got there. What skill, expertise, or mastery did she have to work things like that? I read *Lord of the Rings* quite young, and I really identified with the Elven women there. That was my image of 'witch' – woman of power, prestige, and magic.
>
> (Galadriel)

> I identify with the witch because I see the witch in my childhood and in story books as an outcast in society – she was *considered* an outcast in society. There was always a witch in our neighbourhood, an old woman who lived in a house that had curtains that didn't open very much and she lived behind a hedge. I spent most of my time not frightened of her but very worried for her. I was worried that she wasn't warm enough, and I wondered how she got out to get food. I was worried that the boys in the neighbourhood would attack her. It was very real for me, that worry all the time. I perhaps relate to the witch in the same way as I relate to being a lesbian . . . as an outcast.
>
> (Kez)

> I never see witches as having a 'bad' association for me. I see witches as being in society's terms 'naughty', as are all powerful, so-called 'unruly' women. Identifying as 'witch', and also identifying as a lesbian witch, I feel more fulfilled in this time of my life than I have in any other.
>
> (Sybil)

> It's so interesting hearing people speak, because I'm just realizing how lost all the aspects of being a witch have been to me – like the healing and the wisdom.
>
> (Scarlett)

> I don't know how it happened, because she used to be the one who *delivered* babies – she never *ate* them. That was an image that was held up to us of the witch as being synonymous with the Devil or the harlot. She has feelings and needs and a voice and everything that's quite normal.
>
> (Sybil)

These witches are well aware that they are contesting the popular image of the witch: their self-identification as 'witch' is conditional upon 'witch' being defined in their terms. All would deny 'witch' identity in a context where 'witch' is defined by the dominant culture according to the traditional image of the witch. This explains why some women are ambivalent or reticent about self-identifying as 'witch', and why for most women the decision about whether or not to identify is based on how they judge a particular social context.

The paradox is that while feminist witches are determined that the dominant culture's image of the witch should be transformed in line with a feminist re-evaluation of the witch, and while they believe that reclaiming the name 'witch' themselves is an effective way of assisting this transformation, many are also frightened of the possible repercussions of openly and unreservedly identifying as 'witch'. To re-invent the witch is no mean task. Feminist witches are acutely aware not only of the dimensions of the task, but also of its dangers for them personally. Their fear of a Christian fundamentalist backlash is realistic: such a backlash would not only make individual women vulnerable, it would probably damage the reclaiming process as a whole.

The other reason why some women do not make a point of openly self-identifying as witches is that they are not interested in proselytizing. They are much more urgently concerned about changing people's attitudes towards environmental destruction and social injustices than they are about converting people to a religion called 'witchcraft'.

Most witches draw a line between public and private self-identification. The line is drawn in different places. At one end of the scale there are women who do not claim to be witches even in a private context, but who see some parts of themselves – aspects of their characters, experiences or work – as witch-like. The majority of women in feminist ritual groups do identify as witches within the private context of the group where it is safe to do so and where a common understanding of what being a witch means is shared by group members. One woman said:

> I identify as a 'feminist witch' within the women's circles and in anything that involves the public I call myself a 'ritual-maker'. I don't want to be drawing down negative energies upon me because I want to protect the spiritual process. Part of my protection is not calling myself a 'witch' in the media because for me that's drawing down unnecessary hostile energies towards me. I know there's a lot of fear out there. I've come through the women's movement fighting for abortion and getting the fundamentalist backlash. I have experienced the amount of power they have and the amount of fear they have. I'd get much more noticed if I went round calling myself a 'witch', but I see no value in having that.

Beyond the context of the ritual group, most witches I met judge carefully whom to tell that they are witches. There are several important criteria for public self-identification. First, women only identify as witches in a context where they have an opportunity to explain what such an identification means to them. Thus, public self-identification virtually always goes hand-in-hand with an attempt to deconstruct the stereotypical image of the wicked witch. Noreen said:

> I attempt to explain what I mean when I say I'm a witch if I'm talking to friends who know me well, and I also attempt to explain Paganism to people who are sympathetic. It's really impossible to explain it to people who are antagonistic, but I do try with friends. I certainly

> don't discuss ritual-making or the words 'witch' or 'Pagan' with casual acquaintances – I never mention anything like that because of the impossibility of explaining it to them.

Second, feminist witches usually only disclose their 'witch' identification to people who know them fairly well. Some women expressed the concern that people should have a balanced and rounded view of them *before* finding out that they are witches. Galadriel said:

> Occasionally it can get in the way of how people see you. But if it fits into the context of the conversation, and you're essentially validated as a person, introducing the fact that you're a witch is just adding an extra dimension to your character.

Thirdly, women tell others that they are witches when they judge that it is useful and safe to do so. At the other end of the scale from those who are extremely wary about telling people they are witches are some women who are completely 'out' and openly tell their friends, family and colleagues that they are witches. For these women, publicly reclaiming the name 'witch' is a way of 'moving out of the shadow of the burning times'. If witches become visible, these women believe, people's fear, mistrust and misconceptions about them can be addressed and eventually removed.

However, even women who are publicly relatively open about their witch identification are cautious, and not only because they do not want to become victims of a fundamentalist Christian backlash. As I pointed out in chapter three, the point of publicly adopting the name 'witch' is to expose the historical witch as an invention and to explicate the link between the wise woman and the witch and the process by which the former became anathematized. In short, the only point of publicly self-identifying as 'witch' is to re-invent the witch. Women who are committed to participating in this re-invention process walk a fine line, and they know it. In the following quotation, Sybil speaks of her sense of connection with the historical witches, the political aspect of her public self-identification as a witch, and her pride, tempered with caution, in claiming this identification.

> I'm very proud about identifying as a witch in the fullest sense of the word. I am a healer, a storyteller. I wear very proudly my pentacle around my neck and on my finger as well. Coming out as a witch for me is a very similar process to coming out as a lesbian. There are situations where I won't necessarily say I am a lesbian or I am a witch, but by wearing those symbols proudly, I feel it is easier for other women who also identify as being witches or lesbians to recognize me. It's saying I'm not alone, I'm identifying with a group of women.

> For me it's also quite a political thing too, because I've noticed that all manner of people will actually comment on the symbol I'm wearing around my neck. It's been very interesting. I'm quite happy to talk about it, but I will judge very quickly by their reaction how much to talk about it, and what to say. Some people know immediately what it is. My mother recognized it. She knew I belonged to a women's spirituality group, but she said, 'Oh, you've got the witch's symbol on your finger, dear!' That was absolutely fine.
>
> It's a reclaiming of the name for a start. 'Witch' for me is more than wearing black, more than honouring the banshee side of myself. The witches were actually healers and there were millions of them burnt. Any one of us would have been burnt then.
>
> I think women's reluctance to take on the title 'witch' does come from centuries of stigma being attached to it, and the millions of women who were burnt who weren't necessarily even self-identified 'witches'. It was a label that was put on them. They were the healers. They were any women of power basically. Any woman who owned land. Any woman who wasn't married. Any woman who dared to say more than two words strung together. They didn't have to do much to qualify as a witch.

Near the beginning of this chapter I quoted Joan stating her belief that the terror and tragedy of three centuries of gynocide in Europe have penetrated the cultural and individual psyches of people in Western societies. These 'witch ripples', she says, permeate our cultural knowledge, myths and literature. We might consider the effects of these 'witch ripples' in the psyches of men and women in the little over 200 years since the last witch-killings. For men, the witch is 'other', to be feared, dark, dangerous and voracious. For a woman, the witch is an image of her own dark, dangerous power which she has been taught effectively to fear. The witch is an image of her old age, her aloneness, her sexual undesirability, her woman's knowing trivialized as 'women's intuition' by a male-oriented intellectual tradition. For women, the witch image is more frightening. The witch is a symbol of what she can become and will be damned for becoming.

Joan says that by reclaiming the name 'witch', contemporary women are finding a means of understanding why the witch-craze happened, of meeting and healing their fear of the witch, and of retrieving women's power, knowing and healing. By self-identifying as 'witch', they are reclaiming and re-instating the crone as the third aspect of the Goddess. In doing so they are reclaiming an alienated part of themselves and identifying themselves as Goddess. Remembering the 'witch' – the Crone Goddess – is a way of remembering themselves.

8

THE ATTRACTION OF THE GODDESS

Witches' worldviews

> I believe women must develop a theory of symbol and thealogy congruent with their experience at the same time as they 'remember and invent' new symbol systems.
>
> (Christ 1982: 77)

> Somewhere along the way the Goddess got taken away from us and put *out there*. We had to earn it. I don't understand why that was necessary.
>
> (Kez)

A sceptic I met at a party several years ago, having listened to a potted account of my research, pronounced that feminist witchcraft/Goddess spirituality was a 'designer religion'. It was a flippant and patronizing remark, but also fairly astute. While I would agree with Greenwood (2000a: 121) that 'magic is often viewed by practitioners as a way of healing the individual from the effects of a fragmented rationalist and materialist world', magical beliefs and practices are themselves an assemblage of fragments from numerous diverse sources. Goddess spirituality draws on prehistoric, classical, Celtic, ancient Egyptian, Nordic and Near Eastern goddess images, and invokes a wide range of goddesses from contemporary non-Western cultures with a vigorous and unabashed eclecticism. It draws on a range of philosophical perspectives and religious traditions: the holistic, cosmological worldview of the Greek philosophers, the Romantic view that nature is an organic totality, the Hegelian view which sought to transcend dualisms, the Hindu concept of karma with its recognition of continuous cycles of change (Morris 1987: 8), Jungian ideas about the collective unconscious and archetypes, and poststructuralist ideas about the collapse of metanarratives and the legitimacy, or inevitability, of pastiche. It draws on the women's movement, the ecology movement, the peace movement, indigenous peoples' myths and rituals, alternative healing, and aspects of New Age philosophies and therapies. It attracts women who are smart, arty, left-wing, right-brained, into recycling and rebirthing, tofu and the tarot, who are committed to both personal empowerment and social transformation.

'Designer religion' is apt in so far as the intellectual and the aesthetic are neatly integrated in Goddess spirituality. Participants in the movement are highly literate and articulate about their beliefs, and are used to, and comfortable about, examining the intellectual basis of their spirituality. Yet they place equal – possibly more – emphasis on the aesthetic. Rituals are carefully designed to have sensuous appeal: incense and fragrant oils are used; candles are lit; flowers, beautiful cloths and symbolic objects are arranged to create an altar befitting the ritual's theme; poetic invocations to the Goddess are written and spoken; music is played and made; and each ritual concludes with delicious food.

In the sense that it is trendy, creative, eclectically constructed and highly self-conscious, Goddess spirituality can be seen as a designer religion. But women in the movement are not self-indulgent opportunists or poseurs preoccupied with image whose rhetoric, beliefs, values and commitment are superficial. To dismiss it with a chic label is to misunderstand and underestimate what the movement is about.

Like all religions, it is socially constructed, but unlike other religions, its participants are not only aware of, but also emphasize and celebrate its constructedness and their own role in this process. Joan, one of my interviewees, sees it as quite possible for individuals to passionately hold particular religious beliefs while understanding that all such beliefs are meaningful only because those who hold them charge them with meaning. She said:

> I think that human beings create the notion of the sacred; I think it's a human artefact. I think we create the sacred because life's too horrible otherwise. I have quite a functionalist view of it.
>
> It's great to feel that there are supernatural things, and I think it's fine to invent them. Because when you're actually *doing* the rituals, you do believe in it. The fact that you know you're creating it doesn't take away from the sacredness of it or stop you fiercely believing in something. It's never been a contradiction to me, and I don't think a lot of women have a problem with it either. I think it's wonderful to have an imaginative world of tuning into the earth and the landscape.
>
> I think magic is marvellous. There's got to be more to life than watching television and eating McDonalds. There's got to be a spiritual dimension, and I think Goddess spirituality is a brilliant way of doing it. It doesn't hurt anybody. It brings women together – which is why, of course, they used to burn us for doing it – and I also think it has terrific potential for helping the environment. You can't fault it really.

As well as borrowing a plethora of goddesses from various sources, women in Goddess spirituality sometimes invent entirely new goddesses with new names. In a continuing education workshop I attended at the University of Waikato a woman who had just moved into the Waikato area commented that she would like to create some new goddesses to help her to familiarize herself with and 'feel connected' to her new environment. Several others in the group agreed heartily that this was a good idea, and someone suggested that a 'goddess of fog' could be a useful start.

The concept of Goddess is not restricted to a number – even a very large number – of named goddesses, whether ancient, non-Western or newly created, who are worshipped or invoked as if they existed in some transcendent sense 'out there'. Sometimes women speak of, or pray to, goddesses in this way, but mostly goddesses are thought of as archetypes or images of womanhood. The Goddess or goddesses are not worshipped in the way that the Judaeo-Christian God is worshipped in those religions. The concept of Goddess includes all these archetypal goddesses along with the paramount idea that the earth is the sacred body of the Goddess. Goddess is also a synonym for the creative energy, the life source, the ultimate reality, the sacred feminine, the Great Mother, and the cycle of life and death. Underlying all these meanings is the particular view of the world shared by women in the movement: 'the vision of life as a living unity' (Baring and Cashford 1991: xi).

So while Goddess spirituality can be seen as a designer religion created out of apparently disparate ancient and contemporary fragments, the worldview of the movement is essentially and fundamentally holistic and claims deep roots. In some introductory notes I was given at one of her Goddess workshops, Lea Holford writes:

> The central theme of the Goddess religions concerns the wholeness and continuity of life, encompassing the transformations between birth and death, light and dark, pain and pleasure. Known as the 'myth of eternal return', this recurring order of fixed forms constitutes a miracle of continuous arising and dissolution . . . All living things go through cycles of transformation and return to repeat them again and again. Thus, the mother gives birth to a daughter, her body having transformed into another of like kind. The harvest of the season dies in the winter only to be reborn in the spring through the dormant seed. The vessel itself is that which contains this transformation, the womb of life itself.

This emphasis on the holistic, cyclic nature of life is frequently contrasted with the dualistic Christian worldview, which one contributor to the *Women's Spirituality Newsletter* (Brigid issue, 1991) claimed, 'divides the cosmos into two halves – the good, active, pure, light of the heavenly father and the evil, passive, impure dark of the earthly mother'. This woman, and many others in the movement, wants 'somehow to turn these notions on their head and clear the way for a different cosmology'. Thus 'darkness' is re-invented: instead of being associated with sin and danger, it becomes 'the womb where everything is conceived and generated . . . the place where all brilliance and enlightenment gestates'. Another contributor to the *Newsletter* urges women to seek 'endarkenment', saying, 'Wonderful things happen in the dark – embryos are conceived and grow, seeds germinate, and people dream'.

Women in the Goddess movement want to move beyond dualistic ways of thinking, which lead to dualistic ways of organizing society, and replace what Eisler (1988) calls the 'dominator model' of social relations with a 'partnership model'. 'In this model,' Eisler (1988: xvii) writes, 'beginning with the most fundamental difference in our species, between male and female – diversity is not equated with either inferiority or superiority'. Eisler's ideas are well known among New Zealand feminist witches. In an interview, one workshop facilitator told me:

> The partnership model as opposed to the dominator model is a much more useful way of looking at it than 'matriarchy versus patriarchy', which makes matriarchy look like patriarchy in reverse, which is another dominator model. The partnership model, which revolves around the Goddess, means espousing partnership with the earth, partnership with other human beings – they all go together.

'If we are to survive,' writes Starhawk (1988: 4), 'the question becomes: how do we overthrow, not those presently in power, but the principle of power-over?' She sees the principle of 'power-over' as permeating Western economic, social and religious institutions, as informing our treatment of ethnic groups and cultures other than our own, as shaping relationships between women and men, and as pertinent to issues ranging from rape and war to pay equity legislation and environmental destruction. The model for 'power-over' structures, says Starhawk, derives from the Judaeo-Christian belief in a transcendent God who has power over humanity and who, in turn, gave humanity power over plants and animals and, to men, power over women, thereby implicitly sanctioning gender inequality and environmental exploitation.

This line of thinking puts feminist witches and the Goddess movement very close to an eco-feminist perspective. Van Gelder, for example, says that eco-feminism is 'a philosophy that takes on not just the domination of the earth by polluters, but domination *itself*, in all its forms . . . In an eco-feminist society, no one would have power over anyone else, because there would be an understanding that we're all part of the interconnected web of life' (van Gelder 1989: 60–1). Feminist witches, it would seem, are even more concerned about environmental issues than other kinds of witches. Greenwood (2000a: 135) found this to be true in England, and I have certainly found New Zealand feminist witches to be ardent environmentalists in both theory and practice (although I am not in a position to compare them with practitioners of other witchcraft traditions in New Zealand).

The women I worked with have no illusions about the huge scope of the task of, as Starhawk puts it, 'overthrowing the principle of power-over'. They envision such a fundamental change in Western cultural values as being slow, requiring, as one woman told me, 'a change of the whole mind-set and energy that's out there', but as being crucially important and ultimately possible. Through individuals and groups learning to see the world differently and gradually having an influence on people around them, they envisage the dominant cultural mind-set eventually changing.

In contrast with the patriarchal construct of power as 'power-over', feminist witches conceive of it as 'power to do or to be' (Griffin 1995). Power is not conceived of as a limited commodity to be competed for, fought over, possessed or wielded. 'Power from within' (the title of Juliet Batten's first book) is available because divinity – alternatively called 'the Goddess', 'the life force' or 'creative energy' – is immanent in every person: power is simply a function of being. When witches talk about 'contacting their inner power', as they frequently do, they are not referring to some paranormal ability or magical power, they are simply acknowledging, perhaps reminding themselves, that they have the right to choose their own lives and can achieve what they choose, and that the strength and resourcefulness to do this comes from within themselves. Starhawk (1988: 12) explains:

> Immanent power, power-from-within, is not something we *have* but something we can do. We can choose to cooperate or to withdraw cooperation from any system. The power relationships and institutions of immanence must support and further the ability of individuals to shape the choices and decisions that affect them. And those choices must also recognize the interconnectedness of individuals in a community of beings and resources that all have inherent value.
>
> It is challenging to try to envision a society based on that principle. The implications are radical and far-reaching, because all of our present society's institutions, from the most oppressive to the most benign, are based on the authority some individuals hold that allows them to control others.

The business of contacting, affirming and working with one's 'power from within' is a central preoccupation of the women I met during fieldwork. It is this preoccupation which has undoubtedly given rise to the accusation that women in the movement are self-engrossed and apolitical. It is true that most of the ritual work done in the workshops I attended and in the ritual group with whom I worked closely has related to women's personal psychological and emotional processes; to issues in their domestic, social and working lives;

and to problems, decisions or transitions they are facing. But, as I have noted, these women are not inept, wimpish or megalomaniacal. The issues they deal with using ritual are the ordinary issues and problems that many people come across in the course of their lives. Through ritual these women confront, gain an increased understanding of, and find a way of coping with, solving, or moving through a problem, issue or transition.

My observation is that women in feminist ritual groups do not have more problems and are not more obsessed with these problems than anyone else in society. In fact, they probably spend less time fretting about and returning to problems in their lives than other people, because through ritual they have an efficient, structured means of dealing with whatever arises in their lives. As one woman wrote in the April 1987 *Women's Spirituality Newsletter*:

> For myself, spirituality begins with psychic healing, for I believe one cannot touch the inner Goddess or the outer Universe unless one has met one's own demons. They test our sincerity and commitment to change. Therefore, I feel one very important aspect of spiritual work is dealing with our shadow aspects. For myself, this has occurred most fruitfully in group sharing situations where members are willing to risk being honest and where mutual respect of differences is well tolerated.

Rather than seeing women's concern with their inner processes as an unhealthy and apolitical self-absorption, I see it as being motivated by a desire for personal autonomy and responsibility, which in turn motivates and sustains their activity in the 'outer world'. The importance of personal autonomy extends to women's belief systems. Feminist witchcraft/Goddess spirituality has no fixed doctrine which all participants believe, or are required to believe, and participants strongly resist the idea of developing one. Women are free to work out their own beliefs and values. To those who have left the Church, the absence of a rigid, restrictive, imposed doctrine is particularly attractive. Megwyn, for example, said: 'What got me about Christians was the arrogance of thinking that theirs was the only religion, that this was the only way to go. I just became so fed up with that.'

There are only two laws or principles in feminist witchcraft, and these are shared with other witches. The first is the Wiccan Rede which states: 'And ye harm none, do as thou wilt'. The Rede gives witches the freedom to do as they please according to their personal morality, so long as their actions do not adversely affect another person or deprive another of the same right. Some believe that this law is a remnant of ancient witchcraft which has been passed down through the centuries and possibly millennia, while others believe that Gerald Gardner invented it. Whatever its origin, the Rede is taken seriously by feminist witches as the principle which encapsulates and combines the important principles of personal freedom and social responsibility. Noreen said:

> Our creed is: 'Do what you will and harm none', which means, of course, that you have that control that you're not going to harm anyone, no matter what you do. After saying that, you then choose how you behave.

Joan said:

> The old witches' maxim is: 'Do what thou wilt and harm no one', and that's my motto, that's my theology. I'll do what I like, but I'm not going to be hurting anyone in the process. I wish to God . . . if that became a universal golden rule round the world, that would be the beginning of a real New Age.

The Rede outlaws hexing. Another sanction against hexing is the second principle of witchcraft: the three-fold law. This states that whatever one sends out will return three-fold. It expresses a belief in karma and is a stronger version of the Christian 'Do unto others as you would have them do unto you'. Witches believe that if they think and act positively in relation to themselves and their own lives, and towards others, they will reap the benefits. Conversely, by thinking negatively about oneself or others, and especially by hexing, one generates, attracts or lays oneself open to 'negative energies'. Thus, however bitter or angry witches might feel towards another person, they are obliged, in their own interests, not to hex that person. They may do a self-protection ritual, but not invoke harm on another person. In 13 years of attending feminist witches' rituals in New Zealand, I have never witnessed or heard anyone express an intention to hex.

When I asked Noreen about her worldview, she began by contrasting her present beliefs with those of the Church with which she had been intensely involved for much of her adult life. She emphasized the importance of personal choice and responsibility for one's actions and the importance of caring for the planet:

> There is no male God in our cosmology, no male-only God. There are no hierarchies, so we don't have 'Lords' and 'masters' and so on. Nobody is above, and so there is no one below either. There is no sin/repentance idea, no idea that somebody is coming to judge. And there's no searching for immortality as a reward.
>
> So, therefore, the opposite of those negatives . . . there's the idea of 'Goddess' or 'woman energy' or self-empowerment as being the force we're interested in and looking for. All people are equal, so nobody tells someone else what they must do, and nobody would necessarily ask someone else to tell them what to do.
>
> We're interested in joyousness in life on this earth. We're interested in celebrating life here and now, every day, every minute of every day,

> so therefore conservation is very important to us – all kinds of conservation – care for all life and care for this earth.

Bonney also stressed the importance of spiritual autonomy and personal responsibility and the urgent need to avoid further environmental destruction. She emphasized the implications of her belief in the immanence of the divine, whereby the familiar spirit/body split dissolves and all human experience – including sex, menstruation, pain and our relationship to the earth – becomes sacred. Bonney said:

> Christianity and many other religions have taken away the personal responsibility of people to perform their own rituals and to make their own connection with their own God. By having official ritual-makers in churches – priests and ministers – you are denied the opportunity of setting up those conditions yourself for wisdom to come to you and for personal knowledge to come through you.
>
> The other thing they've really ignored is responsibility to the planet. For a long time through Christianity we've just embraced heaven and tried to deny our physicality, deny our menstruating, our pain, our birth-giving, our love-making, and deny our relationship to the earth. Every time we gather together our compost and throw it in a plastic bag to put in the rubbish dump where it won't decompose for 400 years, we're raping the soil of its goodness for the food we eat, but not returning anything.
>
> We need to realize that unless we are taking from the earth, offering it to the Goddess in some way by being thankful for it and being aware of what a beautiful gift it is, and then returning the waste products to the earth, we haven't completed the cycle of being fully integrated spiritual beings. I think being spiritual is a two-way thing – it's spiritual and physical, and we've got to have the integration of the two in order to progress – or even survive – as a human race. We've got to complete a circle that's been broken for a long time. So I see myself as an ecofeminist as well as a spiritual feminist.

Feminist witches' practical concern with caring for the environment and their deep sense of a sacred connection to the earth and all other life forms are very *this-worldly* preoccupations. This distinguishes them from the English witches Greenwood (2000a: 30) writes about, whose central concern is to communicate with the *otherworld*, 'to engage with the beings therein and mediate the forces bringing back knowledge and wisdom to ordinary reality'. New Zealand feminist witches do not refer to an 'otherworld' inhabited by spirits, deities, other beings, forces and energies which is distinct from, and co-existent with, their own everyday reality. Their goal is to engage as intimately as possible with the sacred energies of *this* world and their own inner worlds. One occasionally hears reference to 'power animals' and 'spirit guides' (borrowed from Native American traditions) but much less frequently than among American spiritual feminists, who incorporate numerous spiritual beings along with goddesses in their pantheons: disembodied spirits and spirit guides, elementals, ancestors, power animals and, occasionally, malicious spirits (Eller 1993: 146).

A central aspect of any religion is its beliefs about death. As we have just seen, a key feature of Goddess spirituality is that it fully embraces human physicality and is committed to 'celebrating life here and now'. Just as this world is more important than an otherworld, the focus is on *this* life, not on an afterlife. The numerous books on feminist witchcraft/Goddess spirituality, while reiterating a general belief in the cyclic process of life, death and regeneration (not explicitly reincarnation), do not spell out any specific beliefs about what happens to an individual after death. Nor did I hear any discussions in workshops or very much informal talk among ritual group members about what happens after death, despite the fact that witches, at least those I came to know, talk quite comfortably and openly about dying and the importance of death rituals to mark the 'final passage of the body'.

I have never heard anyone claim to believe in heaven or any form of paradisiacal land, real or metaphorical. Some believe in the immortality of the individual soul and some, especially those with an involvement in Eastern philosophies and religions, believe in reincarnation. There is a more widespread belief, sometimes very vague, that upon death a person's spirit or life energy is absorbed back into the great pool of cosmic creative energy which is the source of all life forms. Some women have formed no clear idea about what happens after death and the question does not figure very importantly for them. Death itself is acknowledged as important in Goddess spirituality, for both the dying and for those who will mourn, but life after death is not a particular concern.

Goddess myths widely known and invoked in Goddess spirituality present death as a phase in the continuous cycling of life: the Greek Persephone, the Egyptian Nut, the Polynesian Hina, the Sumerian Innana, and the Babylonian Ishtar are all goddesses who journey to the place of the dead and back to the world of the living. Their journeys are taken to represent not only the cycle of life and death, but all the cycles which constitute our lives – the cycle of day and night, the cycling of the seasons, women's menstrual cycles, the moon's cycle, and so on. For the women I worked with, the belief that death is a natural part of the cycle of life and the absence of any belief that death is followed by divine judgement remove much of the fear and anxiety which death evokes in our society. Juliet said:

> I think for me the Goddess is about affirming the life and death cycle. Death is still very untalked-about in our society – very much a taboo subject. The Goddess gives us permission to talk about death

> again because it is just part of a cycle. It's not that line. I remember once in a workshop we did lifescapes and a woman drew this line, and she had a cliff, and death was falling off the cliff at the end, and she was devastated by this. This was how she saw death.
>
> But the moment you get the Goddess, you get the cycle. It gives death a place again. It's very empowering because we know about cycles as women. We know about the cycle of the seasons and the cycle of the moon, and the more we learn to respect cycles, the more respectful we're going to be of each other and the earth. And even our view of history might be different. So it's a very empowering model.

Lea said:

> We have to die in order for new life to come forth. It's not a tragedy; that's just the cycling of life – that's just the way it is. Next time you might be a waterfall, a butterfly, or a really nice rock. You don't have to believe in other *lives*; all these transformations happen to us in *this* life.

Joan said:

> I think one of the neatest things personally since I've got into this is that I've lost my fear of death. I think that's been the bonus. And I think a lot of other people feel the same, because you're tuning into something beyond yourself. It takes down the importance of the ego; it takes down that feeling of being alone that patriarchy gives us. I don't actually believe in the existence of individuals; I think it's a bit of a myth. I think the individual itself is a modern construct; it's very Western and incredibly destructive. If you were an Aboriginal or something you just didn't feel like an individual. Your consciousness is much more tied into that of the group.

The emphasis in Goddess spirituality on fully experiencing and celebrating this life is tied to women's intense concern with preserving the environment. Carol Christ's essay, 'Finitude, death and reverence for life' in *Laughter of Aphrodite* (1987: 213–27), written on the Greek island of Lesbos shortly after the Chernobyl disaster, deals very powerfully with this theme. She sees the threat of global destruction as a result of 'the failure to acknowledge our own finitude and death and the potential finitude and death of the earth' (p. 213). This denial stems from our religious and philosophical traditions which have, since Plato, 'prevented us from fully comprehending our connections to this earth'. The traditional Christian theological position in which God transcends all of his creation has led to the view that the earth, our bodies, and carnal, finite life are to be despised and ultimately transcended. The denial of death is, paradoxically, our culture's failure to affirm this life on this earth in these bodies. Christ writes (pp. 214–15):

> It might be argued that the denial of death expresses an affirmation of life. But life bounded by mortality is the only life we know, the only life we can know. We must learn to love this life that ends in death. This is not absolutely to rule out the possibility of individual or communal survival after death, but to say that we ought not live our lives in light of such a possibility. Our task is here.

Christ asserts that the spirituality we need for our survival is not one which denies our physicality and mortality, but one which encourages us to recognize limitation and mortality, and calls us to celebrate all that is finite. She claims that it is destructive of the finite, embodied reality we know to focus on some imagined 'higher reality' (p. 226). The introduction to her essay points to the crucial and inextricable link between spirituality and politics:

> I feel deeply that the flight from finitude and death is at the root of the problems we face. It seems so simple: if we truly love this life which ends in death, then however could we destroy it? It must be that we do not love earth and life enough. Maybe something went wrong, massively wrong, when Platonism and Christianity became the dominant symbol systems of our culture. Maybe the return of the Goddess can help us to re-member ourselves, to re-member this earth, which is our home. Maybe she can help us to turn away from our quest for immortality, our quest to escape change, our quest to control the conditions of our lives. Perhaps she can help us to love a life that ends in death.
>
> (p. 210)

The ritual group I joined held a special workshop to address issues surrounding death. A funeral celebrant who was deeply involved in Goddess spirituality was asked to facilitate the day-long workshop. The purpose was to explore the practical issues surrounding death and possible funeral ceremony options. The practical information covered everything from the physical changes which take place at death, the legal requirements for dealing with the body, the embalming process and cremation and burial procedures to the variety of headstones available and the prices of plots. In the centre of the workshop area a simple altar was set up with symbols of the four elements, and the facilitator began the day by lighting white and black candles to symbolize the cycle of life and death. It was emphasized that death, as one of the greatest transitions people experience, needed to be honoured and marked with carefully thought-out rituals. As part of the day we visited a funeral director's premises where we examined a range of caskets, toured the embalming room and rooms where viewings and ceremonies are held, and asked questions of the funeral director.

Later in the day we discussed the significance of the funeral as a ritual and watched two videos on the subject, and women were encouraged to begin to think about what they would like to happen at their own funerals. We discussed ancient Celtic funeral rituals and the possibility of adapting and using them. Some women became enthusiastic about designing and making a pall to be used at group members' funerals. In the weeks following the workshop, women continued to discuss the issues that had been raised, and one or two planned their own funerals in considerable and creative detail. A follow-up discussion evening was held.

There was nothing in the least morbid about the workshop or women's attitudes towards death. In choosing to organize the workshop and hire someone to lead it, group members were seriously and practically addressing the issue of their own mortality. Several had been recently involved in helping with the funerals of friends or relatives, or were soon expecting to be involved, and they felt they needed to prepare for this. Just as thought, care and time are given to planning and conducting all sorts of life-transition rituals within Goddess spirituality, participants also expect to devote thought, care and time to planning and carrying out death rituals which mark, arguably, the most important transition a person faces.

In the remainder of this chapter, I look at what the Goddess means for some of the New Zealand women with whom I worked closely. In chapter four I explored the meaning of the Goddess in the movement more generally and as presented in the literature on the subject (mostly from the US), emphasizing that for contemporary women the Goddess is a symbol, and as such is given different meanings by different women. All meanings are deemed valid and are embraced within the movement's holistic worldview. The women I met described their images of the Goddess in a great diversity of ways: as a voluptuous, heavy woman surrounded by energy and movement; as a very old, wise woman; as a woman wearing a faded blue sweatshirt and cut-off jeans; as an unseen presence. For the women I quote below, the Goddess has a multiplicity of meanings, and women feel free to choose any particular meaning at any time. They also demonstrate an awareness that they are constructing these meanings.

In their highly flexible ways of conceptualizing the Goddess and their tendency to confound any attempts to pin down their theology, New Zealand feminist witches closely resemble the American spiritual feminists about whom Eller (1993: 130) writes:

> Do spiritual feminists believe in one goddess or in many goddesses? Both, they answer, both at the same time. Is their goddess within them, a part of them, or is she completely outside of them, looking

> in? Both, they answer, both at the same time. Does this goddess exist independently of human beings or did spiritual feminists invent her? Both, they answer, both at the same time.

Megwyn's reply to my question: 'Who is the Goddess?' was:

> You are the Goddess and I am the Goddess. Starhawk really sums it up for me. At times I think of the Goddess as my real self; it's the real me becoming balanced and whole. At times it's all of nature. And then at times it's just what I'm needing when I don't feel I've got a lot inside. I want to think of a symbol outside myself, and so I think of a Goddess outside myself. So it's outside and within and through the whole of creation. That's really how I see the Goddess.[1]
>
> There's no judgement, no reproach. There's nobody telling you off and saying you haven't done the right thing. I can feel silly and disappointed about what I've done, but I don't feel that I'm reproached. It's always loving and caring and supportive and helping me to get back to a centre of balance.
>
> There's the wonderful idea that you are linking in with every other person's idea of Goddess as well. The trite phrase is the 'Universal Consciousness'. In a way it's like that. I do think there is a common knowledge and we can link in with each other.

Sybil's response to 'Who is the Goddess?' was similar:

> I definitely think of the Goddess as being within myself, within every woman whether she accesses that or not. But I also see the Goddess very much in the elements – they give me a physical, tangible sense of her being in the earth, the air, the water and fire. I also get her spirit sense from the feeling I have of an 'Other' other than myself, and other than what I can see. I do very much feel her presence in this spirit sense, something that's much bigger than me and than any of us, and yet something that resides in all of us. It's that feeling very much that the Goddess is everywhere.
>
> I talk to her, and sometimes that will be getting in touch with the Goddess in myself, and sometimes she will be the inner child, and sometimes she'll be my inner guide or wise woman or my mothering self. At other times I'll be very much talking to someone 'out there'. Sometimes that will be in praise almost, and other times it might be sheer desperation and despair.
>
> And then I feel very much like I'm talking to her when I go for walks somewhere like Te Henga, or through the Waipoua forest, or go for a sail in a boat, or sit around a big fire, or any of those situations where I feel very much connected.

I asked Sybil whether she thought about the Goddess as a deity who inhabited her in the way that Christians say God can enter and live within them, or whether she thought of *herself* as being the Goddess. She replied:

> I think they're both correct. It's an all-pervasive sensation for me. At times it can feel like getting in touch with different parts of myself. But sometimes it can feel like the Goddess resides in me. I don't have a sense that I invited her to enter me. When I invoke her in rituals, I get the sense that we're just acknowledging her, because her presence is already there. It's just focusing that energy and increasing our awareness of something that already exists.

Scarlett's concept of the Goddess echoes Megwyn's and Sybil's:

> For me, the Goddess is in me and in each one of us and in everything, in the sea and in the elements. I pray to her a lot and meditate, and she's like a friend to me or she's whatever I happen to be needing. It makes it very easy. I know she's not going to be anything other than exactly what I need. So if I need a friend, she's a friend. If I need all-pervasive protection, then there she is. If I'm desperate, she's there then.

What is notable here is the apparent paradox between conceptualizing the Goddess as someone to whom one prays, implying that she is an anthropomorphic and transcendent entity, and seeing her as 'whatever I happen to be needing', implying that the Goddess can be constructed and reconstructed in a variety of ways by an individual person. To say, 'She's whatever I happen to be needing' is quite a different statement from, 'She gives me whatever I happen to be needing'. The former carries the idea of the Goddess as continually changing and ever changeable: her form is not static or bounded. She does not simply bestow on the supplicant a solution to a need: she becomes the fulfilment of the need.

When Sybil referred to the Goddess as 'sometimes . . . the inner child, and sometimes . . . my inner guide or wise woman or my mothering self', she was not conceptualizing the Goddess as an entity *out there* which can transform Herself or an individual person, she was referring to various aspects – parts or forms – of herself as Goddess. Galadriel explained her understanding of the Goddess in a similar way, employing Freudian terms.

> In psychology, I read about us each having within ourselves a child, an adult and a parent, and also the id, ego and super ego. I was introduced to the idea of the super ego as being your 'God-consciousness'. When I left Christianity I resented the idea of having a God-consciousness, so I looked to the idea of my super ego being

> my 'Goddess consciousness'. In other words, a part of me. That fitted in nicely with the idea of the maiden, the mother and the crone.
>
> When I did a spell, I looked on it as contacting the child part of me, a younger self. I thought it was a very nice dialogue between my 'inner child' and my parent 'Goddess-consciousness' or super ego. It bypassed the adult, which is very rational in interacting with the everyday world. That's part of what the Goddess is to me.

In referring to various parts, forms or aspects of themselves as 'Goddess', or aspects of the Goddess, Sybil and Galadriel echo an American feminist witch, Hypatia, whom Griffin (1995) describes. During a weekend workshop ritual held under a full moon in the mountains, Hypatia presented herself to 60 women as the goddess Diana, dressed in green cape and pants, bare-breasted, carrying a bow and arrow, and wearing deer horns and a mask of fur and dried leaves. Hypatia told Griffin later that in this dramatic self-presentation she had neither 'become' nor 'invoked' Diana – phrases which would suggest that the Goddess was an external entity. Rather, Hypatia had 'manifested that part' of herself that was Diana.

The way in which these feminist witches think about the Goddess in relation to themselves is significantly different from the way that Wiccans – whether American, British or Australian – think about the Goddess. In Wicca, one of the central mysteries is the ritual of 'drawing down' the Goddess into a priestess, who thus incarnates or is temporarily possessed by the deity (Adler 1986: 109, Hume 1997: 127, Greenwood 2000a: 95).[2] The priestess may enter a trance and speak on the Goddess's behalf, perhaps blessing other members of her coven. I have never witnessed or heard mention of such a 'drawing down' ritual being practised among New Zealand feminist witches, and I suspect the notion would sit rather uncomfortably with them. Rather, they think of all women as goddesses, as equally, inherently and permanently divine. They may, however, at times invoke the archetypal qualities of a particular goddess which they consider may be helpful in dealing with a certain situation.

For a number of women quoted in this chapter, Goddess spirituality is attractive because it contains no concept of sin, repentance or divine judgement. Kez said:

> One of the big problems for me with other religions was that I never felt I was good enough to have God in me. No matter how many times I went to church and tried to do what I was supposed to do, I never actually felt God came into me. It was an incredible trauma for a long time. One reason I left the Pentecostal church was that I never felt I got it right.
>
> The Goddess I discovered one day – someone led me in a visualization in a counselling session, actually – I discovered she was my

> strength and wisdom. She was there even though I'd done all those naughty things. It was very powerful for me all of a sudden. It was such a relief that I didn't have to be good to get her. I didn't have to go through pearly gates to get there.

Writing in the *Women's Spirituality Newsletter* (Winter Solstice, 1990), an Auckland therapist and Goddess workshop facilitator makes a connection between patriarchal religions and socio-political structures that oppress women, saying that in her experience 'women in such structures often internalize a punitive male God/Father whose approval is usually withheld. Seeking his approval means they strive hard to be perfect, reinforced by a lot of cultural expectations.' She echoes Mary Daly (1979: 1), who states that patriarchy does not 'exist simply "outside" women's minds, securely fastened into institutions we can physically leave behind', but it is 'also internalized, festering inside women's heads'. This 'internalized Godfather' must be exorcized, Daly says, if women are to discover and create a world other than patriarchy.

Women in Goddess spirituality relish the idea that the Goddess incorporates a dark, destructive aspect as well as her creative, nurturing aspect. In a group discussion I recorded, it became clear that the Goddess acts as a role model for women, enabling them to accept the 'dark' or 'naughty' parts of themselves.

- 'The thing I love about the Goddess is that she is all those naughty things we do as well. The first "goddess", as it were, that I ever encountered was Hecate. She came to me in a time that was very dark and when I was very depressed and suicidal. I've always honoured that dark side of myself and that dark side of her because of that. She isn't *only* the virgin. She's wildness and she's running about screaming, and she's all those things that are not allowed to be God.'
- 'I really like that thing of her being Hecate and being all the negativities as well.'
- 'Yeah, for a long time we only had the Blessed Virgin held up to us as something to strive towards. She didn't have a voice. She didn't have a character. She didn't have anything going for her much. Powerless!'
- 'Worshipped for her unreachable qualities.'
- 'She never lost her temper or had a fit.'
- 'What's very important about women's ritual groups for me is that I have my womanhood sanctioned by what we do.'

The Goddess is attractive to these women because she sanctions their womanhood. She affirms not only women's procreative and nurturing aspects, but also helps them to reconnect with the 'dark feminine': she is the nurturing mother and the destructive crone. She affirms women's sexuality and allows them to be unruly. She is a symbol of woman's wholeness. For women who have grown up in a society where divinity is imaged singularly as an omnipotent, punitive male, and where woman is imaged as the temptress Eve, or as the pure, powerless Mary, discovering the Goddess is enormously liberating. Christ (1982: 84) writes:

> As women struggle to create a new culture in which women's power, bodies, will, and bonds are celebrated, it seems natural that the Goddess would re-emerge as symbol of the newfound beauty, strength, and power of women.

The absence of any imposed doctrine in Goddess spirituality, and the fact that it accords women autonomous control over their spiritual practices and their lives, contribute to the Goddess's attraction. Above all, the Goddess is attractive because she is an all-encompassing symbol of the holistic nature of life, the central, essential element of witches' worldview. She opens up new options for reorganizing gender relations; she is a reminder of the interconnectedness of humanity and the rest of the natural world; she gives death a place as part of the celebration of life.

9

WHAT WITCHES DO

> In Witchcraft, we define a new space and a new time whenever we cast a circle to begin a ritual. The circle exists on the boundaries of ordinary space and time; it is 'between the worlds' of the seen and unseen, of flashlight and starlight consciousness, a space in which alternate realities meet, in which the past and future are open to us. Time is no longer measured out; it becomes elastic, fluid, a swirling pool in which we dive and swim. The restrictions and distinctions of our socially defined roles no longer apply; only the rule of nature holds sway . . . Within the circle, the powers within us . . . are revealed.
>
> (Starhawk 1989: 71–2)

This is the first of four chapters dealing with feminist witches' rituals. In this chapter I describe the various categories of rituals, their structural framework, and the variety of ways in which seasonal rituals and rites of passage are marked. In the next chapter, I again take up the idea that feminist witchcraft is a constructed spirituality, and show that witches' rituals, like their belief systems, are artefacts constructed self-consciously using various sources. In chapter 11 I discuss anthropological ideas about the function of rituals along with witches' own ideas about how magic works. Finally, in chapter 12 I show how women, through ritual performance, embody the symbolic meanings of 'witch' and 'goddess' in an attempt to collapse the separation of these polarized images of female power, and thereby re-member their own power.

Two broad groups of rituals are celebrated in feminist witchcraft: those connected with the earth's changes during the annual cycle, including the eight Sabbats (seasonal festivals) and moon rituals, and those connected with the changes, transitions, problems and occasional crises in women's personal life-cycles. Not only is the cycle the dominant and recurring metaphor in witches' worldviews, but the earth's cycles and women's life-cycles, what Starhawk calls 'the inner and the outer cycles', are analogously connected.

> Winter, Spring, Summer, Autumn – birth, growth, fading, death – the Wheel turns, on and on. Ideas are born; projects are consummated; plans prove impractical and die. We fall in love; we suffer loss; we consummate relationships; we give birth; we grow old; we decay.
>
> The Sabbats are the eight points at which we connect the inner and the outer cycles; the interstices where the seasonal, the celestial, the communal, the creative, and the personal all meet. As we enact each drama in its time, we transform ourselves. We are renewed; we are reborn even as we decay and die. We are not separate from each other, from the broader world around us; we are one with the Goddess, with the God.
>
> (Starhawk 1989: 181)

Because of the link made between 'the seasonal, the celestial, the communal, the creative and the personal', the two broad groups of rituals outlined above often merge – a Sabbat festival often incorporates human processes and transitions. At a Winter Solstice ritual I attended (described in the next chapter), for example, women were invited to face their own inner darkness (Winter Solstice being the longest night) and contemplate what they wanted to 'sacrifice' to fire – outmoded, negative or unconstructive thoughts, attitudes, or behaviour patterns, and so on. Sticks of firewood became symbols of what women wanted to get rid of from their lives and were thrown on a fire in symbolic acts of sacrifice. At Candlemas, the Festival of First Light which follows Winter Solstice, women may be invited to contemplate what is just beginning in their lives and where they want to direct their energy. Spring Equinox is a time to say farewell to the dark, to prepare for growth, to indulge one's playful self. Beltane is a time to celebrate both the burgeoning of the earth's new growth and human sexuality. At Lammas, the first harvest festival, women celebrate their achievements and successes. At Autumn Equinox they contemplate the approach of winter and consider what personal resources they will need to sustain themselves through the darker months. At Hallowe'en or Samhain, the veil between the seen and unseen worlds is said to be thinnest and human psychic powers are considered to be most acute.

The dates of the Sabbat festivals given in all the British and American manuals on Paganism and witchcraft relate to the seasonal cycle as it is experienced in the northern hemisphere. In the southern hemisphere, of course, these seasons are reversed, and so, too, are the dates of Sabbat rituals, at least for feminist witches. In Australia, Hume (1997: 116) says, some Wiccans transplant the northern hemisphere calendar in its totality; others reverse the seasons, and yet others use a combination of northern and southern dates. This may also happen among New Zealand Wiccans, but New Zealand feminist witches, in my experience, all use a ritual calendar attuned to the southern hemisphere, probably because of the wide use of Juliet Batten's book *Power from Within* (1988), which sets out a 'Wheel of the Year' revised for the southern hemisphere.

Each year I am reminded of this reversal of the northern hemisphere calendar as I prepare to celebrate Beltane with the ritual group I joined 13 years ago. Until about a decade ago, the commercialized celebration of Hallowe'en enjoyed especially by American children was not practised in New Zealand. In recent years, however, it has become quite popular in some areas, and is celebrated, as it is in the US, at the end of October. Now, each year as I drive off to a Beltane ritual to celebrate the beginning of summer with maypole-dancing and bonfire-leaping, I see flurries of small, black-caped witches and the odd ghost with wonky eyes clutching bags of sweet booty swooping about our neighbourhood. If they (and my household) are lucky, I have remembered to stock up on sweets while preparing my Beltane greenery and maypole ribbons. These little 'witches' are, of course, ignorant of the incongruity of celebrating Hallowe'en, the festival which marks the beginning of the 'dark season', on a bright early summer evening in Auckland.

The Pagan annual cycle has two solstices, two equinoxes, and four cross-quarter days between the solstices and equinoxes. These eight festivals fall at intervals of about six weeks throughout the year. I set out below the dates (as they are given in Batten's *Power from Within*), and a brief description of the importance of each of the Sabbats as they are celebrated by feminist ritual groups in New Zealand. The symbols listed are also taken from those suggested by Batten; they focus on the New Zealand natural environment and may be used as a starting point for creating an altar for a particular ritual.

The wheel of the southern year

Winter Solstice (also known as Midwinter and Yule) 20–23 June

Symbols: caves, fires, rocks, drums, branches, sun symbols such as oranges and other citrus fruit.
Colours: black, red, yellow, gold.

This is the longest night/shortest day of the year, a time to acknowledge the Goddess in her crone aspect, to turn within to face one's inner darkness, a gestation period for new projects. At Winter Solstice 'the Great Mother again gives birth to the Divine Child Sun' (Starhawk 1989: 182). Thus, this is also a turning point after which light begins to increase, a time to celebrate the 'rebirth' of the sun and rebirth from our own darkness, to give gifts, make merry and plant garlic to harvest at Summer Solstice.

Brigid (also known as Candlemas and Imbolc) 1 August

Symbols: fires, candles, first buds, new spring bulbs, jasmine, daphne, freesias.

Colours: white (initiation, new beginnings), green, orange (along with white, Irish national colours), yellow, red (fire).

This is the fire festival of increasing light which foreshadows the beginning of spring, named after Brigid, Irish (Celtic) goddess of fire, inspiration, smith crafts, poetry and healing. Brigid is often a time to initiate new ritual group members, to set new directions, to nurture new projects, to let go of winter's darkness, to celebrate and share creativity, to spring-clean.

Spring Equinox (also known as Eostar) 20–23 September

Symbols: coloured eggs, spring flowers, balancing scales, pictures of children.
Colours: pastels.

Days and nights are equal in length; the light is increasing. This is a time of joy, freshness and playfulness, and a time to contemplate the theme of balance in one's life. The primary symbol is the egg, symbol of new life and fertility. Eggs may be coloured, decorated, exchanged. In Greek myth, Persephone returns from the underworld: this is a time to reclaim childhood and the child within.

Beltane (May Eve in the northern hemisphere) 31 October

Symbols: high airy places, maypole and ribbons, flute music, bonfires, garlands of flowers.
Colours: red, rose, pastels.

Beltane is a celebration of the earth's fertility, rising energy, sexuality. May Eve (celebrated on November Eve in New Zealand) was once the time of the maypole dance and heralded 'the merry month of May' in European villages, according to contemporary Pagans. Traditionally the maypole was a phallic symbol planted in Mother Earth; in Goddess spirituality it is taken to represent sexuality generally, since a high proportion of participants are lesbian. Beltane is a time to make and wear garlands of flowers and greenery, to weave a maypole with coloured ribbons, to leap over bonfires and make wishes, to make love spells, to feast, to pour energy into projects. It is also a time to honour mothers and daughters and to make rituals for young women to celebrate menarche.

Summer Solstice (also known as Midsummer and Litha) 20–23 December

Symbols: sun, pohutukawa flowers, karaka berries,[1] red roses, fire.
Colours: red, green, gold, yellow, white.

ıgest day/shortest night of the year, after which light begins to
nmer Solstice is a time to celebrate, usually outdoors, the God-
ℓother aspect at the height of her strength, sexuality and fertility.
to celebrate the year's achievements, appreciate success, harvest
.ed at Winter Solstice, acknowledge that after the peak comes the

Lammas (also known as Lugnasad) 1 February

Symbols: flax seeds, herb flowers, stone fruit, corn on the cob, grains.
Colours: dark green, yellow, golden, orange.

Lammas was once the festival of the wheat harvest, the 'Feast of Bread'. It is a time to celebrate the first fruits of the harvest, to bake and share fresh bread, to make a corn dolly, to acknowledge the fruits of one's labours and lessons learned, to celebrate personal harvests. It is also a time to make rituals to honour women passing through menopause.

Autumn Equinox (also known as Mabon) 21–23 March

Symbols: late vegetables such as capsicum, aubergine, tomatoes; grapes, seeds, nuts; autumn leaves; balancing scales.
Colours: autumnal.

Like Spring Equinox, this is a time of balance where days and nights are equal in length. 'It is a time to let go, to plough the fruits of experience back into the earth, to revert to essence' (Batten 1988: 45). It is a time to light the first fire, to do what is necessary to achieve balance in one's life, to plant a seed/wish to gestate over winter, to focus on one's inner life. The mother has become the crone: this is a time to acknowledge the wisdom and life experience of older women.

Hallowe'en (also known as Samhain) 30 April

Symbols: pumpkin lantern, egg-shells, cauldron, pine cones, nuts.
Colour: black.

The end of the annual cycle but also its beginning, Hallowe'en is the witches' new year – the time when the worlds of the living and the dead draw closer together. It is a time to remember the dead by lighting black candles, to make pumpkin lanterns symbolizing the full harvest moon and Hecate's fire, to burn symbols of fears in Hecate's cauldron, to destroy the unwanted, to clear out the old to make way for the new. At this Sabbat feminist witches often adopt the archetypal witch's image, dressing in black costumes and applying macabre make-up (see chapter 12).

As well as celebrating these eight festivals, groups may also regularly or occasionally hold rituals to mark various phases of the moon, especially full moon, 'dark moon', and new moon. These phases are said to represent the Goddess in her various aspects: the waxing moon symbolizes the Goddess as maiden, at full moon she becomes the mother, and when waning she is the crone. Ancient moon goddesses from numerous cultures are invoked: Selene (Greece), Isis (Egypt), Izanami (Japan), Shakti (India), Tiamat (Near East), Yemaya (Yoruba West Africa), Kwan Yin (China), Hina (Polynesia) and others (Stein 1990: 69).

The moon is held to be intimately connected with women because their menstrual cycles are approximately the same length as the 28½-day lunar cycle. In Goddess spirituality menstruation represents the procreative power of women, their sacred connection to nature: menstrual blood is called 'moon blood'. Menstruation is not 'the curse', but a time of 'psychic opening' and heightened intuitive powers. I have been in rituals where pieces of red wool have been passed round for menstruating women to take and tie around their wrists so that their special state can be acknowledged and honoured by the other women present.[2] Rituals are held to celebrate menarche and menopause, symbolizing respectively initiation into womanhood and initiation into 'cronehood'.

'Moon Lodges', workshops for women to 'honour the mysteries and the symbolism of the bleeding cycles, to reclaim the sacredness and to heal the pain of the womb' have been advertised in the *Women's Spirituality Newsletter*. These workshops, run jointly by a naturopath and a ritual-maker, cover myths and traditions surrounding menstruation, diet and herbs as self-healing aids, ritual, art and movement, and provide a context in which women can share their experiences of menarche, menstruation and menopause.[3] The concept of the Moon Lodge is borrowed from the feminist spirituality movement in the US, which in turn borrowed and adapted it from the Native American menstrual hut, to which menstruating women withdrew from their daily routines and chores and communed with other women (Eller 1993: 86).

Moon rituals may also be done for more general purposes. Each phase of the moon is associated with a different 'energy': the waxing moon with waxing energy; full moon with intense, abundant energy; the waning moon with banishing or relinquishing energy. A ritual held while the moon is waxing is likely to be focused on putting energy into a new project. Full moon rituals celebrate achievements, fulfilment, the consummation of projects and plans. In waning moon rituals women usually focus on letting go of, banishing, or healing the effects of negative influences in their lives.

As well as these calendrical rituals tied to the seasons and moon, witches perform a great variety of rites of passage which are held whenever a woman or a group wishes to do so. Such occasions include birthdays; baby blessings and namings (to replace christenings); trysts or marriages; leaving a home, job or relationship; blessing a new home; starting a new job or relationship; completing a course of study, an important personal project or life phase; making the transition from maidenhood to motherhood or from motherhood to cronehood; funerals or any other important transition a woman is facing.

All rituals, both seasonal and rites of passage, follow the same prescribed structure. This structure derives from the Wicca tradition, but has been simplified in feminist witchcraft, and in New Zealand seems to be even less tightly prescribed than elsewhere. Nevertheless, New Zealand witches are very strict about adhering to a basic format, a simplified version of the one set out in British and American manuals. To begin with, there is a purification, the circle is cast, and the directions and elements are invoked. Next there may be a guided meditation or visualization, followed by the body of the ritual which will include symbolic activity related to the ritual's theme, chanting, singing, sometimes dancing and occasionally the raising of a 'cone of power'. Finally the circle is 'opened'. Rituals conclude with a shared meal and socializing.

In New Zealand, and in many overseas feminist groups, there are no prescriptions for what is said or done at any stage of a ritual – that is decided by the women responsible for organizing the ritual. The only part of a ritual with a set verbal form is the opening of the circle at the conclusion of the ritual. This blessing has been used in all the rituals I have attended. There are no set prayers or invocations which must be included in rituals, although the many manuals available are full of ones for women to use if they wish. Most women borrow, adapt or create their own invocations. I discuss the various components of ritual structure, beginning with the preparation of a ritual, below.

Preparation

In New Zealand, as elsewhere, ritual groups are fairly small – usually between five and 15 members – and quite autonomous. As in many (but not all) feminist covens overseas, but different from gender-mixed Wiccan covens, New Zealand feminist groups use no special status designations such as 'priestess', 'high priestess', 'apprentice' or 'initiate'.

In the group I joined, the responsibility for organizing a particular ritual passes around the members of the group – usually two people plan and facilitate each ritual. A roster is constructed at the annual AGM of the group.[4] While the dates of the Sabbats are tied to the Wheel of the Year, and every effort is made to hold the ritual on the 'correct' date, practical considerations, such as whether the date suits most people, are taken into account when deciding on the date to hold a ritual. During my fieldwork the group took into account my difficulty in getting to Auckland during the week, and a ritual would sometimes be shifted from the 'correct' date so that it would be easier for me to attend. However, women are reluctant to shift rituals more than a day or two from the prescribed date, because the energy is believed to be strongest on the proper date.

Occasionally a ritual will not be planned, beyond deciding on a time and place for the group to meet. Such rituals take shape as women tune in to the theme of the particular seasonal celebration, listen to their intuition, and spontaneously set up an altar, cast the circle, invoke the elements, lead a meditation, and suggest symbolic acts to perform. In the group I joined, Summer Solstice has always been a spontaneous ritual held at a beach because women have felt too busy with end-of-year activities to plan it in detail beforehand.

Preparing for a ritual involves the women who have offered to organize it meeting for a planning session, then posting (nowadays sometimes e-mailing) invitations to other group members detailing where to meet and what to bring (perhaps a candle, cushion, symbols, flowers, food to share). At planning sessions women spend time brainstorming, consulting a variety of manuals, debating the virtues of various venues, delegating responsibility for facilitating various parts of the ritual, making lists of materials to be collected and brought to the ritual, constructing an outline for the ritual, writing the invitation, and consuming a lot of tea and cake. During my fieldwork it was always easy to tell when mail held an invitation to a ritual – the envelopes were typically recycled and decorated with pentacles and spirals, and, when opened, it was not unusual for little gold stars, hearts, glitter, pressed flowers or bright autumn leaves to fall out.

Rituals are usually held in group members' homes or gardens, in community buildings hired for the occasion, in parks or public gardens, on mountains or beaches. Privacy is an important consideration to enable women to concentrate fully on the ritual. It is rare for a ritual to be held in a house when other members of the household are at home. If the ritual is to be held outside in a public place, the organizers will visit the site to find a suitable spot, and, if necessary, prepare it on the day of the ritual by tidying the space, clearing stones, thistles, cow-pats, and so forth. While privacy is important, secrecy is not. In this respect New Zealand feminist witches' rituals differ from the English witches' rituals Greenwood (2000a: 135) and Luhrmann (1989) describe. An outdoor location does not need to be entirely hidden from public view, but a place will be chosen where the public will not stumble upon the ritual.

Preparing the space/setting up

Before the ritual, the room to be used is carefully prepared, usually by the organizers. It is cleaned and, as far as possible, signs of the room's mundane functions are removed or concealed (with silk scarves and batik cloths, for example). Extraneous furniture is removed and the curtains are closed. Candles are placed around the room if the ritual is to be held at night. At one Winter Solstice I attended the organizers had wanted to hold the ritual in a cave, but could not find one suitable, so built a simulated cave in a bedroom using indigo-dyed bed-sheets.

In the centre of the room an altar is created on the floor, or occasionally on a low table, around which the participants will sit on cushions in a circle. The altar is the focus of the ritual and reflects its theme. A circular or square cloth is spread out, the colour often chosen for the ritual's theme (for example, black at Hallowe'en, gold at Lammas, white at Candlemas, red or flowery at Beltane). Symbols of the four elements are placed on the cloth in the appropriate directions: air in the east, water in the west, fire in the north and earth in the south (a compass may be used to check the orientation of the room). The element/direction correlations for water and air are the same as those used by witches in the northern hemisphere, but those for earth and fire have been reversed for the southern hemisphere.[5]

Incense, ready to be lit when the elements and directions are invoked, is often placed in the east, along with other symbols of air, for example, feathers, ornamental birds and butterflies, seed pods, *toetoe*,[6] fans and bells. The ritual sword, the *athame*, is an air symbol commonly mentioned in British and American witchcraft manuals, but I have very rarely seen it used by New Zealand feminist witches and never in the group I joined. A chalice or bowl of water, preferably fresh spring water or sea water, is placed in the west, along with water symbols: shells of all kinds, a starfish or sea urchin, an ornamental dolphin, mermaid or other sea creature. A candle to be lit during the invocation of the elements is placed in the north along with other fire symbols: a wand (symbol of the witch's will) and perhaps red flowers, berries, leaves or red-skinned fruit. Examples of symbols of earth placed in the south might include pentacles, a pot-plant, flowers, a sheaf of wheat, bulbs, fruit, herbs, crystals, stones, ceramic sculptures, a dish of salt, a dish of earth.

Various goddesses from a plethora of pantheons are associated with different elements and their images or symbols may also be placed in the corresponding directions: the Hawaiian Pele and Maori Mahuika, for example, are fire goddesses; Artemis, Persephone and Hine-titama are associated with the east; Gaia, Demeter and Papatuanuku are earth goddesses; Aphrodite and Ishtar are associated with water. A special symbolic object relating to the theme of the ritual is often placed in the centre: an orb, a goddess image or sculpture, a flower arrangement, a candle. A tarot card relating to each of the elements may also be placed on the altar.

Altars are always artistically created and beautiful. The symbols are intended to help women contemplate the theme of the ritual. At a Candlemas ritual I attended, for example, the altar was a blaze of candles forming a pentagram on a gold-coloured cloth. (We spent quite a long time after the ritual ironing the carpet with brown paper to remove the puddles of wax.) At Lammas the altar is often stacked with symbols of the harvest: fresh breads, corn cobs, grapes, grains, fruits and vegetables. At Beltane the altar is festooned with flowers. For outside rituals the altar is much simpler, partly because the whole outdoor environment is evocative in itself, and partly because it is difficult to carry a lot of gear to an outdoor site.

It is important that rituals are prepared with meticulous attention to detail to avoid technical hitches which would interrupt the ritual's flow and women's concentration. Taped music must be ready to go, matches conveniently located, water on hand to dowse a fire if necessary, a torch or candle handy so that a guided visualization can be read comfortably, and so on. Once the circle is cast, women should not leave it except in the case of an emergency.

Entering sacred space

The boundary of the ritual space is consciously marked by the women planning the ritual, and frequently symbolic acts are performed by those attending as they cross this threshold. Shoes (but not clothes as in many Wiccan rituals) are removed if the ritual is held indoors.[7] The door to the ritual room is kept shut until the organizers invite the other participants to enter. If the room has no door, a makeshift curtain may be used to create a symbolic veil between the ritual space and the everyday world. Women are usually greeted at the entrance by the organizers with a kiss or hug. A description of a Winter Solstice ritual in the *Women's Spirituality Newsletter* (Brigid 1991) describes how women were symbolically birthed into the ritual space:

> Each woman came up the stairs and was greeted by two women, hands joined, arms forming an arch. As they walked through the arch, the arms fell to encircle them. 'From woman you were born into this world. From women you are born into this circle.'

After entering the room, each woman chooses a place to sit around the central altar, sets down her candle, symbols and so on, and waits quietly for everyone to be seated. This is a time to 'become centred' – to relax, to become aware of one's physical, emotional, mental and spiritual state, to focus on the purpose of the ritual. Music, instrumental or Goddess chants, may be playing quietly. Once everyone is seated, the atmosphere has stilled, and there is an air of expectation – all of which are judged by the organizers – the ritual begins.

Welcome

One of the organizers welcomes the women and may speak briefly about the ritual's theme. This is not a time, however, for lengthy explanations, and, in fact, at no point during a ritual is there any sermonizing. 'Ritual is a "right brain" activity,' Batten (1988: 16) says, where women allow the creative, emotional, intuitive aspects of themselves free rein. Music, dance, drawing, trance, meditating on symbols and symbolic acts are all regarded as 'right brain activities'. Language and rationality belong to the left brain and are downplayed in ritual. An example of a simple welcome to an Autumn Equinox ritual I attended is set out below:

> Welcome to Autumn Equinox everyone! This Sabbat is also called Mabon after Queen Mab of the Faery People or Maeve of the Celts. Mabon is the harvest festival. It is a time of balance and poise: light and dark are equal, and the dark is about to increase. We meet to celebrate our personal harvests, to rediscover balance in our lives, to fuel our inner fire as the darkness increases. The Mother has become Crone. We honour the wise women in our lives. Welcome!

Purification

Batten (1988: 11) says that 'the transition from outer world into sacred space is not always easy to make, and attentiveness to the need for clearing opens the way for the inner journey'. The purification may take place as women cross the threshold into sacred space, or it may occur before or immediately following the welcome. During the purification women symbolically clear away worries or preoccupations which might prevent them from concentrating fully on the ritual – from being 'fully present'. 'Purification means letting go of the earthplane in readiness for entering between the worlds, the place of connection with Goddess' (Stein 1990: 49).

Purification is not meant to represent a purging from sin (sin not being a relevant concept in this religion) – the things women symbolically leave behind are simply those which might distract their concentration: tiredness, busyness, nervousness, self-doubt, guilt about leaving children or partner for the evening, physical aches and pains, worries about work or money, preoccupation with a domestic issue. The purification involves each woman in the circle performing a symbolic act and sometimes articulating what she is 'leaving behind'. Examples of purifications, using different elements, are:

- A bowl of water (perhaps scented and containing floating flower petals) is passed around the circle for women to wash their hands or sprinkle or flick water around their body.
- Each woman strokes the aura of the woman next to her with incense, a

stalk of wheat (Autumn Equinox), a long-stemmed flower (Spring Equinox), a wand or a feather.
- Each woman shakes maracas around her body and then passes them to the next woman.
- A large stone is passed around the circle. Each participant projects into the stone everything she wants to leave behind, then the stone is plunged into a bucket of sea water.

Casting the circle

The casting of the circle is critically important to all witches' rituals. It explicitly and symbolically marks their separation from the everyday world and entry into a liminal state. It is 'a gesture of unification that marks the enclosure of sacred space' (Batten 1988: 12). The circle is a place where women are free to be themselves, where they can expect loving acceptance and can address issues in their lives in a safe, confidential and supportive context, and where they can perform symbolic acts of self-transformation.

But the cast circle is more: it is seen as an 'energy form' which contains the positive energy the women generate. It is this energy which helps make the ritual a more powerful experience for participants, and which, they believe, helps them achieve the transformations they seek. Because the circle is seen as a container of energy, it is crucial that once the circle is cast no one enters or leaves it. If someone arrives late to the ritual, and the group agrees to admit her, the circle must be recast.

In the southern hemisphere the circle should be cast in an anti-clockwise direction, following the direction of the sun's movement, according to American writers (Starhawk 1989: 75; Stein 1990: 50). However New Zealand feminist witches do not consistently follow this practice and Batten does not mention it: the direction for casting varies.

Some methods of casting the circle are:

- An object (candle, crystal, fruit or symbolic object) is passed around the circle. Each woman, as she passes it on, says to the woman next to her, 'Welcome to Beltane [for example], —— [woman's name]'. Or a dish of perfumed oil may be passed around, with each woman anointing her neighbour's forehead with a crescent moon or pentagram.
- Women join hands and a squeeze is passed around the circle three times. Women visualize energy swirling around the circle.
- At Lammas a chalice of grape juice may be passed around the circle, each participant welcoming and toasting the woman to whom she passes the chalice.
- Each woman in turn chants her name into the circle and the others echo it back to her three times.

After performing one such symbolic act, all participants join hands, close their eyes, and contemplate their connectedness within the circle of sacred space.

Invoking the directions/elements

According to Starhawk (1989: 75), the concept of the quartered circle which is basic to witchcraft is a feature of many worldviews and religions.

> This concept is common to Native American, African, East Indian, Tibetan, and many other spiritual systems, as are the four elements of air, fire, water, and earth. Of course, we know that these are not elements in the same sense as are hydrogen, helium, and carbon, but they are the basic necessities for sustaining life.
>
> (Starhawk 1989: 226)

Juliet Batten calls this phase of the ritual 'orientation'. If the ritual is held outside, and sometimes when it is held inside, the *tangata whenua* are honoured, 'acknowledging other layers of experience of this land and deep identification with it' (Batten 1988: 12).[8]

The directions and corresponding elements are invoked verbally, along with the qualities of each element and any goddesses associated with particular elements or directions whose presence or 'energy' the women wish to invoke. The invoking may be done by the organizers or by four different women, each one seated in one of the directions (in this case, the invocations may be written on cards and placed at the edge of the altar in the appropriate direction). In groups where women are experienced ritual-makers, the invoking may be done spontaneously. The qualities or associations connected with each of the elements are set out below (compiled from Batten 1988 and Starhawk 1989).

> *Fire/North*: spirit, energy, power, will, passion, opening, manifesting, destruction, summer.
> *Earth/South*: body, depth, withdrawal, inner journey, nurturance, darkness, fertility, winter.
> *Air/East*: mind, dawn, beginnings, newness, freshness, knowing, intuition, rationality, clarity, spring.
> *Water/West*: emotions, flow, return, surrender, daring, autumn.

The centre is the fifth 'direction' and is invoked last. It is seen as the catalyst, the point of transformation, 'the place where magic happens'. An example of what might be said during the invocation is set out below. It was used in a ritual for a woman who was about to leave New Zealand on an overseas trip (hence the incorporation of Maori deities).

> Hine-titama, goddess of the east and the air, the dawn maiden, you are the mother of us all and you greet us in death. Come and be with us now.
> Mahuika, goddess of the north, the one who gave the world fire, you warm us with your energy. Come and be with us now.
> Taranga, goddess of the west, who gave birth to Maui in the ocean, you keep us alive with the water of life. Come and be with us now.
> Papa-tuanuku, goddess of the south, who came forth from Te Po, the darkness, you are our mother earth. Come and be with us now.
> Hine-ahu-one, the essence of all living things, breathe with us now and energize us with your power. Centre us now.

Guided meditation/visualization

Almost all witches' rituals include a guided meditation or guided visualization designed to invoke a state of trance. The meditation takes the form of an imaginary journey in the course of which each participant receives new energy, insight, a symbolic gift, or a message from a Being or the Goddess who may take a variety of forms (including the form of the woman imagining the journey).

One of the organizers prepares the meditation, either by taking one from a manual or by writing her own. Taped music may be played softly in the background. Meditation tapes or gentle classical music are used most often.

Before the meditation women are asked to make themselves comfortable – they may wish to lie down. The woman leading the meditation asks them to close their eyes, then takes them through a full body relaxation sequence. The journey may begin with women imagining themselves in a beautiful or wild place in nature, usually one familiar to and loved by them – it may be a beach, a forest, a mountain-top, a field of flowers. Or the journey may begin by women discovering an entrance – to a cave, a magical garden, a labyrinth. In some journeys women travel back in time, either to another stage of their own lives or to a past era.

Once the goal of the meditation experience has been reached, the person leading the meditation guides the women back to the journey's starting point – back to the gate, the garden, the entrance to the cave, or the field of flowers. This is important, as some women fall into trance easily and deeply and may find it difficult to return to normal consciousness. Starhawk (1989: 157) describes the point of trance thus:

> Trance unlocks the tremendous potential inherent in our unused awareness. We can augment our sensitivity, growth, and creativity.
>
> In trance we are more suggestible – a fact that underlies the most common uses of hypnosis . . . The Craft teaches the use of suggestion to help us consciously direct our own minds . . . [W]e increase our awareness of the functioning of suggestion and learn to use it

> deliberately on ourselves . . . The unconscious is no longer split off, but is in constant communication with the conscious mind.
>
> We can use our own suggestibility for both physical and emotional healing. Mind and body are linked, and our emotional state contributes to disease, whether it is purely physical or psychosomatic. Suggestion can aid learning, increase concentration, and further creativity. It can also open up new forms of awareness and awaken the psychic senses.
>
> Trance stimulates vision and imagination and opens up new sources of creativity. When the barriers between the unconscious and the conscious are crossed, ideas, images, plans, and solutions to problems arise freely. As the right-hemisphere, holistic vision is awakened, it becomes a rich source of insight, of new and original approaches to situations.

Guided meditations are based on the idea of 'power from within' – that each individual is her own ultimate source of knowing about herself and her life, and has within her the power to know and meet her own needs and to realize herself fully. By passing into an altered state of consciousness, women believe they gain access to this self-knowledge and discover the tools they need to use the knowledge effectively in dealing with and directing their own lives. Whatever is brought back from the imaginary journey may be applied to specific issues or situations in a woman's life: her 'deep self' gives her conscious self insight on the situation.

My understanding of how guided meditations or visualizations work for New Zealand feminist witches is rather different from Luhrmann's understanding of their function for English witches. In England, the guided visualization is called a 'pathworking' and constitutes the most important component of a ritual. English witches believe that as the participant imagines the pathworking, power to bring about a desired change is released and produces the change. The power is seen as a kind of force which can be generated or activated by, but also moves beyond, the individual or group. The greater the ability of the participants to visualize powerfully, the greater the power. Luhrmann writes (1989: 194):

> A pathworking is the paramount form through which power is supposedly generated, gathered and released as the story develops and climaxes. The standard explanation for a ritual is that as the story is being told, the power is flowing, stimulated by the participants' imaginations. At the climax of the story, the power is released through the final images in the rite.

Most of the witches I have worked with do not seem to believe that, as they are sitting in a room imagining a journey and an encounter with a powerful

Being, power is released 'out there' on their behalf. Rather, they believe that the experience of the guided meditation enables them to contact their own inner power and knowledge and gain insight on how to use these effectively.

In one meditation I participated in, we were asked to imagine ourselves in a beautiful garden, to discover a path and follow it, to enter a warm enveloping mist, and then to emerge on the other side of the mist where we met the Goddess. The Goddess gave us each a gift which we took back with us along the same route. Following the visualization we were invited to make statements to the group about the experience beginning: 'In my trance . . . '. Here are some of them:

> In my trance the Goddess gave me a book. It was the story of my life and it was only half written. It was for me to write the rest.
>
> In my trance I saw the Goddess, and she was me.
>
> In my trance the Goddess gave me a stone which was many times heavier than its size.
>
> In my trance the Goddess became very old and turned into a Crone before my very eyes.

The guided meditation usually takes place before the central enactment phase of the ritual. It opens women to a new state of consciousness, gives them a sense of connection with their inner or 'deep self', enhances their sense of the sacred through the imagined meeting with the Goddess, and provides an intense imaginative and emotional experience which prepares them for the transformation work which occurs during the next phase of the ritual.

Enactment

'Enactment' is Juliet Batten's name for the heart of the ritual where its central purpose is enacted. It usually incorporates two main parts: a sacrifice and a constructive, constitutive component. The sacrifice often involves participants identifying what is preventing them from moving forward in their lives and then performing symbolic actions to leave behind, destroy or banish these things from their lives. Having cleared away negativities or obstacles, women are then ready to 'bring in the new' (Batten 1988: 14). Here, participants affirm their new goal, acknowledge new learning or insight, make a commitment to themselves, pledge an action, or prepare to embark on a new phase. Again, a symbolic act is performed.

In their heightened state of awareness as a result of the guided meditation, or a period of silent meditation, participants seem to discover what they need to sacrifice relatively easily. They may be invited to write down or draw a symbol of these negativities and then burn the bits of paper in a cauldron or on an open fire if one is available. A metal rubbish bin, old pot or wok serves just as well. Sacrifices can be quite dramatic. As each woman steps forward, names what she is burning, sets it alight and drops it in the cauldron, the rest of the group may stamp and shout and beat drums to demonstrate their support. They may chant repetitively something like: 'Banish, burn, go!' The burning may also be done in silence, but in a highly charged atmosphere.

Fire, as in many religions, is regarded as a highly potent form of sacrifice, but other methods are also used. Symbols of what is to be sacrificed may be buried in earth or sand or thrown into the sea. Cords representing what is binding a woman to the past may be cut. Clay may be moulded into a symbol of an obstacle and then pounded.

At a birthday ritual for one of the women in the group I joined, the woman whose birthday it was had pinned a red paper heart to her top and suspended a 'cage' cut from a cardboard box around her neck covering the heart. She explained that she had been finding it difficult to get emotionally close to friends and people she loved, and wanted to change this. She took off the cage, cut it up, and burnt it in the fireplace, symbolically freeing her emotional self. She also wore a skirt made of strips of paper. Each strip represented something she wanted to leave behind or an issue which needed resolving. Each of these was named, ripped off the waist-band, and thrown into the fire. In the weeks following the ritual the woman concentrated on resolving these issues and conflicts.

After the symbolic sacrifice, the woman reported feeling 'lighter and better'. She felt, though, that her heart was too exposed and needed some protection and so, during the constructive phase of the ritual, she placed garlands of different coloured ribbons around her neck, each symbolizing an aspect of her life which would be important during the coming year – career, friends, ritual, health, home, 'lots of fun' and so on. She arranged some of the ribbons to fall across the heart so that it would 'feel less exposed'. Everyone in the group gave her a gift to symbolize what we wished for her in the coming year: a black lace garter for sensuality, a bulb of garlic for good health, a badge bearing the woman's symbol to remind her of her strength, a bracelet woven from eleven strands representing the love of group members, a bracelet of shells with various symbolic meanings including wisdom and protection. The ritual concluded with feasting and celebration.

The key elements in the constructive phase of the ritual are healing, resolution, change and transformation. The planting of seeds is a common symbolic act used in this part of the ritual. Examples of other constructive symbolic acts are set out below.

- In a Beltane ritual participants made garlands of spring flowers to be worn during the maypole dancing. Each flower was chosen to represent a quality or something new they wanted to bring into or foster in their lives.

- In an Autumn Equinox ritual women plaited girdles from carpet wool, weaving in symbols of their personal harvests or qualities they wanted to carry forward into the dark, lean period of winter.
- At the conclusion of a series of Goddess workshops, we were invited to choose two of the goddesses we had studied whose qualities we especially wanted to invoke in our lives. The facilitator produced containers of glitter in different colours – each representing a different goddess: yellow for Hestia, blue for Artemis, green for Aphrodite, red for Demeter and so on. We each sprinkled glitter from the two containers representing our chosen goddesses into a bowl of water and stirred them together with a wand so that they swirled and sparkled in the candlelight.
- In another workshop we were encouraged to think of something we wanted to request of Artemis. Each woman in turn placed 'Artemis's crown', a grand headdress of peacock feathers, on her head, made her request, and beat on a drum saying: 'Artemis, hear my call'. The requests included: vindication for a shamed daughter, help to find a focus in life, help to explore creativity, help to care for oneself better, help to deal with a bureaucratic institution. One woman invoked Artemis the huntress by stating: 'I want to become the arrow, the bow and the target!'

Chanting

Chants, the simpler and more repetitive the better, are said to help induce a state of trance. The effect of 'droning music', says Shekhinah Mountainwater (1991: 93), is enchanting and hypnotic, and has a powerful effect on consciousness. American witchcraft manuals give the words to numerous chants, mostly written by women and some men over the past three decades, but including Sumerian chants and chants borrowed or adapted from other religious traditions. Only a few of these are used in New Zealand, probably because women do not know the tunes to most of them.[9] New Zealand feminist witches frequently say they wish they knew more chants. Apart from a handful of well-known and often-used chants, chanting in New Zealand witches' rituals tends to be spontaneous and lacking in established lyrical and melodic forms.

Chants may be incorporated into any part of a ritual. A 'names chant' may be done at the beginning to acknowledge each woman and to welcome her. In a large group, all women may simultaneously sing, say or chant their names repeatedly into the circle; the sound builds to a crescendo and then dies away. The process is guided by all participants listening and tuning in to one another. In a smaller group, each woman may in turn chant her name in a way which expresses how she is feeling, then the group echoes the chant back to her. The elements may be invoked by members of the group spontaneously chanting the qualities of each element in a way which evokes the energy of the element.

I noted above that during the sacrifice phase of the ritual women may repetitively chant a simple phrase such as: 'Banish, burn, go!' accompanied by drum-beat. Chanting may also be used in the constructive phase of the ritual. During the first workshop I ever attended with Juliet Batten, each participant plaited a 'magic cord' using three strands of twine in different colours, each representing a quality we wanted to weave into our life (for example, serenity, spontaneity, self-trust, creativity, toughness, healing, joy, faith, opening and self-love). The cords were tied around our waists or wrists or wound into headbands or necklaces, then we held hands and spontaneously chanted together the three qualities we each wanted to invoke. On each successive workshop evening the magic cords were worn to remind us of the qualities we had named.

The most powerful and dramatic chant witches use is the 'cone of power'. Stein (1990: 61) says that in the US raising the cone of power is done in almost every Dianic group ritual in some way, and Eller (1993: 97) declares it 'the simplest and most common ritual practice'. The point of raising the cone is to concentrate the group's energy and to direct it towards furthering the purpose of the ritual and bringing about the inner transformations each participant seeks.

Batten (1988: 21) describes the technical aspects of raising the cone, at least as it is commonly practised in New Zealand:

> The group begins with linked hands, relaxes and breathes together, until there is a sense that the group is one whole. Then the breath becomes a simple quiet hum. It builds in strength, throats open and vowel sounds emerge. The notes build. Consonants, words may be added, or the notes may simply rise, higher and higher, building in both pitch and intensity as the visualised cone builds to a peak. A drum or other percussion instruments may join the chant. When the energy has built to its highest point, the leader cries out 'Now!' The sound is cut, and everyone grounds, palms to the earth, allowing the energy to return to the source. They breathe, in trance. The energy flows through them strongly, clearing and purifying, carrying with it tears from released pain, anger, tension, blocks and resistances. By relaxing into the energy flow and trusting the process, the women experience a letting go. They feel energised and clear.[10]

In my experience the raising of a cone of power is done much less frequently in rituals in New Zealand and has rather different purposes from those described in the US. Starhawk (1989: 237), Stein (1990: 61) and Eller (1993: 98), for example, talk about the cone as a concentration of energy which can be directed towards the achievement of a specific goal, either related to the women in the ritual or to a goal outside, such as the healing of a person. The success of the exercise depends on the women visualizing their intent very clearly. Among New Zealand feminist witches, however, the point of the raising of the cone has more to do with its general therapeutic value for participants.

Dance

Dancing with or without music, either free and unstructured accompanied by whooping, drumming or chanting, or simple circle dancing, is a part of many rituals, especially the more light-hearted Spring Equinox, Beltane and Summer Solstice ones. In circle dances women retain their place in the circle, often link hands, and perform simple steps which take them towards the centre and out again and move them to left and right in the circle. Because the steps are so simple and repetitive, permitting the dancers to close their eyes, a state of light trance may be induced. Circle dances include traditional dances from various countries (for example, Greece, Ireland and Germany) and dances which the ritual-makers themselves create to suit the mood and theme of the ritual. Dance may be included at any stage of a ritual.

Opening the circle

At the conclusion of every ritual I have attended, the circle is opened with the singing or speaking of the traditional Wiccan blessing:

> The circle is open, but not broken
> May the peace of the Goddess go in our hearts.
> Merry meet and merry part, and merry meet again!
> Blessed be.

The opening of the circle marks the formal conclusion of the ritual. Candles are blown out, lights are switched on, women retrieve their symbols and the altar objects are put away.

Re-integration

The passage between the sacred space of ritual and woman's everyday lives is facilitated by the sharing of food and drink, talk and music. This is said to 'ground' women and bring them back to 'everyday awareness' before they go home (Batten 1988: 15). During this period of socializing, arrangements for the next ritual may be discussed.

As well as the fairly elaborate rituals I have described, witches do spells. A spell is a mini-ritual usually performed by one woman. It may be incorporated within the framework of a group ritual, or it may stand alone. In the latter case, the woman who is doing the spell will prepare and perform it largely on her own, while the others sit in the circle with her as witnesses and providers of moral support. They may join in during part of the spell, but only if the spell-maker requests it. Sometimes a group will gather for a special evening of spells, and time may be set aside during workshops for women to do spells if they wish. Spell-making is discussed further in chapter 11.

Most feminist witches' rituals, whether they are rites of passage or seasonal festivals, conform to the structure I have described in this chapter. I have emphasized here the separate components of this structure; however in rituals these components often flow into one another and may not be explicitly announced as they occur. They are, however, usually readily identifiable to anyone familiar with Batten's *Power from Within* or with US manuals by, for example, Starhawk, Diane Stein or Barbara Walker. In the next chapter I begin with a description of a Winter Solstice ritual to demonstrate how a ritual works as an organic whole, albeit one constructed of segments borrowed from diverse sources.

10

RITUAL AS ARTEFACT

Winter Solstice, Te Henga

We pulled into the near-empty car park backing on to the dunes at Te Henga just before 11:30am. A few other car-loads were arriving and unloading – I didn't recognize anyone, but it was easy to tell they were here for the same reason – all women, well wrapped up, mostly in black or dark colours, some in heavy cloaks, lugging bags of firewood, jar lanterns, kits containing vacuum flasks and rugs.

Unsure of what to do or where to go, we made for a sandy path between the dunes and were met and greeted by two women I faintly recognized from last year's Solstice. They were updating the *Women's Spirituality Newsletter* mailing list and collecting donations towards Luisah Teish's visit. We were told to go further along the path where another woman would meet and brief us on the ritual.

With this third woman we formed an 'information circle' and were told the procedure for the first phase of the ritual – the journey to the cave – and the chants to be used in the ritual itself. After the briefing, we climbed higher into the dunes to join women who had already been inducted in similar circles.

By noon close to 100 women had gathered, were sitting talking quietly in small clusters with friends (presumably many belonging to the same ritual group), or alone in meditation overlooking the sea. The sky was heavy but the rain held off; there was a light, salty breeze off the Tasman, a strong sense of anticipation, excitement.

Finally a woman holding a tall staff signalled that we were about to begin the journey to the cave. We stood and filed after her in silence. We had been told that this was a time to 'ground and centre' ourselves in preparation for the ritual, and to leave spaces of several metres between each other to facilitate this. The line stretched out in front of me and behind, disappeared into the sand-hills and re-emerged snaking between the dunes.

The cave is at the south end of the beach. Over the brow of a hill I saw in the distance a woman standing very erect in its entrance holding a staff, watching us. At our approach she dramatically raised the staff and a drumming began deep inside the cave, echoing out to us over the sand-hills above the sound of the surf. We climbed down over mussel-covered rocks and, between in-rushings of the tide, scuttled into the cave.

We lit our lanterns (mostly candles standing in sand inside a large jar with a string handle) and stowed any extra gear against the cave walls beyond the reach of the tide. The cave was deep and domed high overhead. Towards the back, in the centre, a fire had been lit and an old woman in a purple cloak sat tending it. A circle of women had begun to form towards the back of the cave. We joined it, arranging ourselves cross-legged on the damp sand on bits of plastic with our candle lanterns in front of us.

As the last of the women entered the cave and the circle of lantern-light closed, the drumming intensified. Other drummers joined in and the rhythm changed. Women on the other side of the circle began beating maracas. The sound reverberated around the cave walls, seemed to swirl around the circle, became engulfing.

Light from the cave mouth illuminated a pall of smoke hanging above us. The woman who had led us to the cave walked anti-clockwise around the circle, then stationed herself between us and the cave mouth to stand as guardian (to stop curious members of the public from coming in to the cave).

The drumming stopped. The woman by the fire stood and said, 'Welcome everyone! Welcome to Winter Solstice! We celebrate the long dark and welcome the return of the sun.' She moved to face each of the four directions and repeated the welcome, beginning in the west, and then took her place in the circle among members of her ritual group.

Another woman stood and walked to the centre of the circle facing the mouth of the cave. She gave its full Maori name and acknowledged the *tangata whenua* of the area and our gratitude for their blessing on the holding of the ritual.

It was explained that we would invoke the elements first with a 'walking meditation'. We all stood and walked or danced anti-clockwise in the circle chanting repetitively, accompanied by percussion instruments, 'The earth, the water, the fire and the air; Returns, returns, returns, returns'. Then four women performed an invocation to the four directions, chanting the words loudly and slowly:

> West, water, water, west, water, water
> Turn the ocean tide . . . LISTEN
> North, fire, fire, north, fire, fire
> Turn us to the dark . . . WATCH
> East, air, air, east, air, air
> Breathe the winter wind . . . FEEL
> South, earth, earth, south, earth, earth
> Hold us in the dark . . . TOUCH

We were invited to 'bring our energy into the circle' by chanting, singing or shouting our names into the circle. Women began immediately to do this – the chanting tentative at first, then building to a crescendo and ebbing away.

The old woman who had welcomed us stood and invited the Goddess to be with us, concluding the invocation with, 'Help us to dream our lives again'.

We were told that there was to be a time for personal meditation, accompanied by drumming, during which we were to ask ourselves, 'What are you ready to sacrifice to fire?' We were asked to let any images or words come into our minds; the slowing of the drum-beat would bring us back from the meditation. We closed our eyes and again the drum-beat began swirling around the circle, this time created by one woman drumming while walking quickly around the perimeter of the circle close to us.

The drumming slowed and stopped. We were invited to sacrifice whatever we felt we no longer wanted or needed in our lives by leaving our places in the circle, taking sticks of wood from one of four piles to symbolize what we wanted to destroy, and casting them into the central fire. Women did this as they felt ready, usually several at a time. Most were solemn, some stood a moment in front of the fire before casting in their piece of wood. The wood-piles gradually emptied and the refuelled fire blazed.

The sacrifice ended and a chant began, which we all joined in, singing it several times:

> We all come from the Goddess
> And to Her we shall return
> Like a drop of rain
> Flowing to the ocean.

Another short meditation followed. This time we were encouraged to go within and find our own 'inner sun', a personal strength to celebrate. When we opened our eyes after perhaps five minutes, one of the facilitators had changed into a long, bright yellow dress. She announced that the shortest day had passed; it was time to welcome the sun's return. We were each given a yellow balloon to symbolize our personal 'inner sun'. The balloons were blown up, knotted, waved, batted or thrown into the air amid whoops of celebration.

The ritual group which had organized and facilitated the ritual formed a circle in the centre holding hands, facing outwards (towards us). They led the final blessing:

> The circle is open but not broken
> May the peace of the Goddess go in our hearts
> Merry meet and merry part, and merry meet again
> Blessed Be!

Someone announced, 'Let the feasting begin!' Women fetched hot soup and muffins, chocolate and fruit and shared it in groups. There was laughter and embracing as women met up with others from their ritual groups or women they had met at ritual workshops. A few took a mid-winter swim.

We finished our picnics, packed up and trekked back along the beach to the car.

This account of a Winter Solstice ritual held at Te Henga (Bethell's Beach on Auckland's west coast) comes from my field notebook dated 22 June 1991. Rituals fairly similar to this are still held every year at Te Henga, although the responsibility for organizing them has since passed to other ritual groups which have each introduced their own unique elements and energies. The rituals have always been open, meaning that all women are welcome to participate, irrespective of whether or not they belong to a feminist ritual group. Open rituals like this provide an opportunity for interested women to taste ritual without having to commit themselves to taking a course or becoming a member of an established group. Each year the ritual is advertised in the *Women's Spirituality Newsletter* (timing is arranged to fit in with low tide) and attendance ranges between 80 and 130, including a sprinkling of girl children. Following the particular Solstice ritual described above, a number of accounts and poems about it appeared in the *Newsletter* (Brigid 1991). Here are extracts from three of these:

> Senses totally stimulated – the power of the sea calling me inside myself. The safety of the cave and the sense of love and belonging drawing me close to the other women. Feeling my baby stirring within my womb, and knowing I have come home.

> Moving in silence with many other women, serpent-like over the soft, undulating body of the Great Mother – entering the darkness of her womb and exploring my own darkness. Feeling connected to nature and safe to face my fears. Yearning for the light.

> The journey beginning with oneself
> Among the dunes of Bethell's
> Being in one's inner darkness
> Letting go unwanted thoughts, feelings
> Being there . . .
> At home in the bosom of the Great Mother
> The Spirit of Te Henga
> Papatuanuku[1]

I begin this chapter by describing this Winter Solstice ritual to demonstrate that feminist witches' rituals, like their belief systems, are collages constructed of borrowed, adapted and invented elements. Luhrmann (1989: 244) has made this point very clearly (and apparently disapprovingly) about English witches' incorporation of diverse mythologies and symbolisms within their magical practices, saying: 'They poach from the past in the interests of the present and plunder the world's mythology for their symbolic goods'. I will return to the issue of appropriation below; first I discuss further the phenomenon of witches' invention of ritual.

In *Secular Ritual* Moore and Myerhoff warn of the potential danger that those carrying out rituals will glimpse themselves as the inventors of those rituals, as the makers of their meaning, and as the creators of their own culture, and will thereby discharge the rituals of meaning. They write:

> And underlying all rituals is an ultimate danger . . . the possibility that we will encounter ourselves making up our conceptions of the world, society our very selves. We may slip in that fatal perspective of recognizing culture as our construct, arbitrary, conventional, invented by mortals.
>
> (Moore and Myerhoff 1977: 18)

This 'danger' is clearly not one which troubles feminist witches. They are well aware that their rituals are deliberately and self-consciously constructed. Moreover, they know that all rituals are. Barbara Walker, a well-known author in the Goddess movement, writes: 'The practice of religion is ritual, and every ritual *is* a human invention' (Walker 1990: 3). It is relevant here that a large proportion of the women involved in feminist witchcraft/Goddess spirituality have university degrees (see chapter six), many in the social sciences, and I met many who had studied at least some anthropology and had some familiarity with the role of ritual cross-culturally. Starhawk regularly draws on anthropological knowledge in her writing. Understanding that not only their own beliefs and rituals, but all religious rituals in all cultures, are invented leads them not to reject all rituals as meaningless, but to recognize a universal importance of ritual in the lives of human societies past and present. Interestingly, whereas mainstream religion in Western society is often criticized for being narrow-minded and convinced of its own unique access to truth, Pagans are sometimes criticized for indiscriminately embracing aspects of many religions in order to create their own pastiche.

The Winter Solstice ritual described above was clearly designed by the ritual group that organized it to evoke what they imagined an ancient pagan ritual might have been like. The venue was a cave – according to participants in the modern Goddess movement, archaeological evidence indicates that caves have been used as sites for venerating the Goddess since the Palaeolithic. The fire, the drumming, the invocation of a trance-like state, and the crone tending the fire were all carefully calculated images intended to assist women to imagine that they were participating in a ritual which had ancient roots.

There is a paradox here – there seems to be a notion among contemporary witches that any claims to authenticity for their spiritual practices require some claim to historicity. Luhrmann (1989: 244) also makes this point, stating that English witches 'make an effort to ground their myth and symbolism in history'. 'Yet,' she says, 'magicians free themselves from the need to prove their historical accuracy and the cultural pertinence of the appropriate mythology by arguing that history can serve the role of personal metaphor or myth'. It is true that Starhawk concludes her account of the 'history' of witchcraft by saying:

> Witchcraft has always been a religion of poetry not theology. The myths, legends, and teachings are recognized as metaphors for 'That-Which-Cannot-Be-Told', the absolute reality our limited minds can never completely know.
>
> (Starhawk 1989: 2)

The details of the history of witchcraft are regarded as less important than the broad outline of the 'history' and its symbolic importance. While on one hand ancient historians, art historians, classicists and archaeologists are building and debating a body of scholarship intended to shed light on the issue of ancient goddess-worship, on the other hand women in the Goddess movement often say that they do not require this kind of authority in order to claim that their new/old religion is valid. It is as if they know that religious traditions typically lay claim to a 'history' which acts to authenticate the tradition primarily for insiders but also for outsiders; thus, in their re-creation of Goddess religion, they have constructed for themselves what they sometimes call their 'history' and 'traditions', sometimes their 'mythology', and sometimes a poetic narrative which has metaphoric significance.

Realistically, as most modern witches know, we can have little idea about how Winter Solstice was celebrated thousands of years ago, but the legitimacy and success of feminist rituals do not require this knowledge. It is enough to invoke an imaginative connection, a connection women 'intuitively feel' they have with early goddess-worshipping societies. It is clear from what the three women who participated in the Winter Solstice ritual wrote about it afterwards in the *Women's Spirituality Newsletter* (quoted above) that the ritual's imagery had evoked in them an imaginative, emotional response – they talked about the cave as the womb of the Great Mother and saw the dunes as her soft, curvaceous body. The poignancy of this imagery heightened the women's experiences of the ritual. They felt closer to other women, connected to nature, and safe to face personal fears and inner darkness.

Moore and Myerhoff (1977: 7) argue that certain formal properties of collective ritual or ceremony lend themselves very well to making ritual a 'traditionalizing instrument', and that collective ceremony can traditionalize new material as well as perpetuate old traditions. The means by which new ritual forms become traditionalized, according to Moore and Myerhoff, include: repetition (either of occasion, content or form), acting (rather than behaving spontaneously), 'special' behaviour or stylization (the use of actions and symbols in a way that sets them apart from mundane uses), order (the imposition of a prescribed structure), evocative presentational style (including the manipulation of symbols and sensory stimuli), and the 'collective dimension' – the very occurrence of the ritual contains a social message. They claim:

> In the repetition and order, ritual imitates the rhythmic imperatives of the biological and physical universe, thus suggesting a link with the perpetual processes of the cosmos. It thereby implies permanence and legitimacy of what are actually evanescent cultural constructs. In the acting, stylization and presentational staging, ritual is attention-commanding and deflects questioning at the time. All these formal properties make it an ideal vehicle for the conveying of messages in an authenticating and arresting manner.
>
> (p. 8)

Feminist witches' rituals in general and the Winter Solstice ritual I described in particular contain each of the traditionalizing properties Moore and Myerhoff list. The structural form of rituals, detailed in chapter nine, is orderly, repetitive and prescribed, although there is room within rituals for spontaneity and improvisation. The Winter Solstice ritual included the qualities of acting and staging – we were told before the ritual the words of the chants to be included, and the whole ritual, in fact, had the quality of a theatrical performance. (This is less obvious, however, in smaller rituals where only a few women who know each other well participate.) The invocation of the elements and directions by the four women, in particular, was a staged performance with carefully rehearsed and synchronized movements, words and sounds. The combination of invoking an imaginative, emotionally-charged connection with ancient pagan rituals through the use of particular images along with the employment of the traditionalizing properties Moore and Myerhoff describe contribute to the tradition-like quality of feminist witches' rituals.

I have noted that a component of many rituals is the adaptation of elements from non-Western spiritual traditions, especially those of so-called 'nature religions'. In the US Native American spirituality, in particular, is a popular source, and various practices have filtered into New Zealand. Workshops devoted to shamanic drumming and the shamanic journey have been held in Auckland and other centres.[2] The use of particular drumming rhythms in the Winter Solstice ritual recalled shamanic drumming used to induce altered states of consciousness.

Another Native American technique sometimes used in the purification stage of a ritual is smudging. This involves setting alight a container or tied bunch of a special combination of dried herbs and wafting the smoke (sometimes with a feather) from the smouldering herbs all around the body, the palms and the soles of the feet. This is believed to remove any negative energies or thoughts.

Other elements used in the construction of feminist witches' rituals are concepts and techniques derived from New Age therapies and those adapted from psychotherapy. I have noted that the best known facilitators of Goddess workshops during the 1990s also worked as psychotherapists, and one was particularly inclined towards Jungian thinking. Thus working with personally meaningful symbols was extremely important in the rituals she developed. In an interview she told me: 'Symbols represent collective experiences of the feminine that go through time, and so connect us to our ancestors and the whole continuity of female experience throughout time'. Working with symbols is an enormously important part of New Zealand witches' rituals and will be discussed further in chapter 11.

Terms such as 'grounding' and 'centring' are popular New Age jargon which have spilt into feminist witchcraft/Goddess spirituality and are beginning to spill into the everyday speech of New Zealanders unconnected with either movement. Central concerns of New Age therapies are self-awareness, self-healing, self-development and self-transformation. In the Winter Solstice ritual the invitation to 'bring our energy into the circle' by chanting, singing or shouting our names was inspired by New Age self-affirmations. Creative visualization and guided meditation, components of most feminist rituals, are techniques borrowed directly from New Age manuals.

In creating their rituals by assembling elements from diverse borrowed sources, especially from the religions of non-Western peoples, contemporary witches and Pagans lay themselves open to the accusation that they are appropriating cultural resources which they have no right to, often from indigenous peoples who have already suffered from having their resources appropriated by white colonizers. Moreover, it could be argued, the extraction of religious elements from the cultures in which they are embedded may rob not only the original 'owners', but also the meaning from the religious element – whether it is a myth, deity, chant, religious tool or ritual practice.

Contemporary witches and Pagans have a range of takes on this matter. Some see the borrowing as unproblematic, claiming that there is universal value in a great diversity of spiritual traditions which offer insights and benefits desperately needed by today's world beyond the confines of their cultures of origin. Indigenous cultures, in particular, they say, are frequently the repositories of valuable spiritual knowledge which has been lost and needs to be retrieved by Western societies. In these people's view, religions are bigger than cultures and are not the property of specific cultures. Answering the accusation that their appropriating behaviour could be seen as perpetuating a colonialist or imperialist impulse, these Pagans insist that they treat others' sacred beliefs, rituals and sites with reverence and indigenous societies with respect. They would see themselves as learning respectfully, rather than poaching, from other cultures. Starhawk (1989: 214) has stressed the responsibilities which accompany such learning from indigenous cultures:

> Any real spiritual power we gain from any tradition carries with it responsibility. If we learn from African drum rhythms or the Lakota sweat lodge, we have incurred an obligation to not romanticize the people we have learned from but to participate in the very real struggles being waged for liberation, land, and cultural survival.

Starhawk herself has a long history of dedicated political activity in these and other vital areas, but it cannot really be said that the movement as a whole mobilizes for such causes, especially in New Zealand (although individuals within it have done and still do). Whatever Starhawk says, one senses a mix of romantic nostalgia for the primitive or exotic with cultural ignorance or naivety when Pagans and witches proclaim the potency of, for example, their power animal or dream-catcher.

Some women in the movement defend and even celebrate their borrowing of religious elements from ancient and indigenous cultures, seeing the resulting collage of decontextualized beliefs, deities, and ritual practices as legitimate in a postmodern and increasingly globalized world where cultural resources are considered part of the universal human heritage.[3] Others, however, are troubled by the issue of appropriation. Asphodel Long describes how, as time has gone on, the focus of the Goddess movement in Britain has shifted away from South American, African and other traditional religions to 'home goddesses' – those of ancient Britain and northern Europe. She tells of the dilemma she faced when asked to teach a postgraduate course on African goddesses, which she refused to do because she did not want to take up a 'colonialist' position (Long 1995: 26–7).

A number of New Zealand women are uncomfortable about or critical of the way in which elements of Native American religions in particular (for example, ideas and practices relating to Shamanism) have been appropriated by the US Goddess movement. At worst, this is regarded as cultural theft by a more powerful social group (mostly white, middle-class women), as well as being a phoney decontextualization of religious cultural elements. There is a hyper-sensitivity in New Zealand about appropriating any kind of cultural property from indigenous peoples because of the challenges which Pakeha New Zealanders have faced and still face from Maori, particularly in relation to land, but also in relation to all kinds of cultural knowledge. Because of this, the Goddess movement in New Zealand, largely a Pakeha phenomenon, while respectful of Maori spirituality, does not attempt to pursue or incorporate it to any great extent. At most, well-known *atua wahine* (female deities) associated with particular points of the seasonal round may be verbally acknowledged at the beginning of a ritual, and when a ritual is held outdoors in a public place, as at the Winter Solstice at Te Henga, the tribe associated with the area, the *tangata whenua*, are often honoured.[4]

In her book *Celebrating the Southern Seasons: Rituals for Aotearoa* (1995) Juliet Batten explicitly addresses the issue of multicultural rituals and beliefs in relation to the New Zealand setting. Rather than focusing on questions of cultural ownership and appropriation, she focuses on what both Maori and Pakeha have in common, their connection with the New Zealand landscape and the seasonal cycle as it is experienced in this country. She acknowledges the colonization process which resulted in the importation of the Roman calendar 'without any adjustment to the fact that Aotearoa/New Zealand is a Southern Hemisphere island in the Pacific Ocean' (p. 11), and the need to inquire into indigenous practices and attitudes to the seasonal cycle. Her hope is that by offering information and stories about the ancestral traditions of both Maori and Pakeha – traditions from ancient Maori, Pagan Europe (especially Celtic) and Christian Europe – 'it will be possible for the different spiritual traditions to meet; that we will be held by a deep love and respect for this land, for each other, and for the heights and depths of human consciousness' (p. 12).

As well as incorporating borrowed and adapted elements from many sources, rituals include highly original elements. They are both derivative and creative. Women responsible for organizing a ritual are free to include any activity they see fit. I asked Juliet Batten how she decides what to do in a ritual. She replied:

> I get my ideas for rituals by meditating – I tune into the morphic field and let the ideas come. I really just work very intuitively. Whenever I'm planning a ritual workshop I open myself in a particular way and I get the ideas. Even when I'm working with a group I'll be totally open and I'll get messages: 'Don't do that. Do this'. Things will come to me. I tune in to the group and I tune into the season and what's needed here. It's a matter of trusting and staying open.

A number of the other women I interviewed talked about using various manuals (Batten's and books by Budapest, Stein, Starhawk and Walker) as well as making up their own ideas.

I concluded chapter four by saying that feminist witchcraft is unique as a religion not only because it is self-consciously created, but also because this fact is openly articulated, heartily celebrated and, at the appropriate moments, deliberately forgotten. When women are fully engaged as actors within the rituals they have created, they do not question the authenticity of what they are doing, and are convinced of its value, efficacy and power. They know that they have made up the ritual, but they also talk about the ritual as, in some way, having its own power. The ritual process is believed to entail more than a participant proceeding through a series of chants, invocations, prayers, statements of intent and commitment and symbolic acts: the participant is not simply 'doing' the ritual. The ritual itself is perceived as a dynamic whole capable of having a powerful impact on the ritual actor and of taking a turn which she does not expect. In the course of a ritual, unimagined and unexplainable things may happen. Lea Holford described to me her first experiences of this:

> We'd come with these symbols and then, after casting the circle, creating that sacred circle, it was just amazing what would come out! All of us were absolutely overwhelmed with the power of it. So often it would bypass rationality. We all came in there with these belief systems – 'This is the way the world is' – and yet when we went to that deeper level of work, a whole different wisdom came out that we didn't know about. It was much more profound and had a much greater truth than anything we'd come in there with. Every time I'd go home and think, 'What was this power we contacted?' Obviously it was in all of us. We all tapped into it. It was present for two or three hours and it was something we could feel ourselves taking home every time and building something quite new, a new psychic structure.

Many other women I talked with also spoke about 'contacting' or 'tapping into energy' through ritual – I return to this in the next chapter where I discuss how women believe magic 'works'. Here, my point is that women's acknowledgement of the constructedness of their rituals does not prevent them from attributing to rituals a power which is greater than human artefact.

11

HOW MAGIC WORKS

> Rituals are ceremonies which evoke the sacred through shared experience. Ritual can be used to reveal the ineffable aspects of ultimate reality, to reinforce a felt sense of the sacred, to mark important events and life mysteries, and for personality transformation.
>
> (Lea)

One of the first definitions of magic I heard as an anthropology student was the classic Victorian one: 'Magic is primitive man's science'.[1] The social evolutionist, Edward Tylor, viewed any practice of the 'magical arts' or 'occult sciences' as a survival from a barbarous past, while James Frazer declared that magic was in some ways a precursor of science, but 'was its bastard sister' (Tambiah 1990: 45, 52).[2] Today, still, modes of experiencing and understanding which fall outside 'ordinary' rationality and consciousness are often viewed, especially by those working in the fields of science and medicine, as blighted by befuddled or regressive thinking (Winkelman 2000: 3).

And yet at a time of unprecedented advances in scientific knowledge and accomplishment, magic's popularity is simultaneously flourishing, both in popular culture (witness the stupendous success of the Harry Potter books and *The Lord of the Rings*) and as the central ritual practice of the growing global neo-Pagan community. Those in Western societies who embrace magical systems of thought are also adept at operating within a scientific paradigm, and a great number of those who trust implicitly in science probably also 'lapse' into magical thinking (ranging from everyday superstitious beliefs and practices to prayer and other non-scientific religious practices) from time to time. This suggests to me that the relationship between science and magic is not what it has been thought to be, that magic and science are not contrasting epistemologies – or at least they are not mutually exclusive epistemologies – and to rank them on an evolutionary scale (with magic on the 'primitive' end) is simplistic.

Despite the longstanding cohabitation of magical and scientific ways of thinking within Western societies, theories about magic and ritual have long been dichotomously constructed within anthropology: science versus magic (and religion generally), the symbolists versus the intellectualists, structure versus anti-structure, ritual as *action* versus belief as *thought*.[3] What has come to be known as the 'rationality debate' emerged in the wake of Evans-Pritchard's seminal work on Azande witchcraft (first published in 1937). Two broadly opposed camps were established: the intellectualists, who drew on the earlier ideas of Tylor and Frazer, and the symbolists, associated most prominently with Durkheim.[4] The intellectualists claimed that belief in magic arose from a particular view of the way the world operates in which magic is a substitute for science, while the symbolists saw magic and ritual primarily as symbolic systems which express important meanings, often about the social order, through metaphor and analogy.[5]

The intellectualists emphasized the instrumental, technical aspect of ritual. Frazer had claimed that magical thought relies upon an implicit faith in the order and uniformity of nature, and that magicians rationalize a causal connection between things which resemble each other or are contiguous in time and space: through magic an object can influence that with which it is symbolically associated. He divided magic into two categories: homeopathic magic, based on the law of similarity between objects, and contagious magic, based on the law of contact between objects (Frazer 1994: 26–37).

On the other side of the rationality debate, the symbolists, who have come to dominate anthropological thinking, emphasized the expressive function of ritual.[6] Tambiah (1985), for example, saw rituals primarily as performances generated by a society to convey to itself messages about its social norms and structure. Turner (1974a, 1974b) was also interested in rituals as social dramas or performances, but he saw them (rites of passage in particular) as being generated out of conditions of 'liminality, marginality and inferiority', and the bonds created between ritual participants as *anti-structural* in that they are undifferentiated, equalitarian and direct as a result of participants having signs of their social status removed from them. A number of other anthropologists have also concentrated on the performative, dramatic aspect of ritual, notably Richard Schechner, who claimed that ritual shares key characteristics with drama: both deal with crisis, schism, conflict and the resolution of these disruptions. The themes of both centre on sexuality, rebellion, generational conflict and the rites of passage, while the techniques of both drama and ritual concentrate on the transformation of people into other people (Schechner and Schuman 1976).

More recent anthropological theories about magic and ritual have also been dichotomously constructed. Tambiah (1990: 105–10) has proposed that there are two fundamental orientations to the cosmos which people can experience: *causality* and *participation*. The orientation he describes as 'causality' is associated with atomistic individualism, the language of distancing and neutrality of action and reaction, and an emphasis on the causal efficacy of technical acts and the idea that instrumental action changes matter. The characteristics he associates with 'participation', on the other hand, include: the concept of the ego/person with the world and as a product of the world; the language of solidarity, unity, holism and continuity in space and time; and an emphasis on the performative efficacy of communicative acts. There are strong echoes here of the earlier ideas of the intellectualists (who stressed instrumentality) and the symbolists (who stressed expression), however Tambiah saw the two orientations as 'simultaneously available to human beings as complementary cognitive and affective interests' (p. 108).

Greenwood (2000b: 142) suggests that these two orientations parallel Michael Harner's (1990) 'Ordinary State of Consciousness' (corresponding to causality) and 'Shamanic State of Consciousness' (corresponding to participation). Greenwood (2000a, 2000b) herself frequently refers to contemporary English witches' communication with an 'otherworld', a realm of deities, spirits or other beings experienced in an alternative state of consciousness which is distinct from the world of ordinary reality but co-existent with it as part of a holistic totality. The feminist witches I studied do not see things in quite such dichotomized terms as these anthropologists propose; they make no distinction between 'this world' and an 'otherworld', or between an ordinary reality and a non-ordinary reality with different truth values and rules of logic.

Winkelman has recently argued that the instrumental and symbolic functions of ritual are not always separate in practice or in their effects (2000: 233). He points out that symbols and rituals are incorporated within activities regarded as technical, while symbolic, expressive acts also have a technical component in the way that they transform experience and produce physiological consequences (such as healing). Thus, he would want to emphasize not only the psychological, social or symbolic functions of ritual, but also its physiological effects on the bodies of ritual actors. Ritual is instrumental even where its effects are on participants' emotional states and social relations if these are the *intended* technical effects of the ritual process.

Most anthropologists now regard as naive any attempt to understand ritual and magic, especially other people's rituals, in terms of the truth canons of Western scientific rationality, and focus instead on understanding the ritual actors' own logic. Nonetheless much theorizing about ritual still tends to construct it as a homogeneous category with a coherent purpose, and has not often sought theories of ritual action generated by ritual-makers or magicians themselves. Of course, most ritual-makers are probably not very concerned about theories of ritual action: its meaning and effectiveness in their lives is a given, theories about how it works are embedded in their cosmologies and worldviews and are not necessarily articulable, even if they are consciously held.

Gilbert Lewis (1980: 117–19), rightly in my view, emphasizes that viewing ritual only in terms of its instrumental or expressive components is reductive and can never offer more than a partial explanation: the emotional and aesthetic responses of those performing the ritual are crucial to its importance and meaning for them. Ritual, Lewis says (p. 118), 'is primarily action – a way of doing, making, creating, showing, expressing, arousing – a complex form of stimulus to which people respond'.[7] In a similar vein, Luhrmann (1989) argues that among contemporary English witches, beliefs and thoughts sometimes developed *as a result of* magical activity (rather than the other way round);[8] beliefs were not always consistent, coherent or clear-cut; witches' emotional and imaginative involvement in ritual work helped determine their beliefs.

The rituals performed by the feminist witches I studied form a far from homogeneous category: they incorporate diverse purposes and components including performance and play, aesthetic and expressive values, and norm-challenging as well as instrumental functions. At times witches articulate a highly intellectualized understanding of their magic; at other times they claim that the meaning of their rituals cannot be framed in language. Their emotional and imaginative involvement in magic and their embodied experience[9] of a ritual are always important and are usually given priority over intellectual understanding or verbal explanation. It is to contemporary witches' experiences and ideas about magic that I now turn.

Witches' definitions of magic show an unequivocal rejection of the magic versus science dichotomy. Aleister Crowley, whose works have been influential in modern magic, famously defined magic as 'the Science and Art of causing change to occur in conformity with Will', and Isaac Bonewits, a high-profile American witch, has described it as 'an art and science designed to enable people to make effective use of their psychic talents' (both cited in Adler 1986: 8). Starhawk (1989: 202) sees science and magic as 'both quests for truth – they differ only in their methodology and the set of symbols they use to describe their findings. The field of enquiry is the same.' (Tylor and Frazer would have added that magic also differs from science by being wrong – because magicians mistake association for causality – although they agreed about the field of enquiry being the same.) Religion and science are separated, Starhawk continues, when 'God is felt to be separate from the physical world . . . But the Goddess is manifest in the physical world, and the more we understand its workings, the better we know Her.' For Starhawk, the pursuit of scientific knowledge is a spiritual endeavour. Berger says that during her study of American witches she was 'told repeatedly by Witches that they became convinced of magic by seeing it work. They claim it is not a matter of faith but of empiricism' (1999: 24). Echoing Bonewits, Berger (p. 34) says that among witches 'magic is seen, at least in part, as a process of awakening one's own psychological mechanisms'.

Clearly, the instrumental goal of magic is emphasized in these definitions. Working magic requires a mobilization of one's confidence, will, emotion, imagination and concentration. It involves an understanding of psychological and environmental processes (Adler 1986: 8), and relies upon a theory which sees human nature and the external world of nature as interconnected. The 'central tenet of magical practice,' writes Greenwood (2000c: 144), is 'that the microcosm (the individual) is a part of the macrocosm, and that work on the microcosm will have an effect on the macrocosm'. Similarly, changes in the macrocosm, which includes both the material world of nature and the larger social world, can come to influence the individual. One of the ways change can happen is through the use of magical techniques. This theory derives from witches' holistic perception that all matter, energy and consciousness are connected in a dynamic, interactive system. According to this way of thinking, scientific knowledge and techniques are not in opposition to magical knowledge and techniques; both fit under the capacious umbrella of witches' worldview.

The New Zealand witches I studied, like their American and British counterparts, also refer to 'magic' in instrumental terms. All their rituals incorporate magic, even if their stated purpose is the celebration of a personal milestone or a part of the seasonal cycle. At Sabbats the primary purpose may be to acknowledge change rather than to cause it: thus the ritual's function is primarily expressive, it is a social performance of important shared values and beliefs using symbolic activity. However, embedded within any such ritual which has an obvious expressive function, there is also an instrumental magical component.

Thus, as we saw in chapter nine, during a ritual to celebrate Spring Equinox, the earth's greening following the dark, dormant phase of winter, the women will also perform 'magic' in relation to something they want to grow in their own lives (for example, a particular creative project, a new job, material security, a more assertive attitude towards an employer or a partner, or a quality such as patience, boldness or wisdom). The magic might take the form of a guided visualization to focus intent, followed by each woman planting a seed to symbolize what she wishes to grow in her life, chanting to 'energize' the magical project, the sharing of personal stories and a group blessing of each woman's seed. After the ritual, each woman takes her seed home and tends it. Nurturing the seed, which serves both as a symbol and a mnemonic device, helps the woman continue to focus attention on her magical project, thereby 'energizing' it further. Along with the ritual activity of watering the plant, the woman takes practical steps in her life to help realize her project. As the seed grows, her project moves towards actualization. If the seed or the project does not flourish, the woman thinks about the reasons and rationalizes the failure: the timing or the project might be wrong, her commitment to her goal might not be strong enough.

Such magic could be seen as an extension of the power of positive thinking to the symbolic enactment of one's goal in a heightened state of consciousness in the company of a supportive group. Winkelman (2000: 234) has pointed out that 'calendrical rituals are often used as contexts for rites of social transition (passage)'. Through symbols and symbolic activity personal transitions are placed within a cosmological framework. The use of analogy, metaphor and symbols and the extension of associative links to causative links are deemed rational in terms of witches' worldview.

The function of another category of rituals performed by feminist witches is primarily and explicitly instrumental: these rituals are 'spells'. They may be performed by an individual alone, or in the company of her ritual group or coven. In one of the workshops I attended early in my fieldwork, the facilitator handed out some notes she had written about spells. I include the text here because it provides an excellent basis for understanding how these witches believe spells work.[10]

Spells

A spell is a mini-ritual – good practice for full-scale rituals. It is a 'symbolic act done in an altered state of consciousness, in order to cause a desired change' (Starhawk 1989: 124).

How to cast a spell:

1 Get in touch with something you want to change in your life. Keep to *small things*. Don't tackle anything too big. Check out that you are ready to change this position or attitude, that you *want* to let go of it.
2 Get in touch with the *desired end*. See it clearly. See yourself achieving it.
3 Now choose a symbol or action that will encapsulate the change, remembering to keep the desired end clearly in view. Don't bother about how it will happen. Spells can work in unexpected ways!

Some examples

- To gain clarity: pour murky water out of a vessel and pour clear water in. Believe that with the clear water, your mind will clear. You may wish to add words that will help too.
- Banishing anger and putting forgiveness in its place: hold a stone to your forehead. Let the anger pass into the stone. Then hurl it away (do this outside!), chanting suitable words. Then give yourself a gift to symbolize forgiveness/peace or whatever you desire to put in the place of anger. Breathe in the gift, chanting suitable words.

4 Add to the symbol or action ingredients that will help you to achieve an altered state of consciousness so that you will be more

open to the suggestions contained in the spell, e.g. meditate first, use repetition, use chanting, use the presence of others to give energy, use darkness and candles for focusing, use water, use incense to change the atmosphere.

5 Believe, desire and expect that the spell will bring about the desired end. (Your preparation to achieve that state before enacting the spell is often as important as the spell itself.)
6 Enact the spell in the presence of others. Give it your total attention and energy flow. The more you can enter a trance state and link up with the universal energy flow, the more effective your spell will be.

See Starhawk's *The Spiral Dance* for more ideas. Never do a spell to hex or damage another person. Whatever energy you give out will return to you threefold!

These notes make explicit the instrumental purpose of spells, although they could be seen as having an expressive function also: the woman casting the spell is telling herself and others present, both symbolically and verbally, about a decision she has reached, about what is important to her and her life at present, about her concerns and goals in a particular situation, and about what she regards as an effective way of dealing with her situation. As well as giving instruction on how to cast a spell, the notes indicate how spells work. Points one, two and five emphasize the role of the spell-maker's will, desire, imagination, concentration and confidence. Points four, five and six emphasize the importance of conducting the spell in a heightened state of consciousness or trance state which enables the spell-maker to 'link up with the universal energy flow'. Point six stresses the social aspect of ritual, the importance of having like-minded and supportive witnesses present, and point three deals with the crucial importance of symbols and symbolic activity.

Working with symbols in a focused and self-conscious way is usually the most important component of any ritual. Most invitations to rituals ask participants to bring a symbol of something related to the ritual's theme. I have been asked to bring symbols of, for example, a personal quality I have in abundance, my childhood, a personal goal or achievement, my sexuality, an old fear or chapter of my life to be sacrificed, a quality needed to sustain me through winter's dark, and so on. These symbols are woven into the ritual's fabric through story-telling, symbolic action, and art and craft work.

It is significant that the two women most responsible for the early growth of the movement in Auckland are both psychotherapists who work with symbols – one uses a Jungian approach and the other psychosynthesis. During a workshop I participated in, one of them explicitly talked about the transpersonal quality of symbols, their multivocality, their capacity to represent many levels of experience and meaning, and their ability to cope with or incorporate paradox. During my interview with her, this woman referred also to the therapeutic aspect of working with symbols:

> I think for a lot of women, learning to work with symbols is the first step to honoring the depth of their experience and the validity of it. The more women work with symbols, the more they can make sense of their own dreams and their own fantasies, and use those inner powers to develop their intuition.
>
> And I think it empowers women then to face themselves at deeper levels. Often if they don't develop these tools, they're just too terrified to face their personal history and their personal woundedness. It's essential work because otherwise power remains 'out there'. Working with symbols helps women to find the power is actually within themselves. The symbols help them see it more clearly and work with it more effectively, focus it.

She emphasized that the power to bring about change lies within, rather than outside, a person. She sees the symbolic enactment as 'like making a vow in front of a group of people', saying 'yes' to possibilities, and putting that commitment in motion. Similarly, in the workshop notes about spells, it is clear that the symbols used in spells are not *in themselves* thought to be responsible for causing the desired change; they have no inherent magical power. Symbols are used to represent what the spell-maker wants to happen. Her expectant attitude, will and commitment to change, and belief in what she is doing are crucial if the spell is to 'work'.

Winkelman, in his discussion of ritual healing, says that 'symbolic acts elicit associations and beliefs that transform experience, as well as physiological responses, and enhance positive expectations and commitment', providing a powerful stimulation of one's intentionality (2000: 233, 246). This is also true in feminist witches' magic. By bridging the iconic and verbal domains, symbols, along with other ritual behaviours and myth, integrate previously unconscious material into the conscious network, which may bring about profound changes in the individual's experience of self and world, including her behaviour and personality (p. 245). Symbols are tools – tangible, visible and real – which women can use as a focus in their efforts to understand their psychological processes, face their personal histories and seek healing, insight and power. Luhrmann makes the same point in relation to English witches:

> Magicians use symbolism to capture, express or articulate their experience, and in its mixture of precision and evocation it becomes tremendously important to them. Ultimately it can become a means of therapy.
>
> One way that symbolism forms a magician's hermeneutic is by

> providing an apparently objective medium in which to talk about one's quite subjective self.
>
> (Luhrmann 1989: 245)

I have noted in previous chapters that feminist witches' ritual-making is a highly creative enterprise. As Eller (1993: 89) says, 'Variety and inventiveness in ritual are encouraged in all the major texts of the feminist spirituality movement'. From my reading and experience, it seems that New Zealand feminist witches may be especially inventive, flexible and given to improvisation.[11] They are not particularly concerned about using any prescribed, hallowed or hereditary tools, ingredients or procedures. Most consider that it is impossible to make a dangerous mistake, or any mistake, while doing a spell. Anyone may do a spell for any purpose she chooses (except to harm someone) and may invent the spell herself, choosing the symbolic objects, words and actions she wants to use.

I have noted that one reason for this high level of creativity is that in its early days the movement in New Zealand attracted a number of feminist artists who helped determine the nature of ritual-making and influence the development of the movement. Other reasons have to do with New Zealand's diasporic and extremely isolated geographic location, the fact that feminist witchcraft and Wicca became established as two quite separate traditions in New Zealand, and the national character. The modern witchcraft movement in New Zealand, being only two decades old, cannot claim deep indigenous roots or genealogical links with ancient Wiccan covens, and New Zealand witches simply do not have access to a lot of the ritual paraphernalia described in overseas manuals. New Zealanders in general have always taken pride in their ability to improvise, which they claim derives from their relatively recent pioneering roots. When feminist witches make love spells, for example, the ingredients are much more likely to be gathered from their pantries and gardens than a witches' supply shop, and symbolic associations are assigned to ingredients on a personal basis: for example, salt for faithfulness, zesty good health or preservation; rose petals for romance, kindness or beauty; dried chillies for excitement, exotic travel or passionate sex.

New Zealand feminist witches' understandings about the working of magic conform in large part to canonical anthropological explanations of magic whereby a causal connection between things which resemble each other (homeopathic magic) or are contiguous in time and space (contagious magic) is rationalized, and the fate of one object is believed to influence that of the object with which it is symbolically linked. Both of the spells given as examples in the workshop notes on spell-making (above) are examples of homeopathic magic: the stone resembles cold, hard anger, and the clear water resembles a clear mind. An example of contagious magic would be where a woman wanting to address her concern about her child might incorporate a toy or article of clothing belonging to the child in her spell.

The symbols used by the witches I studied always have homeopathic or contagious properties. The potency of any symbolic object or action depends upon the woman's conscious acknowledgement of the link she has chosen to make between symbol and referent: symbols are regarded as potent not simply because of their resemblance to or contact with an associated object or person, but because they evoke a potent psychological connection for the woman doing the spell.

Like Frazer's magicians, feminist witches also rationalize that the potency of the symbolic act has to do with a natural energy or force which connects everything: people, objects, nature, the elements, human thought, speech, emotions, motivations and the universe at large. In point six of the notes on spell-making, this force is called 'the universal energy flow'. The manipulation of symbols and symbolic action alone do not produce change, it is believed to come about through a complex interaction of the psychological state of the woman doing the spell, her symbolic acts using symbolic objects, and the creative energy connecting all things in the world at large and beyond.

A spell done within a circle of coven members is often stronger because it is assisted by the *communitas* generated within the group. The group gives its full concentration and support to the woman doing the spell and the psychic energy is intensified. This interaction of and flow between inner and outer worlds, physical and social worlds, emotion, imagination and intent, has some resonance with what Lévy-Bruhl (1985) termed 'mystical participation' and with what Desjarlais (1992) has called 'an ecology of knowledge'. It has been described by many ethnographers of indigenous peoples, from the Inupiat of the frozen North Slope of Alaska (Turner 1996) to the Yarralin of Northern Territory, Australia (Rose 1992). Contemporary feminist witches share this conception of the inter-relatedness of all, where all parts of the system can communicate with and influence all other parts.

I have stressed that knowing they have invented the ritual or spell does not stop these witches from attributing to it a power which is greater than human artefact. While they consider themselves to be personally empowered through doing magic, they also believe that the ritual can in turn have a powerful impact upon them, and may produce unexpected outcomes. In interviews my research participants spoke frequently of 'channelling', 'harnessing' and 'working with' energy. Here are five women's comments from a group discussion:

> I get a sense that ritual concretizes spirit. The group energy focuses on a change we want to bring about, an energy we want to invoke, a time we want to honour. We call upon that spirit energy and bring it into the group and channel it into something that becomes almost concrete. It becomes a physical act. It's no longer something intangible that you're wanting or dreaming or fantasizing about, but something very concrete that you're doing.

> It's a very symbolic act. It's also very creative. It's like harnessing that energy and creating with it, and bringing into being what it is that you're trying to do in a symbolic way.
>
> Ritual begins with creative visualization. You see things in your head. After a while I come to know that they're real, and they're something that feels right for me. By doing the ritual I'm solidifying the visualization and I'm moving it from the unformed into an increasing level of form. That focuses my purpose even more, and it reaches my subconscious so I put myself in the way of opportunities that can lead me to getting my desire or need met.
>
> If you do a ritual on your own, that's very powerful, but the whole idea of doing it in a group is that the energy is increased by more than the women in the group. The sense I get is that you've actually invited the Goddess to become part of the circle and her energy is there. You are calling upon that energy – the Goddess energy. Once when I had my eyes closed in the circle I actually saw four of my favourite goddess images come to the circle, sit down in between us, and join our circle of linked hands. That gave me a sense of what happens when you invoke certain goddesses. That energy does come and join you and become part of the ritual group. So you're working with energy rather than asking that energy to intervene to do it for you.
>
> We're taking it from the intangible and giving it form.

For these witches, energy is present in embodied form in all of nature. It also exists in disembodied form: a house may have 'good energy'; 'healing energy' may be invoked during a ritual. There is energy which is disembodied but has strong links to the physical dimension, such as 'woman energy', 'male energy' and 'earth energy'. Energy is anthropomorphized: it can be gentle or angry. Energy can be invoked, generated, focused, increased or altered either deliberately or unconsciously by people's thoughts or behaviour. A personal goal can be 'energized' by concentrated thought. The distinction between witches' personal energy and the energy outside themselves, between the seen and the unseen, the formed and the unformed, is not a well-drawn line. Witches believe that in ritual they can 'tune in' or 'tap in' to an energy greater than themselves, the creative force which brought and brings all things into being.

The symbolic act performed during a ritual is a concretization of personal intention which helps hold a woman to that intention and activate her will, but this process is made more potent because the woman is aligning her energy with a greater universal energy and working with it. For feminist witches the feminist project of increasing women's agency in their lives needs to be contextualized in terms of this understanding. A woman's personal agency is enhanced and supported by being integrated with the greater energy system which has over-riding agency in bringing about transformation. Thus feminist witchcraft serves a feminist project of self-empowerment, as a first step towards social change.

When the witches I studied do magic, they are seldom looking for dramatic answers to crises in their lives or for miracles. Rituals and spells are mostly done to address the kinds of situations and problems that occur in most people's regular lives from time to time. By performing a ritual, a woman gains a sense of being able to do something practical and useful about a situation or problem in her life. As Starhawk (1989: 125) writes:

> Spells . . . go one step further than most forms of psychotherapy. They allow us not only to listen to and interpret the unconscious but also to speak to it in the language it understands [through symbols] . . . Through spells, we can attain the most important power – the power to change ourselves.

The spell described below, which includes both imitative and contagious magic, was performed by a 20-year-old woman (the youngest in her family) who wanted to cast off her feeling that she occupied an inferior position in her family and to acknowledge herself as an adult equal to the other adults in her family. The group, of which I was a member, was seated in a circle on the floor. The circle had been cast, a purification done, and the directions invoked. Scarlett began by telling us how she felt she was the 'ugliest and boringest' member of her family. (This was astonishing to hear, because Scarlett, to our eyes, appeared attractive and interesting.) She showed us a picture she had drawn of her family with herself as a little, dirty girl at the end of a family of five. She ripped up this picture and put it into a box through a slot in the top, symbolically destroying this image of her place in the family. She then produced a fragment of an old child's garment, telling us that this was a symbol of her childhood; she had always worn dirty, paint-covered clothes (she later completed a Bachelor of Fine Arts degree and is currently doing postgraduate work). The clothing fragment was put into the box with the ripped-up picture.

Scarlett said she had a lot of childish habits which she wanted to leave behind; she did not detail these. She scattered dead leaves representing the habits in the centre of the circle and trampled them. She then announced her new decision to wear clean, bright clothes and pulled a purple silk scarf out through the slot in the box. She produced some new patent leather shoes, bought that day as a gift to herself, and put them on along with the scarf. Finally, she lit a very tall red candle to symbolize the bold adult status she was choosing to claim. The spell finished with all the women in the circle giving her three hearty cheers.

The second spell was done by an older woman, Jean, during a ritual workshop, and was designed to help her 'accept cronehood and ageing'. It incorporated symbols which served a mnemonic function in the telling of her personal story and symbolic gift-giving by the other women in the circle. Jean set out a cloth and placed on it symbols representing different parts of her life. She spoke tearfully about the difficulty of giving up some sports altogether and accepting lower performance levels from herself in other sports as she got older. Jean talked about her fear of becoming less attractive according to society's standards, and her frustration about her waning strength. She asked the women in the circle to give her gifts for her cronehood. Each of us spoke briefly, honouring her age and courage, wishing her well, and giving her a 'gift'; these included wisdom, acceptance, expectation and celebration of her inner beauty.

During the interviews I conducted with witches, they frequently made the point that performing rituals gave them a greater sense of being able to control or direct their own lives, to assimilate change as Jean was attempting to do, or to heal the past and assume greater agency in the future as Scarlett was working towards. Sybil said:

> Ritual does give a sense of being really powerful and instrumental in your own path, rather than just waiting for things to happen or come your way, or accepting that 'What will be will be'. It's more like: 'Hey, I do believe in my destiny, but also I believe that I have the ability to bring about change and be instrumental in that'.

Joan said:

> Ritual creates a feeling that you do have some sort of control, that you're not a mere whim of fate, that *you* are actively going to take steps. Quite often after a ritual a woman will ring up and say, 'Look, after that ritual I bloody well told so-and-so to stuff off!' or 'I did this' or 'I made a decision' that she had been prevaricating about. The fact that she has consciously chosen to conduct this ritual makes it an *active* act.

Through ritual women become the catalysts for their own magical transformation, which begins as a result of 'energy shifts' generated in the course of the ritual and felt in the body. Juliet told me:

> In ritual the container of sacred space is made, energy is raised within it, and energy is moved. There's often something surrendered. I know people do say, 'Something left me'. People really experience something happening – they let go of something and open to something else. Sometimes they might need to do it several

> times. People experience an energy shift and then they go out in their life and they find that spontaneously different things start to happen. Things really have changed and people come back and report change.

The use of witches' rituals for personal emotional and psychological healing has been reported by numerous scholars and practitioners, including all those who have conducted ethnographic studies of contemporary witchcraft in Western societies. Greenwood (2000b: 150) says that ritual may convert feelings of powerlessness into experiences of empowerment, and that 'magical ritual may be a cathartic space of transformation of the social realm' where 'social relationships of power from the ordinary world are negotiated and transgressed'. This may be true, but the quotation (immediately above) from Juliet and my observations suggest that the benefits of witches' rituals are not limited to catharsis: rituals may instigate a process of change which often continues long after the ritual.

In *The Ritual Process* Victor Turner (1974a: 4) argued for the 'extreme importance of religious beliefs and practices for both the maintenance and radical transformation of human social and psychical structures', but his emphasis was on the latter – the way in which ritual represents an 'anti-structure' in opposition to the institutionalized, norm-governed structure of society. For Turner, rituals are generated out of conditions of 'liminality, marginality and structural inferiority' (p. 116). Feminist witches' rituals are such. Through them women assert their right and claim the power to transform firstly their own psychical structures and ultimately their structural inferiority within patriarchal society. Lea told me:

> I believe that how we perceive reality has an awful lot to do with how it happens. Many things are possible if you change your point of view. If you send out, 'I believe this can change. I believe this can be different', I think there's a very good chance it *can* be different. We can see possibilities that we were unable to see before, and move into those very quickly, and work with those very quickly.

New Zealand feminist witches' theories of ritual action are based on a worldview which 'sees things not as fixed objects, but as swirls of energy', and a belief that 'if we cause a change in the energy patterns, they in turn will cause a change in the physical world' (Starhawk 1989: 126). Witches believe that when their own energy is concentrated and channelled during a ritual, it can influence the broader energy currents in the world beyond. The cast circle is a liminal place alive with potentiality. Symbolic objects and visualized images become channels for witches' power, but they are simply props: they have no inherent power. 'Props may be useful, but it is the mind that works magic,' Starhawk (p. 124) says. Similarly, Zsuzsanna Budapest (1986: 1) writes: 'It isn't the tools which make the magic come to pass, it is our own brain'. Symbols and images work through suggestion, implanting certain ideas in the unconscious mind which in turn influence the ritual-maker to actualize those ideas. Causation and participation are both integral to the process of making magic; it is impossible to separate them analytically as 'two orientations to our cosmos' as Tambiah does (1990: 105). Moreover, these witches do not distinguish between this world and an otherworld as Greenwood has proposed for the English witches she studied.

For feminist witches, magic is not anti-science, primitive science or pseudo-science. It sits alongside science as another way of addressing a problem, and is often used in addition to the problem-solving strategies used by people in the rest of society. For example, a woman trying to come to terms with surviving incest might decide to have psychological counselling, to confront her abuser, to enroll in a workshop for incest survivors, and to do a healing ritual with supportive friends. A woman who is afraid of being in a house alone at night might take a self defence course and do a nightly self-protection spell.

Through their rituals these women experience themselves as accessing their inner power and connecting with a power beyond themselves. Even magic whose primary purpose is instrumental incorporates aesthetic, expressive and dramatic components which are integrated with and serve its instrumentality. Magic also serves a larger political goal of personal and social transformation. Stein (1990: 2) says that rituals create a microcosm, a 'little universe', within which women try out what they want to be, and what they want the 'big universe' to be. This is very much in the same vein as Geertz, who said: 'In ritual, the world as lived and the world as imagined, fused under the agency of a single set of symbolic forms, turns out to be the same world' (1973: 112–13).

Magic's continuing allure, not just for those who choose witchcraft as a spiritual path, but also for many in Western society more generally, may reflect a yearning to bring together the world as imagined and the world as lived, an attempt to get in touch with another side of human experience: the reality we are familiar with from dreams, fantasy and myths. Believing in both magic and science apparently presents neither a difficulty nor a contradiction for many people: if it requires switching between two worldviews, this switch is made. For feminist witches, however, magic and science do not imply different worldviews: magic is simply science we do not yet know how to explain. Frazer (1994: 806) put it in similar terms: 'The dreams of magic may one day be the waking realities of science'.

12

RE-MEMBERING THE WITCH AND THE GODDESS

> How can I say it? That we are women from the start. That we don't have to be turned into women by them, labelled by them, made holy and profaned by them. That that has always already happened, without their efforts. And that their history, their stories, constitute the locus of our displacement . . .
>
> How can we speak so as to escape from their compartments, their schemas, their distinctions and oppositions: virginal/deflowered, pure/impure, innocent/experienced . . . How can we shake off the chain of these terms, free ourselves from their categories, rid ourselves of their names? Disengage ourselves, *alive*, from their concepts? . . .
>
> Wait. My blood is coming back. From their senses. It's warm inside us again. Among us. Their words are emptying out, becoming bloodless, dead skins. While our lips are growing red again. They're stirring, moving, they want to speak.
>
> (Irigaray 1985: 212)

What feminist witches and feminists more generally have in common is a virulent antipathy for dualistic thinking – especially as it impacts on gender relations. In recent decades feminist scholars have written a great deal about the symbolic associations connected with the fundamental dichotomous pair: man/woman. In Cixous's view, man in Western societies has been typically associated with all that is active, cultural, light and high – in other words, with that which is positive – while woman has been associated with all that is passive, natural, dark and low – that which is negative. Man is the 'self'; woman is his 'other'. Woman exists in man's world on his terms (quoted in Tong 1989: 224).[1] In *The Second Sex* Simone de Beauvoir (1974: xviii–xix) wrote: 'Humanity is male, and man defines woman not in herself but as relative to him; she is not regarded as an autonomous being . . . He is the Subject, he is the Absolute – she is the Other.'

Not only is woman defined in negative terms and as 'other', the category 'woman' can also be split and assigned polarized meanings and values, as

Ortner (1974: 85–6) has famously pointed out: 'Feminine symbolism, far more often than masculine symbolism, manifests this propensity towards polarized ambiguity – sometimes utterly exalted, sometimes utterly debased, rarely within the normal range of human possibilities'. Thus we get the polarized images of the Madonna and the whore, or the Goddess and the witch.

Feminist witches are among those feminists who have challenged Western constructions of 'woman' and 'the feminine', rejecting woman's designation as 'other' along with any symbolic system in which man constructs woman. Believing that symbolic systems are socially constructed for the political purpose of validating and perpetuating the status quo in a society, they believe that what is now needed is 'a revolution of the imagination to free us from what is a highly complex symbol system continuously reiterated and endorsed by our cultural heritage, by advertisements and the media as well as in schools and churches, in psychology and history books' (Goodison 1990: 4).

In particular feminist witches have challenged the stereotypical polarization of the witch and the Goddess. The witch and the Goddess are one, they say. Before she was diabolized by the Church, the witch was the crone aspect of the Goddess and represented her dark, destructive side. As I noted at the beginning of this book, when I told people that I was studying a religion which went by the names of 'feminist witchcraft' and 'Goddess spirituality', many baulked because of the contrasting images conveyed in these names. They were used to thinking of the witch as evil, frightening, old, ugly, dark and destructive, while the Goddess was beautiful, youthful, desirable, life-giving, protective and perfect. The witch was 'utterly debased', the Goddess 'utterly exalted'.

Yet the meanings of the two images for men and women are rather different. Concluding chapter seven, I said that for men the witch has always been absolutely 'other': loathsome, dangerous, lascivious and voracious or, more recently, pitiable or ridiculous. For a woman the witch may be all these things, but she is also the 'other' within, an image of a woman's own dark, dangerous power which she must fear, an image of her old age, aloneness, sexual undesirability, a glimpse of what she can become and will be damned for becoming. The Goddess, on the other hand, represents for men a combination of the perfect mother – wise and nurturing – and the sexually desirable maiden. For a woman the Goddess symbolizes unimaginable power and the eternal youth and beauty she is doomed to strive for and fail to achieve.

What the witch and the Goddess have in common, recalling Ortner above, is that they both exist outside the normal range of possibilities for women: they are both 'other' in relation to women. The Goddess's qualities place her so far above ordinary women that she is unobtainable; she inhabits the realm of the supernatural. The image of the witch, on the other hand, is repellent because of her association with evil, darkness and death.

The reason why the witch and the Goddess have been designated outside the range of possibilities for women, I suggest, is that both constitute images of independent female power and knowledge. Wherever they appear, from fairy stories to Greek mythology, witches and goddesses are powerful female figures who perform magical or supernatural acts at will. Their power comes from an inherent source; it is 'power from within'.

As well as challenging the dichotomization of the witch and the Goddess, the women I worked with challenge their designation as illegitimate images of womanhood. By choosing to identify as 'witch' and as 'goddess', they are symbolically re-membering the witch and the Goddess, embodying and laying claim to the independent female power which the two symbols represent, and thereby re-membering themselves. By deliberately playing with, deconstructing and transforming the stereotypical meanings of the two images, they are accepting Cixous's challenge to 'write themselves out of the world men have constructed for them by putting into words the unthinkable/unthought' (Tong 1989: 224). In Butlerian terms, they are daring to perform gender differently, acknowledging that gender is socially created through the 'reiteration of norms', produced and reproduced as a bodily practice by repeated 'appropriate' performance (Butler 1993: 10). Feminist witches are transgressing and rejecting the patriarchal norms which define the categories 'woman, 'witch' and 'goddess' by their 'inappropriate' performances in ritual.

Claiming to be a 'witch' and a 'goddess' not only breaches the boundaries of what is permissible for women in this society, it also challenges women's own self-perceptions. It goes beyond being a protest about patriarchal prescriptions for womanhood; it causes women to change the way they think about themselves. 'Witch' and 'goddess' are identities which can take some getting used to. Interestingly, it seems easier for women to identify as witches than to claim they are 'goddess'. Through reading, attending workshops and performing rituals, however, many women in the movement gradually begin to think of themselves as sacred, as divine, as goddess.

The two identities become more comfortable as they are rehearsed and dramatized in ritual. 'In ritual,' says Myerhoff (1986: 268), 'doing is believing, and we become what we display'. Hallowe'en, or Samhain, in particular, is a time for playing dramatically with the witch image. A number of Hallowe'en rituals created by the group I worked most closely with can be interpreted as what Myerhoff (1986) has called 'definitional ceremonies'. In such ceremonies a marginal or 'invisible' group refuses to accept definition by the dominant culture and, by deliberate and cunning use of symbols in ritual, displays its own alternative interpretation of itself. Group participants thus claim the right to define themselves, to become 'authors of themselves' and their own reality (p. 263). Ultimately, if the ceremony is conducted publicly, the marginal group may be able to transform, or at least modify, the way that outsiders see and define them.

One Hallowe'en, for example, the organizers of the ritual invited group members to 'openly celebrate witchiness' by dressing up in hats, masks, costumes and make-up. At the appointed hour we arrived at the venue variously clad in black garb, cloaks, star-spangled scarves, pointed hats and make-up applied to create gaunt, wrinkled faces. We were greeted in the hall of the house by a jolly, life-sized hag (painted and cut from thin board) who directed us to 'park our broomsticks and wait'. When the organizers had finished preparing the room in which the ritual was to be held, they slipped out into the hall and invited us to enter. We removed our shoes and quietly filed into the dark room.

The altar was set out on a circular black cloth on the floor with numerous stereotypical witch symbols: a cauldron in the centre surrounded by a green satin snake, a toy bat, toy cats and frogs, a dainty green-skinned witch doll and black and white candles. We settled ourselves on cushions around the altar and carried out a purification using percussion instruments, after which the circle was cast and the elements and directions invoked. The organizers spoke about the significance of Samhain as a time for facing and letting go of fears, resentments and unwanted parts of our lives, a time for confronting darkness and honouring death as part of the cycle. We were reminded that the theme of destruction in this Sabbat is symbolized by the Goddess in her crone aspect – as Hecate, Kali, Cerridwen, Baba Yaga, Spiderwoman and Hine-nui-te-po. Samhain, it was said, was the time when the veil between the living and the dead was thinnest, and it was therefore a time for remembering those who had gone before. We were invited to light black and white candles in memory of dead foremothers – these could be biological relations or esteemed role models.

An open time followed when participants were invited to say what the word 'witch' meant to them personally. Women spoke about the victims of the witch-hunts and the need to reclaim the 'wisewoman tradition', of personal oppression experienced within the Church, of witchcraft as the door to self-knowing, harmony and healing, of the liberation they felt in choosing a spiritual path which fitted their own beliefs. Next there was a 'sacrifice' where we wrote down any negative influences we wanted to rid from our lives – fears, anxieties, problems and so on – and burnt the papers in the cauldron. This was followed by silent meditation and then some art and craft work which involved using collage materials to construct a symbol of 'the safe place' in our lives. Each woman explained to the group the significance of her symbol and after she spoke, we sang the chant: 'She changes everything she touches, and everything she touches changes'. The ritual concluded with a feast.

The symbols used in this ritual would be recognized even by an infant as being those stereotypically associated with witches. The ways in which the symbols were used and what happened in the ritual, however, confounded the stereotype of the wicked witch. One might reasonably ask why these feminist women should want personally to take on the popular image of the witch: in claiming the right to define themselves, why choose a symbol which expresses so unequivocally patriarchal society's misogyny? Why do women who abhor the process by which women were labelled witches 500 years ago now choose to self-identify as witches?

Partly they are trying to subvert the popular definition of the witch, claiming that the Church first subverted the image of the wisewoman/healer and the crone aspect of the Goddess by re-defining her as a witch. Dressing up as witches is a symbolic act of reclamation, an attempt to re-assign the witch with positive meanings and values, to re-invent her. As Noreen Penny, writing in *Broadsheet*, has stated: 'We do NOT accept the pejorative meaning of witch or coven. These are OUR terms and we use them in OUR way' (Penny 1990: 178). Feminist witches are engaging in what Irigaray has suggested as an effective strategy for dealing with patriarchy: mimicry:

> There is, in an initial phase, perhaps only one 'path', the one historically assigned to the feminine: that of *mimicry*. One must assume the feminine role deliberately. Which means already to convert a form of subordination into an affirmation, and thus to begin to thwart it . . .
>
> To play with mimesis is thus, for a woman, to try to recover the place of her exploitation by discourse, without allowing herself to be simply reduced to it. It means to resubmit herself – inasmuch as she is on the side of the 'perceptible', of 'matter' – to 'ideas', in particular to ideas about herself, that are elaborated in/by a masculine logic, but so as to make 'visible', by an effect of playful repetition, what was supposed to remain invisible: the cover-up of a possible operation of the feminine in language.
>
> (Irigaray 1985: 76)

Mimicry is also fun; it enables these women to indulge in a bit of playful naughtiness. In miming the image of the witch, feminist witches playfully distort and transform it, split it off from the negative meanings and values traditionally assigned to it in a performance which is simultaneously defiance and self-definition. What women said and did during the Hallowe'en ritual obviously bore no resemblance to popular beliefs about witches or to descriptions of the witch's Sabbat current at the time of the witch-hunts. There were no babies boiling in the cauldron and the feast was strictly vegetarian – not a newt's eye or bat's wing in sight. There was no orgy, no flying around the room, and no bare-buttocked Devil. The ritual was a memorial for the 'beloved dead', a women's consciousness-raising exercise, a therapeutic healing exercise and fun. The materials used in the craft work came from women's sewing kits and an art supplies store.

Feminist witches are not prepared to abandon the witch as a hideous invention because to do so would leave the power to define her solely with the misogynists of the witch-craze. By projecting an image of the witch that was in part a reflection of the dominant society's image and in part their own invention, they were exposing the stereotypical witch image as myth. They were revaluing the witch and embracing the independent female power she represents.

I turn now to consider how the Goddess is also embraced, embodied and performed in ritual. Early in my research I was at a dinner party where the topic of conversation came round to my research. After a few minutes, the host became visibly distraught and, spitting with indignation, burst out, 'These women are just turning themselves into gods and worshipping themselves!' As well as deploring the heresy, he seemed to be personally wounded. I have met other men too who are suspicious of a woman-centred spiritual tradition and seem to fear that women's empowerment will undermine or diminish men's power. But women's self-empowerment and apprehension of themselves as goddess is not intended to disempower or sideline men. As Lea said to me, 'We want this to work for everybody because that's what the Goddess is all about – the empowering and inter-relatedness of all beings'. I have also met many men who honour the sacred feminine and welcome equal partnership with women. These men see power-sharing as liberating rather than threatening.

During my research I attended a number of goddess workshops run by two different facilitators. Each evening we would focus on a different Greek goddess; those included were Demeter, Artemis, Persephone, Hestia, Athena, Hecate and Aphrodite. The facilitator talked about the historical importance of the goddess (one also showed slides) and her relevance for contemporary women following the style of Bolen's book *Goddesses in Everywoman: A New Psychology of Women* (1985). After this informal lecture, we performed a ritual which explored the 'energy' of the particular goddess.

We were encouraged to see these goddesses as symbolizing different archetypes or energies which may operate within individual women. Thus, Artemis, the virgin huntress, symbolizes the strongly independent, goal-focused woman who is in touch with the wild, instinctual part of herself. Athena, goddess of wisdom and crafts and warrior goddess who protected Athens, symbolizes the intellectual, rational, practical, self-disciplined, judicious woman whose intellect rules her instincts (unlike Artemis). Artemis and Athena, along with all other goddesses in all cultures which have or had them, are conceived of as aspects of the Goddess. Thus the duality represented by Artemis and Athena – wilderness/civilization – is contained within the Goddess.

The rituals we performed had two intended functions: to help participants understand themselves better by thinking about the various 'goddess energies' which seemed to be operating in their lives and to help women find ways of bringing new 'energies' (qualities, personality attributes) into their lives. For example, a woman who identified closely with Athena, who saw herself as 'an Athena type', might want to bring more of Aphrodite's qualities of spontaneity, creativity and passion into her life.

On the evening we focused on Artemis, part of the ritual was a guided meditation which involved visualizing a meeting with Artemis. Afterwards women talked about how this experience had been for them personally. The ways women imagined Artemis varied: she appeared as a typical Greek goddess, magnificent in flowing robes, as a large woman with burning red eyes, as an invisible presence, as a woman wearing a faded blue sweatshirt and cut-off jeans. Each woman created her own goddess. Several in the group created an image which was very close in appearance to themselves. We were invited to think about a goal we wanted to achieve or something we would like to ask Artemis for. Each woman was given the opportunity to articulate this goal, wish or request. Before she did so, Artemis's crown, a head-dress decorated with peacock plumes, was placed on her head.

Writing about Artemis, Bolen (1985: 49) says:

> The Artemis archetype gives women the innate ability to concentrate intensely on whatever is important to her and to be undistracted from her course . . . Goal focus and perseverance despite obstacles in the way or elusiveness of the quarry are Artemis qualities that lead to achievements and accomplishments.

By putting on Artemis's crown each woman became the goddess. After stating her goal or request she beat a drum and said, 'Artemis, hear my call!' The implication seemed to be that we were appealing to a being, or at least a force, which was in some sense transcendent. Thus each woman became simultaneously the goddess and a supplicant.

It was shown in chapter eight that women in the Goddess movement are quite comfortable with this kind of paradox: they are aware of it, draw attention to it and celebrate it. Christ (1982: 76) quotes Starhawk as saying: 'When I feel weak, She is someone who can help and protect me. When I feel strong, She is the symbol of my own power. At other times I feel Her as the natural energy in my body and the world.' Discussing this quote, Christ points out that these are not the words of a sloppy thinker, but of one who does not believe that a symbol must have a single 'true' meaning: 'The diversity of explications of the meaning of the Goddess symbol suggests that symbols have a richer significance than any explications of their meaning can express, a point literary critics have long insisted on' (p. 77).

On the last night of one goddess course, the facilitator, Lea, had prepared an 'integration ritual' which concluded with a 'women's mysteries initiation'. Lea had brought a lot of little pots containing pansy seedlings. The seeds had been planted six weeks earlier during a ritual focused on Demeter's nurturing quality, and had symbolized something we wanted to 'plant' and nurture in our lives. After the Demeter ritual, Lea had taken the planted seeds home and tended them.

For the initiation we sat in a circle. Women had brought along symbols to express their sense of the sacred, of the Goddess within, or of their spirituality. After the first woman had spoken to the group about her symbol, Lea took one of the potted seedlings and gave it to her, greeted her with a kiss on each cheek and whispered in her ear 'Thou art Goddess'. Then another woman talked about her symbol after which the first woman took a seedling to her, kissed her and whispered the same message to her. Thus the message 'Thou art Goddess' was passed from one woman to another until all 25 had been initiated. Here, women were explicitly taking on Goddess identity and acknowledging one another as Goddess.

Another way that participants in the movement are given the message that they are 'Goddess' is through guided meditation tapes. Here is a quotation from one such tape (*Inner Woman* by Denise Linn, 1983):

> And in this dark and sacred place, let the silence fill and penetrate you. And know that you are Isis as are all women, and that within you her power manifests. You are now in the outer darkness, the darkness before the beginning. Within this darkness you are the creator, the sustainer, and the destroyer. You have entered a vortex of power, a place beyond imagining, where birth and death, dark and light, joy and pain, meet. You have stepped between the worlds, beyond time, outside the realm of human life. Be aware as your old self and ideas and opinions and judgements die. And feel yourself reborn.

In this extract Linn encourages each woman to identify – to 'know' herself, to be reborn – as Goddess and powerful. Women are told that in their new place of power the familiar binary oppositions – birth/death, dark/light, joy/pain and so on – are brought together, it is implied, as part of a single cyclic process. This concentration on holism is at the heart of Goddess spirituality: the Goddess, expressed in every woman, is also expressed in every being and all of nature.

At the level of belief, feminist witches have many of the same goals as people in the ecology movement and the overlap between feminist witchcraft and eco-feminism, in particular, is considerable. In terms of their broad social and political goals, feminist witches have the same goals as other feminists. With respect to their spiritual beliefs regarding the sacredness of the earth and the inter-relatedness of all life, feminist witches fit under the neo-Pagan umbrella. Their worldview has important ideas in common with a number of other groups too. Feminist witchcraft is one expression of what witches and some others call a 'new consciousness' which began emerging in Western societies during the counter-culture of the 1960s – one which emphasizes holism, partnership, self-empowerment and self-determination and sees dualistic paradigms, mind/body splitting and social models based on dominance and oppression as damaging and immoral. Other expressions of this broader movement or 'new consciousness' include civil rights movements, the peace movement, gay rights movements, holistic healing movements and disability rights movements. In various ways all have been challenging what witches call the 'principle of power-over' which has been dominant in Western societies.

Although they have much in common with many such contemporary groups and movements, and indeed participate in these movements, in terms of their religious practice feminist witches' rituals are fairly distinctive. Despite the fact that ritual groups or covens are entirely autonomous, rituals are apparently quite similar whether they are conducted in the US, UK or New Zealand, and I would think New Zealand feminist witches would feel at home among feminist witches anywhere. The links with Wicca in New Zealand are much weaker, however, and so some aspects of feminist witches' practice in the UK and US, which owe a great deal to Wiccan practice, are absent in New Zealand. There is no third-degree initiation process in New Zealand, for example; rituals are seldom (if ever) performed nude; the titles 'high priestess' and 'apprentice' are not used and 'priestess' only occasionally; special tools like the *athame* (the black-handled ritual knife) are not used; the 'cone of power' is raised less often and for a different purpose, and there is more improvisation in the way rituals are conducted. My impression is that New Zealand witches are more open than witches elsewhere about acknowledging that their rituals owe a great deal to invention and pastiche.

The feminist witchcraft/Goddess spirituality movement in New Zealand is amorphous, non-institutionalized, loosely structured, and unbounded: women drift in and out of the movement and around its vaguely defined edges. When I began this study 13 years ago feminist witches were a more distinctive group within New Zealand than they are today. The neo-Pagan movement has since grown in New Zealand and the boundaries between feminist witches and the great variety of other Pagans are now more difficult to determine and less important to participants than they used to be. Groups of feminist Pagan women continue to meet to celebrate the Sabbats all over the country, however, and new groups continue to spring up as others fold. Some ritual groups, including the one I joined at the beginning of my research, have been meeting for many years.

Feminist witches have no interest in winning converts to a religion called Witchcraft; they are much more concerned about achieving the goals of the higher profile movements in which they participate, especially the Green movement, feminism and the peace movement. Along with other Pagans they seek to advance the idea of a sacred universe, believing that this is the only sustainable way to live. The major impact of the feminist witchcraft/Goddess movement in New Zealand will continue to be its impact on individual New Zealand women who, through remembering/inventing a woman-centred spiritual tradition, are re-membering themselves, discovering their power, and inventing new lives.

NOTES

1 INTRODUCTION

1 The names accompanying quotations at the beginning of chapters are those of women I interviewed. Participants selected a name by which they would be known in this research.

2 In her review of Luhrmann's *Persuasions of the Witch's Craft*, Rosemary Dinnage (1989: 3) discusses the 'tremendous charge' carried by the word 'witch' as a result of these particular associations.

3 In the introduction to her essay 'Finitude, death, and reverence for life', Christ (1987: 213–27 at p. 210) sees the symbol of 'Goddess' as having the potential to counteract and heal the effects that Platonism and Christianity, as the dominant symbol systems of Western culture, have had in terms of alienating people from parts of themselves and from the natural world, the potential to 'help us to re-member ourselves, to re-member this earth, which is our home'.

4 Some feminist witches acknowledge that there are many within the Church today who are also working hard towards a re-valuing of the feminine. Others see Christian doctrine concerning the nature of divinity and the nature of women as fundamentally problematic and the institution of the Church as a lost cause.

5 Riane Eisler coined this term. She proposes that 'underlying the great surface diversity of human culture are two basic models of society': the 'dominator model' and the 'partnership model' (Eisler 1988: xvii).

6 See Hutton (1999: 75–6) for a discussion of estimated numbers of Pagans in Britain.

7 Pagans' attitudes towards the earth draw on James Lovelock's 'Gaia hypothesis' formed in the 1970s (Lovelock 1988). 'According to this theory, all organic and inorganic matter on Earth is related in a single, complex organism, with self-regulating capabilities' (Lewis 1999: 115).

8 Griffin (2000c: 14) gives several reasons why academic treatment of Paganism has been fairly scant so far. In some cases, she says, research in this area has been actively discouraged by the academy, the topic is sometimes regarded as 'questionable', funding for such research is often hard to come by, and in the US fundamentalist Christians have actively protested against it.

9 Male witches are also called 'witches'; the terms 'wizard' and 'warlock' are not used by modern witches.

10 Some modern witches say that 'Wicca', an Old English word, derives from the root 'wit' or wisdom. Others trace it to the Indo-European roots 'wic' and 'weik', meaning 'to bend' or 'to turn'. Thus 'a Witch would be a woman (or man) skilled in the craft of shaping, bending, and changing reality' (Adler 1986: 11) or bending unseen forces to their will for the good of all (Eller 1993: 50).

11 See, for example, Adler (1986), Luhrmann (1989), Hutton (1991, 2000), Kelly (1991), Baker (1996) and Hume (1997).

12 See Hutton (1994, 1995, 1999, 2000) for accounts of the various historical elements which have contributed to modern witchcraft.

13 The New Zealand Census results for religion can easily be accessed by going to <http://www.nzpagans.com/> and clicking on '2001Census results for Religion'. This takes the searcher to the official government statistics web-page. The web address for direct access to this page is extremely long.

14 See Farrar and Farrar 1981, 1985, 1987, 1988, 1990.

15 <http://www.nzpagans.com/>is a helpful place to start when seeking online information about New Zealand Pagans.

16 Academic writers follow different practices: Hume (1997) and Greenwood (2000a) use 'Goddess', Eller (1993) and Berger (1999) use 'goddess', Luhrmann (1989) changes according to context.

17 Scholars follow different practices, but most use lower case for 'witch' (Luhrmann 1989, Eller 1993, Hume 1997, Greenwood 2000a). Berger capitalizes 'Witch' (but interestingly uses lower case for 'goddess'). Hume capitalizes 'Pagan' and 'Wicca' and Greenwood capitalizes 'Pagan' but not 'wicca'.

18 The indigenous people of New Zealand, the Maori, settled the country around 1,000 years ago, arriving from central-east Polynesia. European settlers, mostly from Britain, began arriving in the 1850s.

19 However there is still a great deal of fear and damnation of anything to do with 'witchcraft' among many, but not all, fundamentalist Christians in New Zealand. I outline a personal experience which illustrates this in chapter five.

2 APPROACHES TO WITCHCRAFT

1 From the *Canon episcopi*, included by Regino of Prüm, abbot of Trêves, in a collection of instructions for bishops, AD 906 (quoted in Ginzburg 1990a: 90).

2 Burke (1990) and Hester (1992) suggest that the use of the term 'witch-craze' is problematic because it implies that the witch-hunts were 'carried out by crazed individuals in an exhibition of momentary madness' (Hester 1992: 107). I would agree that the inquisitors and demonologists who launched the witch-craze were operating within the 'sanity' of their own worldview, in particular, their view of women, but I think the term 'witch-craze' is valid because it shifts the associations of deviance and madness from the witches to their accusers. In academic treatments of witchcraft it has been the witches who have been typically regarded as suffering from delusions and mental instability.

3 Some authors use 'Sabbat' and some use 'Sabbath'. Russell (1980) uses 'Sabbat'. Ginzburg (1990a and b), who is quoted frequently in this chapter, uses 'Sabbath'. Feminist witches and other Pagans use the term 'Sabbat' to refer to the eight Pagan seasonal festivals: Winter Solstice (Yule), Brigid (Candlemas), Spring Equinox (Eoster), Beltane, Summer Solstice, Lammas (Lugnasad), Autumn Equinox (Mabon) and Hallowe'en (Samhain). These are discussed in chapter nine.

4 In the introduction to her ethnography of American witches, Orion (1995: 10) says: 'I have experienced disapproval of the very idea of studying peoples in my own country and for taking witches so seriously when anthropologists had established long ago that witches don't exist except as figments of the imaginations of the credulous'. I encountered the same objections at the beginning of my research.

5 See also Ginzburg 1983 and 1990b.

6 Ronald Hutton says that these writers were the culmination of a reaction to the Enlightenment idea that witchcraft did not exist and that the witch-hunts, therefore, had been a terrible mistake. Reactionary writers of the early nineteenth century had rejected the Enlightenment idea, saying that the alleged witches were indeed the wicked remnants of paganism. This idea was then taken up and turned around by liberal writers like Michelet who argued that the victims of the witch-hunts 'might indeed have been pagans, but not evil; rather, they stood for religious and social freedom, opposed to a feudal state and intolerant Church' (Hutton 1994: 29).

7 Historians and anthropologists have frequently pointed to these common features (Hughes 1965, Cohn 1970, Marwick 1970, Parrinder 1970, Thomas 1970, Douglas 1973, Hoch-Smith 1978, Russell 1980, Karlsen 1987, Jackson 1989, Ginzburg 1990a).

8 Despite the strong consistency in witchcraft beliefs world-wide, Alan Macfarlane (1970a: 6) emphasizes that 'English witchcraft appears to be very different from that on the continent and in Scotland'. He says that in the county of Essex witches were not believed to fly or meet for Sabbats which incorporated orgies, perverted sexual practices, dancing and feasting.

Hallen and Sodipo (1986: 107–8) caution against treating the witch as a cultural universal in the light of a discussion of the Yoruba *aje*. They find that *aje* do not fit the stereotype of the Western witch in several respects: many are men; many use medicine to achieve their ends (that is, they do not rely exclusively on psychic powers); some *aje* are consulted for advice and medicine as witch-doctors are; an *aje* may be a good person – they are not quintessentially evil. Hallen and Sodipo (p. 117) conclude that 'if scholars still wish to insist that witchcraft is some kind of conceptual and cultural universal, and that the Yoruba conform to it, we would suggest that they reflect upon the lessons to be learnt from [our work]. For it may well be that many people who considered themselves to be witches in the West were also intentionally benevolent, exceptionally talented women and men who, because they constituted an implicit challenge to established ecclesiastical and judicial authorities, and to the established socio-economic order . . . either successfully concealed themselves or were unfortunate enough to be reported, hunted down and exterminated.'

9 According to the Oxford English Dictionary, the Old English was *hægtesse*, and Middle Dutch was *haghetissa*.

10 The number of people killed has frequently been put much higher, especially by modern witches, who usually quote a figure of nine million (Starhawk 1989: 20).

11 See also chapters by Greenwood in several edited books (1996, 2000b, 2000c).

12 I have not included in this review Jeanne Favret-Saada's (1980) study of contemporary witchcraft in the French Bocage because it deals with witchcraft from the point of view of the witch's victim and his or her interactions with an 'unwitcher'. Favret-Saada's study, excellent though it is, is essentially a study of witchcraft beliefs rather than a study of witches themselves, although she strongly resists the scepticism of folklorists, reporters and her own colleagues which reduces the Bocage people's beliefs and activities in relation to witchcraft to the delusions of simple-minded, backward peasants.

3 FEMINISTS AND WITCHES

1 The history I give here is necessarily very brief. Adler's *Drawing Down the Moon*, first published in 1979 and revised in 1986, provides an excellent, detailed history of the origins of modern witchcraft in the United States. Lewis's *Witchcraft*

Today: An Encyclopedia of Wiccan and Neopagan Traditions, published in 1999, is also an excellent source.

2 I can do no more than refer to this literature here. Extensive references are given in works devoted to the subject such as Ruether (1986, 1992, 1998), King (1989, 1995, 1998), Thistlethwaite (1989) and Hampson (1990).

3 In 1980 Zsuzsanna Budapest's *The Holy Book of Women's Mysteries* was published; it was originally published as *The Feminist Book of Lights and Shadows* (Los Angeles: Susan B. Anthony Coven #1) in 1975. Two other influential introductions to feminist witchcraft were published on the same day – Hallowe'en 1979 – in the United States: Starhawk's *The Spiral Dance* and Margot Adler's *Drawing Down the Moon*. In New Zealand *The Spiral Dance* is still the first book many women interested in the movement read. Merlin Stone's *When God Was a Woman* (1976), based on research into prehistoric goddesses and their overthrow, was also very widely read in the early days of the movement and fuelled women's interest in ancient goddess worship.

4 See also Carson's first bibliography of works on feminist spirituality (Carson 1986).

5 See, for example, Morgan (1978), Daly (1979), Goldenberg (1982), Walker (1985), Adler (1986) and Crowley (1989).

6 Early in my fieldwork I met a 92-year-old Welsh woman, Ann, living in Auckland, who told me that her mother had been the local wise woman in her village in Wales. She remembered her mother delivering all the babies in the village (including those of upper-class families), setting broken bones with splints made from a broken-up salt box, and giving out doses of 'brimstone and treacle' as an end-of-winter purge to all the children of the village who lined up outside their house. Ann told me various other healing practices used by her mother, and about the 'pre-sight' or 'fore-sight' she had used as an extra source of knowledge. She said that her mother had inherited her psychic ability and healing role in the village from her father (Ann's grandfather). Ann also told me that she had herself inherited these abilities from her mother – although she had received too much formal education to fully develop her 'fore-sight' – and that her husband sometimes referred to her as his 'Welsh witch' (although she was emphatic that her mother was never called a witch).

4 FEMINISTS AND THE GODDESS

1 The editing and finishing work on Gimbutas's last book, *The Living Goddesses* (1999), was carried out after her death by Miriam Robbins Dexter at the request of Gimbutas's daughter.

2 I have discussed some of the major criticisms of Goddess spirituality in two papers (Rountree 1999, 2001). Much of the discussion in the remainder of this chapter is an abbreviated version of what I wrote in those papers.

3 I should make it clear that Spretnak herself does not criticize the Goddess movement in these terms, she is discussing the views of its opponents.

4 See also Bamberger (1974), Binford (1982), Hackett (1989), di Leonardo (1991), Ortner (1996), Goodison and Morris (1998). Grosz (1990: 334) defines essentialism thus: 'Essentialism, a term which is rarely defined or explained explicitly in feminist contexts, refers to the attribution of a fixed essence to women. Women's essence is assumed to be given, universal, and is usually, though not necessarily, identified with women's biology and "natural" characteristics. The term usually entails biologism and naturalism, but there are cases in which women's essence is seen to reside, not in nature or biology, but in certain given

psychological characteristics – nurturance, empathy, supportiveness, non-competitiveness, and so on. Or women's essence may be attributed to certain activities and procedures (which may or may not be dictated by biology) observable in social practices, intuitiveness, emotional responses, concern, and commitment to helping others, etc. Essentialism entails that those characteristics defined as women's essence are shared in common by all women at all times . . . Essentialism thus refers to the existence of fixed characteristics, given attributes, and ahistorical functions which limit the possibilities of change and thus of social reorganization.'

5 See, for example, Ehrenberg (1989), Hackett (1989), Brown (1993), Conkey and Tringham (1995), Meskell (1995, 1998), Tringham and Conkey (1998) and Westenholz (1998).

6 An exception was at the 'Take Back the Night' marches in 1990, where some women dressed up as witches and incorporated Wiccan ritual into the public demonstrations.

7 Since the 1960s the Coromandel has been associated with alternative life-stylers, and it is still strongly linked with Green politics.

8 See *From the Realm of the Ancestors: An Anthology in Honor of Marija Gimbutas*, edited by Joan Marler (1997), a collection of writings dedicated to the memory of Gimbutas. Since her death, admirers of her work have continued to meet at lectures and conferences to discuss her work. Courses in archaeomythology, which explore the international influence of her work, are offered by the California Institute of Integral Studies in San Francisco. 'Archaeomythology' is a term said to have been created by Gimbutas meaning 'a multidisciplinary approach to scholarship that includes not only mythology and archaeology, but linguistics, comparative religion, ethnology and cultural history' (Cichon 1999: 26).

9 Gimbutas also has critics from other disciplines. Juliette Wood, a folklorist, finds Gimbutas's use of 'ancient beliefs' problematic because she moves 'from period to period and from culture to culture with no indication of context . . . uses analogy and suggestion but offers no supporting evidence', fails to document fully her claims, and (in *The Language of the Goddess*) presents a bibliography which contains 'very little modern and mainstream folklore research, and too much fringe and outmoded nineteenth-century material' (Wood 1996: 20).

10 An extremely heated debate about Eller's work took place at the seventh Annual Gender and Archaeology conference at Sonoma State University in Rohnert Park, California, 4–5 October 2002. Eller gave a presentation titled 'Religious uses of prehistoric material culture: female figurines and the feminist spirituality movement', and was later answered by scholars sympathetic to the women's spirituality movement. Marguerite Rigoglioso challenged Eller with regard to her dismissal of the entire body of women's spirituality scholarship and the derision with which her attack had been launched. She also suggested that Eller should update her reading in this area. In her presentation to the conference, Max Dashu, who has critiqued Eller's book elsewhere (see Dashu 2000), said that a systematic global study of the controversial female figurines had yet to be undertaken.

11 Eller (2000: 148) refers to 'Malta's enormous anthropomorphic statues' which are 15 feet tall. No statues that tall have been recovered from the Maltese Neolithic temples. One statue from Tarxien temple, a skirted figure now displayed in Malta's National Museum of Archaeology, is thought to have originally stood two metres tall, but only the bottom half remains (the top having been quarried away by farmers working in their fields which once lay over the site).

5 RESEARCHING WITCHES: BECOMING ENCHANTED

1 Cook and Fonow (1986: 9) point to the dilemma that '[a]s researchers try to include women as subjects they cannot fail to notice how the practice of sociology [or anthropology] transforms all actors into objects'. Lather (1989: 12) says that even to 'make something available for discussion is to make of it an object'.

2 I agreed to teach these courses not because I thought I was an expert on the subject but because it seemed to be a way of giving something back to the movement, and contributed to witches' consciousness-raising goals. I facilitated courses between 1992 and 1996 in Hamilton, Wellington, Rotorua, Tauranga, New Plymouth, Te Awamutu, Matamata and Ohope Beach. They were organized by the continuing education departments of the University of Waikato and Victoria University of Wellington, or by groups of women who approached me because they had heard about my research.

3 At each subsequent series of workshops I participated in over the next two years, I explained my reasons for being there and these were always accepted. No one ever raised doubts or objections with me or the facilitator. If they had, I would have left the group. I regarded myself as a full participant as well as an anthropologist in these workshops.

4 Because I kept a diary of group life, as it were, based on highly attentive observations of the group's rituals, I have been able to recall (with the help of my notes) dates and events which happened during the group's infancy more than a decade ago.

5 Pakeha are New Zealanders of European (mostly British) descent. It is a Maori word which has been adopted widely in New Zealand.

6 In the 'Principles of professional responsibility and ethical conduct' of the national Association of Social Anthropologists of Aotearoa/ New Zealand (ASAA/NZ), first priority is given to the researcher's responsibility to research participants. The first principle states that it is axiomatic that the rights, interests and sensitivities of research participants be safeguarded; that the aims of the investigation should be made clear to research participants; that the group to be studied should approve the proposed research and has the right to decline to continue participation at any point; and that fieldwork should be based on a collaborative and equal relationship between the anthropologist and research participants. This principle, along with others in the code, was an important ethical guide during my fieldwork.

7 If an interviewee wanted something changed, I changed it. This happened in only a few cases. One woman changed a transcript to make her point more clearly; another wanted something negative she had said about her family removed; another corrected factual details. My purpose in giving women the opportunity to make changes was to give them the power to make the quotations say what they wanted them to say, although in my role as 'writer', I chose which quotations would be used.

6 FEMINIST WITCHCRAFT IN NEW ZEALAND: ORIGINS AND DEVELOPMENT

1 I wrote to the *Women's Spirituality Newsletter*, a newsletter for Pagan women published in New Zealand four times a year, asking permission to quote extracts from it. I received a reply saying this would be fine so long as I did not identify the authors of quotations.

2 Pagan publications include: *New Pentacle*, *Under-the-World*, *The Enlightenment*, *Gypsy*

Caravan, Nymphs, Queens and Crones, Rainbow News, Inspiration Input, Pentacles Psychic Adventures Newsletter.

3 The rules of witchcraft are discussed in chapter eight. Briefly, there are two rules or principles: the 'Wiccan Rede' and 'the three-fold law'. The Rede says: 'And ye harm none, do as thou wilt'. The three-fold law is: 'What you send returns three times over'. This is a version of 'Do unto others as you would have them do unto you' (Starhawk 1989: 27). Both rules are severe cautions against hexing.

4 Hume (1997: 90) notes that in Australia, also, witches were not suddenly converted to the religion; rather they gradually re-oriented themselves towards Paganism.

5 One famous example of the spontaneous spread of a new habit concerns the opening of milk bottles in Britain by blue tits (Sheldrake 1988: 177). The birds were observed to attack the bottles minutes after their delivery, tear open the foil caps, drink up to five centimetres of milk and, occasionally, drown head first in the bottles. The phenomenon was first recorded in Southampton in 1921 and thereafter spread, at an accelerated rate as time went on, to locations throughout the British Isles and also to Sweden, Denmark and Holland. The tits were not learning the practice from each other because the practice reappeared in locations well beyond the birds' home ranges. Sheldrake (p. 180) says that the morphic field (of bottle-opening) was 'progressively reinforced by the cumulative effects of morphic resonance from previous milk-drinking tits'.

6 In the 1970s James Lovelock proposed the hypothesis that Earth is a self-regulating, living organism with the capacity 'to keep our planet healthy by controlling the chemical and physical environment' (Lovelock, cited in Sheldrake 1991: 154). Lovelock named this living system 'Gaia' after the oldest Mother Goddess in the Greek pantheon. The 'Gaia hypothesis' contradicts mechanistic science and humanism.

7 *Women's Ministries and Spirituality Conference: A Resource Book for Women: Reports, Resources and Reflections arising from the Third National Ecumenical Feminist Women's Conference held at Rangi Ruru Girls' School, Christchurch, August 31 to September 4, 1988.* The book was edited by Margie Lovell-Smith *et al.* and published by The Planning Group, Women's Ministries and Spirituality Conference, 1988.

8 In 1987 Yolanda Wisewitch completed an MA thesis in religious studies at the University of Canterbury titled 'Women's rites: a study of fifteen Christchurch women's thoughts and feelings about their involvement in Women's Spirituality'. This represents the first academic study of neo-Paganism in New Zealand. Wisewitch conducted interviews with 15 women from five Christchurch ritual groups, asking questions about their religious backgrounds, their reasons for leaving these religious traditions, their reasons for becoming involved in neo-Pagan ritual groups and the importance of ritual in their lives. Other MA theses are those by Paula Whitelock (2000) in sociology at the University of Canterbury, Susan Wesney (1997) in social work at Victoria University of Wellington, and Emma Ramsay (1997) in anthropology at the University of Otago.

9 Aotearoa, meaning 'Land of the Long White Cloud', is the indigenous Maori name for New Zealand.

10 Just as Batten's book looks to Maori spirituality to see how the landscape was sacralized and the seasonal round celebrated locally, Hume (1997: 119) reports that in Australia Pagans 'look to Aboriginal spirituality for guidance' on the seasonal festivals. And of course in the US many Pagans adopt or adapt ideas and practices from Native American spirituality, while in Britain Celtic deities and spiritual ideas are particularly important.

11 See also the edited interview with Juliet Batten conducted by Céline Kearney and

reproduced in *Faces of the Goddess: New Zealand Women Talk about their Spirituality* edited by Kearney (1997).

12 The Treaty of Waitangi was signed on 6 February 1840 by a number of leading Maori chiefs and Lieutenant-Governor William Hobson, representing the British crown. New Zealand thus officially became a British colony. While the Treaty is frequently referred to as the founding 'partnership' document for New Zealand as a nation, it has been the focus of bitter dispute and protest ever since it was signed, and, indeed, it was hotly debated among the chiefs gathered at Waitangi before it was signed.

13 *Womanscript* magazine, based in Christchurch, was begun in 1990 and continued publication until mid-1992 when it collapsed, as many little magazines in New Zealand do, because of insufficient subscribers to offset publication costs. Subtitled *Journal of Wellbeing for/by Women of Aotearoa*, the magazine was not focused explicitly on spirituality, but much of the content had to do with this theme. *Womanscript* had approximately 350 subscribers and was sold in women's and university bookshops, Pathfinder bookshop in Auckland, and a few other bookshops and health-food shops.

The fact that *Womanscript* was available for sale in bookshops meant that women who chose to 'come out' in the magazine did so knowing that they might be identified as neo-Pagan beyond the neo-Pagan community. The association of the magazine with feminist witchcraft was an issue for the editors and subscribers to consider. The first issue contained more explicit references to witches than subsequent issues – some women did not feel comfortable supporting a magazine with a centre-page entitled 'Broomstick' where they were invited to 'write to Broomstick for spells & hexes, cures and curses, recipes & remedies, chants, invocations, incantations, herb & weed lore, magic potions, signs & symbols, lunar lore, any magic, mystery or myth you want to explore'. Issue six, entitled 'Ceremonies and symbols', contained a lot of material about feminist rituals and ritual groups, but without the explicit references to witches (although one group profiled called itself a coven).

14 The only large-scale political ritual I attended during my doctoral fieldwork was one organized by Juliet Batten as part of the 1990 commemoration of the signing of the Treaty of Waitangi. This ritual was for Pakeha to focus on what the Treaty meant for them and to make a commitment to some form of action to honour the Treaty. People were asked to bring young trees to donate to the Ngati Te Ata tribe's replanting programme at Waiuku. There were over 100 men and women present. At the time of the 1991 Gulf War several ritual groups held peace rituals and some women were involved in organizing large peace rallies in Auckland.

15 In 1992 Luisah Teish, who is well known internationally in Goddess circles as a writer and ritual-maker, visited New Zealand. Teish is of Yoruba (West African) ancestry, although she was born and raised in New Orleans. She was the guest facilitator at residential weekend workshops in Auckland and Hamilton dedicated to exploring sensuality and creativity in ritual contexts. Her book *Jambalaya: The Natural Woman's Book of Personal Charms and Practical Rituals* (1985) is well-known among feminist witches in New Zealand. In 1996 Zsuzsanna Budapest visited and held workshops in Christchurch. Her publications are also well known among New Zealand witches.

16 It should be noted, however, that women's spirituality workshops in New Zealand cost a small fraction of what some New Age courses and seminars cost. Facilitators make very little money out of them.

17 In the group I joined, all the current 11 members have a tertiary qualification, and more than half have more than one university degree.

18 See Griffin (1995) for a description of an American group's croning ritual.
19 The idea of the Auckland Young Witches Group is to provide a support network for young witches who follow different paths – it is not a coven, although a core of 12 members celebrates the Sabbats together.
20 However, whenever *The Craft* or a new series of *Buffy the Vampire Slayer* plays on television the organizer of the Young Witches Group gets an increase of e-mails, mostly from 12- or 13-year-olds, wanting to know how they can become a witch. When they learn it is 'not about invoking demons and floating in the air' most get bored with the idea.
21 See Trevor-Roper (1969), Douglas (1970: xxvi), Macfarlane (1970a: 222), Thomas (1970: 64–5) and Levack (1987: 15).

7 THE ATTRACTION OF WITCHCRAFT

1 They seem to do this relatively effectively. When I compare my friends who are witches with women friends who are not, the latter seem rather more likely to 'get stuck' when dealing with decisions, transitions or crises in their lives. They find it more difficult to isolate issues which need to be addressed, harder to 'know what to do', and harder to act on decisions. It seems to me that through learning to work with ritual, witches are able to gain insight on issues and problems in their lives and on practical ways of dealing with them. Ritual provides women with a tool for processing transitions. I discuss how ritual 'works' in detail in chapter 11.
2 Women leave for different reasons. The most common reason is that they are moving to live in a different part of the country, where they may or may not join another group (if they can find one). Sometimes women consider they no longer have the time to put into the group. Occasionally women say that their life or spiritual path is moving in a different direction. On one occasion a woman left the group I was a member of because of a falling out with another group member. This difficulty in their relationship made it too painful for her to participate any longer. The falling out did not occur because of events connected with the ritual group; it was to do with their friendship outside the group.
3 Longer versions of these stories and additional accounts can be found in my doctoral thesis (Rountree 1993).

8 THE ATTRACTION OF THE GODDESS: WITCHES' WORLDVIEWS

1 Eller (1993: 140) reports that many of the American spiritual feminists she interviewed also cited Starhawk (see chapter four) and gave similar answers to this question.
2 In Wiccan rituals the God may similarly be 'drawn down' into a priest of the coven.

9 WHAT WITCHES DO

1 The pohutukawa, a large, protected, native tree, produces red, soft-bristled flowers which bloom during the month leading up to Christmas. Karaka berries are orangey-red and grow on another native tree.
2 Griffin (1995) describes a ritual in which the menstruating women – those 'on their Moon Time' – were each given a sprig of herbs tied with a red ribbon to wear as a symbol of pride.

3 In 1983, at Winter Solstice, Juliet Batten facilitated a 'Menstrual Maze Performance Ritual' designed to 'break the taboos that have been laid upon us and reclaim our power' (Batten 1988: 62). The ritual began with women reciting warnings from the patriarchal mythology surrounding menstruation: 'A menstruating woman will turn the meat bad'; 'She will contaminate the crops'; 'Don't walk under a ladder – a drop of red paint will fall on you and you will die' and 'If a man looks upon a menstruating woman, his bones will soften and his weapons will be rendered useless'. The final part of the ritual was a celebration of a young woman's first menstruation which concluded with all the women present being given sprigs of rosemary with the words: 'We bring you rosemary, for remembrance. Remembrance of your pain. Remembrance of your strength. Remembrance of your ancient power. Take it, and enter the Maze. We give you the gift of your selves.'

4 The AGM is also a time for 'stock-taking' – for each member to reaffirm her commitment to the group or to tell the group that she would prefer to take a lower-key role or to leave altogether. (This may also happen at other times of the year.) The group also discusses aspects of its functioning, for example, expectations of members may be reiterated, such as arriving promptly for rituals and letting the organizers know whether or not one is able to attend.

5 In Britain the correspondences used are always: east/air, south/fire, west/water and north/earth (Greenwood 2000a: 36).

6 *Toetoe* is a New Zealand plant similar to pampas grass, with tall feathery plumes in cream or mauve.

7 New Zealand feminist witches very seldom work 'sky-clad' (nude) as is common for practitioners of Wicca.

8 *Tangata whenua* is a Maori phrase meaning literally 'people of the land'. *Tangata whenua* are those people, often a particular tribe or sub-tribe, who have a strong ancestral affiliation and reciprocal sense of belonging with a particular tract of land. Guests to their area are called *manuhiri.*

9 The two chants used most frequently by the group I joined are 'We all come from the Goddess' and 'She changes'. Both have actions. The theme of the first is the holistic connection and the cyclic nature of all life; the theme of the second is transformation and the ever-changing nature of life. The words are as follows:

We all come from the Goddess
And to Her we shall return
Like a drop of rain
Falling to the ocean.

Hoof and horn, hoof and horn
All that dies shall be reborn
Corn and grain, corn and grain
All that falls shall rise again.

She changes everything She touches
And everything She touches changes.

10 In the US dancing and drumming may accompany the chanting and singing (Eller 1993: 97).

10 RITUAL AS ARTEFACT

1 Papatuanuku is the name of the Maori earth goddess.

2 During my fieldwork I attended a workshop in which participants were led on a 'shamanic journey'. To begin with, all participants sat in a circle, linked hands, and closed our eyes. Beating her drum and using maracas, the facilitator 'called in' all the animal spirits from the four directions. Then she asked us to lie down in a space in the room, cover ourselves with a blanket, and place a covering over our eyes. We were told that we would be taken on a shamanic journey to meet our personal power animal which would then remain with us as our spirit guide. The journey took the form of a guided visualization accompanied by a steady drum beat. The visualization involved finding an opening in the earth and journeying deep into the earth where, it was said, an animal would show itself to us four times. This animal would then become our spirit companion providing guidance and protection.

After emerging from the journey, we were provided with thick cardboard, wood, and collage materials with which to make a shield to symbolize our power animal. Later we danced with our shields inside sacred circles, danced freely around the room with our shields, and made affirmations in which we identified as our power animal – for example, 'I am Bear. I let no one into my lair'; 'I am bison. I am wild and untamed.' The animals included several tigers, a tuatara, a stingray, a bison, an eagle, a lion, a bear and a bird. At the end of the day the facilitator suggested that we ask the dream-maker to give us a dream of our power animal that night.

3 I have discussed these issues in Rountree (2001 and 2002b).

4 Members of the group which organized the first seven Winter Solstice rituals in the cave at Te Henga contacted the Maori tribe associated with the area to check that there was 'harmony of intention' between themselves and the Maori in relation to the cave. For the Maori the cave was linked with a significant female ancestor and they were happy for the cave to be used for the Solstice ritual. A *koha* (donation) was given each year to the tribe to acknowledge their special relationship with the site.

11 HOW MAGIC WORKS

1 An earlier version of this chapter, titled 'How magic works: New Zealand feminist witches' theories of ritual action', appeared in *Anthropology of Consciousness*, published by the American Anthropological Association in 2002 (Rountree 2002a).

2 Frazer's famous thesis postulating an evolutionary progression from an Age of Magic through an Age of Religion to an Age of Science was developed in his multi-tomed *The Golden Bough*, first published in 1890, with a second edition in 1900, and a third (in 12 volumes) published 1906–15. Frazer would have seen the contemporary Western interest in magic as a 'relapse' which, while fit for scientific examination, was an anachronism which ought not to be indulged (see 'Introduction' to the 1994 edition of *The Golden Bough* by Robert Fraser, p. xxiii). Frazer was influenced by Tylor, whose first volume of *Primitive Culture* (1871) included a discussion of magic. Tylor saw elementary religion as employing a 'personalized causation theory', while science employs the concept of 'impersonal causation' (Tambiah 1990: 50).

3 Catherine Bell (1992) provides a comprehensive discussion of theoretical descriptions of ritual which have tended to dichotomize ritual and belief (as the

major components of religion), conceptualizing their structural relationship as parallel to the relationship between action and thought.

4 See Skorupski (1976) for an account of the symbolist traditions.

5 See Luhrmann (1989: 345–8) for a succinct summary of this debate.

6 However the instrumental component of ritual has not been ignored altogether by, for example, scholars such as Firth, Beattie and Leach (Lewis 1980: 16–17, Luhrmann 1989: 348).

7 Lewis acknowledges the difficulty of ritual actors articulating meaning in relation to his study of puberty rituals among the Gnau of the West Sepik (New Guinea), arguing that sometimes rituals are the best or only medium for expressing something important: 'We must expect our informants to be at times inarticulate or silent about part of what ritual means to them, or does to them, or makes them feel' (Lewis 1980: 24). I would suggest, and I think Lewis implies, that silence or 'not being able to say' is not the same as 'not knowing'.

8 Frazer had seen magic as schematized thought and ritual as thought-in-practice (see Fraser's introduction to 1994 edition, p. xxxix).

9 Greenwood (1996: 114) similarly commented that bodily experience is the 'very essence' of English feminist witches' spirituality.

10 These notes were reproduced in my doctoral thesis (Rountree 1993) with the author's permission.

11 However, it may be that New Zealand feminist witches' rituals are not more inventive than the rituals created by Goddess groups in the US – indeed those described by Griffin (1995, 2000c) are highly creative and full of dramatic intensity. There has not been a great deal written by academics specifically about feminist witches' rituals in Britain so a comparison is difficult to make.

12 RE-MEMBERING THE WITCH AND THE GODDESS

1 Tong is quoting Hélène Cixous's essay 'Sorties' in *The Newly Born Woman*, trans. Betsy Wing (Minneapolis: University of Minnesota Press, 1986), pp. 63, 65.

REFERENCES

Adler, Margot (1982) 'Meanings of matriarchy', in C. Spretnak (ed.) *The Politics of Women's Spirituality: Essays on the Rise of Spiritual Power within the Feminist Movement*, New York: Anchor Books, 127–37.

—— (1986) *Drawing Down the Moon: Witches, Druids, Goddess-Worshippers, and Other Pagans in America Today*, Boston, MA: Beacon Press; first published 1979.

—— (1989) 'A response', *Journal of Feminist Studies in Religion*, 5(1): 97–100.

Ankarloo, Bengt and Henningsen, Gustav (eds) (1990) *Early Modern European Witchcraft: Centres and Peripheries*, Oxford: Clarendon Press.

Baker, James W. (1996) 'White witches: historic fact and romantic fantasy', in J. R. Lewis (ed.) *Magical Religion and Modern Witchcraft*, Albany, NY: State University of New York Press, 171–92.

Bamberger, J. (1974) 'The myth of matriarchy: why men rule in primitive society', in M. Z. Rosaldo and L. Lamphere (eds) *Woman, Culture and Society*, Stanford, CA: Stanford University Press, 263–80.

Baring, Anne and Cashford, Jules (1991) *The Myth of the Goddess: Evolution of an Image*, London: Viking.

Baroja, Julio (1965) *The World of the Witches*, Chicago: University of Chicago Press.

Batten, Juliet (1988) *Power from Within: A Feminist Guide to Ritual-making*, Auckland: Ishtar Books.

—— (1995) *Celebrating the Southern Seasons: Rituals for Aotearoa*, Auckland: Tandem Press.

Bell, Catherine (1992) *Ritual Theory, Ritual Practice*, Oxford: Oxford University Press.

Benland, Catherine (1990) 'Women's spirituality movement', in P. Donovan (ed.) *Religions of New Zealanders*, Palmerston North: Dunmore Press, 238–52.

Ben-Yehuda, Nachman (1989) 'Witchcraft and the occult as boundary maintenance devices', in J. Neusner, E. Frerichs and P. V. McCracken Flesher (eds) *Religion, Science and Magic: In Concert and In Conflict*, Oxford and New York: Oxford University Press, 229–60.

Berger, Helen A. (1999) *A Community of Witches: Contemporary Neo-Paganism and Witchcraft in the United States*, Columbia, SC: University of South Carolina Press.

Binford, Sally (1982) 'Myths and matriarchies', in C. Spretnak (ed.) *The Politics of Women's Spirituality: Essays on the Rise of Spiritual Power within the Feminist Movement*, New York: Anchor Books, 541–9 and 558–9.

Bolen, Jean Shinoda (1985) *Goddesses in Everywoman: A New Psychology of Women*, New York: Harper and Row.

Boyer, Paul and Nissenbaum, Stephen (1974) *Salem Possessed: The Social Origins of Witchcraft*, Cambridge, MA: Harvard University Press.

Bridenthal, R., Koonz, C. and Stuard, S. (1987) *Becoming Visible: Women in European History*, Boston, MA: Houghton Mifflin.

Brown, S. (1993) 'Feminist research in archaeology: what does it mean? Why is it taking so long?', in N. S. Rabinowitz and A. Richlin (eds) *Feminist Theory and the Classics*, New York: Routledge, 238–71.

Budapest, Zsuzsanna (1980) *The Holy Book of Women's Mysteries*, Berkeley, CA: Wingbow Press.

—— (1982) 'The vows, wows and joys of the High Priestess, or what do you people do anyway?' in C. Spretnak (ed.) *The Politics of Women's Spirituality: Essays on the Rise of Spiritual Power within the Feminist Movement*, New York: Anchor Books, 535–40.

—— (1986) 'The slothwoman and ancient magician', *Thesmophoria* 7(7): 1.

—— (1993) *The Goddess in the Office: A Personal Energy Guide for the Spiritual Warrior at Work*, San Francisco: HarperCollins.

Burke, Peter (1990) 'The comparative approach to witchcraft', in B. Ankarloo and G. Henningsen (eds) *Early Modern European Witchcraft: Centres and Peripheries*, Oxford: Clarendon Press, 435–41.

Butler, Judith (1993) *Bodies that Matter: On the Discursive Limits of 'Sex'*, New York: Routledge.

Carson, Anne (1986) *Feminist Spirituality and the Feminine Divine: An Annotated Bibliography*, Freedom, CA: The Crossing Press.

—— (1992) *Goddesses and Wise Women: The Literature of Feminist Spirituality, 1980–1992 An Annotated Bibliography*, Freedom, CA: The Crossing Press.

Christ, Carol (1982) 'Why women need the Goddess: phenomenological, psychological and political reflections', in C. Spretnak (ed.) *The Politics of Women's Spirituality: Essays on the Rise of Spiritual Power within the Feminist Movement*, New York: Anchor Books, 71–86.

—— (1987) *Laughter of Aphrodite*, San Francisco: Harper and Row.

—— (1992) 'Symbols of Goddess and God in feminist theology', in C. Olson (ed.) *The Book of the Goddess Past and Present: An Introduction to Her Religion*, New York: Crossroad.

—— (1997) *Rebirth of the Goddess: Finding Meaning in Feminist Spirituality*, New York: Routledge.

Christ, Carol and Plaskow, Judith (eds) (1979) *Womanspirit Rising: A Feminist Reader in Religion*, San Francisco: Harper and Row.

Cichon, J. (1999) 'Archaeomythology conference: deepening the disciplines', *Goddessing Regenerated*, 10: 26–7.

Clifford, James and Marcus, George (eds) (1986) *Writing Culture: The Poetics and Politics of Ethnography*, Los Angeles, CA: University of California Press.

Cohn, Norman (1970) 'The myth of Satan and his human servants', in M. Douglas (ed.) *Witchcraft: Confessions and Accusations*, London: Tavistock Publications, 3–16.

—— (1975) *Europe's Inner Demons*, New York: New American Library.

Coleman, K. (2001) 'Review article: matriarchy and myth', *Religion*, 31: 247–63.

Conkey, M. W. and Tringham, R. E. (1995) 'Archaeology and the goddess: exploring the contours of feminist archaeology', in D. Stanton and A. Stewart (eds) *Feminisms in the Academy*, Ann Arbor, MI: University of Michigan Press, 199–247.

Cook, Judith and Fonow, Mary (1986) 'Knowledge and women's interests: issues of epistemology and methodology in feminist sociological research', *Sociological Inquiry*, 56(1): 2–29.

Crowley, Vivianne (1989) *Wicca: The Old Religion in the New Age*, London: The Aquarian Press.

Currott, Phyllis (1999) *Book of Shadows: A Modern Woman's Journey into the Wisdom of Witchcraft and the Magic of the Goddess*, Sydney: Bantam Books.

Daly, Mary (1979) *Gyn/Ecology: The Metaethics of Radical Feminism*, London: The Women's Press.

—— (1985) *Beyond God the Father: Toward a Philosophy of Women's Liberation*, Boston, MA: Beacon Press; first published 1974.

Dashu, Max (2000) 'Review of *The Myth of Matriarchal Prehistory: Why an Invented Past Won't Give Women a Future* by Cynthia Eller (2000)'. Available online at <http://www.suppressedhistories.net/articles/eller.html> (accessed 16 October 2001).

Davis, Elizabeth Gould (1972) *The First Sex*, Harmondsworth: Penguin.

De Beauvoir, Simone (1974) *The Second Sex*, trans. H. M. Parshley, New York: Vintage; first published 1949.

De Blécourt, Willem (1999) 'The witch, her victim, the unwitcher and the researcher: the continued existence of traditional witchcraft' in B. Ankarloo and S. Clark (eds) *Witchcraft and Magic in Europe: The Twentieth Century*, London: The Athlone Press, 141–219.

Demos, John Putnam (1982) *Entertaining Satan: Witchcraft and the Culture of Early New England*, Oxford: Oxford University Press.

Desjarlais, Robert (1992) *Body and Emotion*, Philadelphia, PA: University of Pennsylvania Press.

Dexter, Miriam Robbins (1990) *Whence the Goddesses: A Source Book*, New York: Pergamon Press.

di Leonardo, Micaela (1991) *Gender at the Crossroads of Knowledge: Feminist Anthropology in the Postmodern Era*, Berkeley, CA: University of California Press.

Dinnage, Rosemary (1989) 'Review of *Persuasions of the Witch's Craft: Ritual Magic in Contemporary England* by T. M. Luhrmann', *The New York Review of Books*, 12 October 1989: 3–6.

Douglas, Mary (1973) *Natural Symbols: Explorations in Cosmology*, London: Barrie and Jenkins; first published 1970.

—— (ed.) (1970) *Witchcraft: Confessions and Accusations*, London: Tavistock Publications.

Duerr, Hans Peter (1985) *Dreamtime: Concerning the Boundary between Wilderness and Civilization*, New York: Basil Blackwell.

Dworkin, Andrea (1974) *Woman Hating*, New York: Dutton.

Ehrenberg, Margaret (1989) *Women in Prehistory*, London: British Museum Publications.

Ehrenreich, Barbara and English, Deirdre (1973) *Witches, Midwives and Nurses: A History of Women Healers*, New York: Feminist Press.

Eilberg-Schwartz, H. (1989) 'Witches of the West: Neopaganism and Goddess worship as enlightenment religions', *Journal of Feminist Studies in Religion*, 5(1): 77–95.

Eisler, Riane (1988) *The Chalice and the Blade: Our History, Our Future*, San Francisco: HarperCollins.

Eller, Cynthia (1993) *Living in the Lap of the Goddess: The Feminist Spirituality Movement in America*, Boston, MA: Beacon Press.

—— (2000) *The Myth of Matriarchal Prehistory: Why an Invented Past Won't Give Women a Future*, Boston, MA: Beacon Press.

—— (2001) 'Response', *Religion*, 31: 265–70.

Evans, J. (1995) *Feminist Theory Today: An Introduction to Second Wave Feminism*, London: Sage.

Evans-Pritchard, E. E. (1976) *Witchcraft, Oracles and Magic among the Azande*, Oxford: Oxford University Press; first published 1937.

Farganis, Sondra (1986) 'Social theory and feminist theory: the need for dialogue', *Sociological Inquiry*, 56(1): 50–67.

Farrar, J. and Farrar, S. (1981) *Eight Sabbats for Witches*, with notes by D. Valiente, London: Robert Hale.

—— (1985) *The Witches' Way: Principles, Rituals and Beliefs of Modern Witchcraft*, with notes and appendix by D. Valiente, London: Robert Hale.

—— (1987) *The Life and Times of a Modern Witch*, Custer, WA: Phoenix Publishing.

—— (1988) *The Witches' Goddess: The Feminine Principle of Divinity*, Custer, WA: Phoenix Publishing.

—— (1990) *Spells and How They Work*, Custer, WA: Phoenix Publishing.

Favret-Saada, Jeanne (1980) *Deadly Words: Witchcraft in the Bocage*, Cambridge: Cambridge University Press.

Finch, Janet 1984, '"It's great to have someone to talk to": the ethics and politics of interviewing women', in C. Bell and H. Roberts (eds) *Social Researching*, London: Routledge and Kegan Paul.

Foltz, Tanice G. (2001) 'Women's spirituality research: doing feminism', in N. Nason-Clark and M. J. Neitz (eds) *Feminist Narratives and the Sociology of Religion*, Walnut Creek, CA: Altamira Press, 89–98.

Foltz, T. G. and Griffin, W. (1996) '"She changes everything she touches": ethnographic journeys of self-discovery', in C. Ellis and A. P. Bochner (eds) *Composing Ethnography: Alternative Forms of Qualitative Writing*, Walnut Creek, CA: Altamira Press, 301–29.

Frazer, James (1994) *The Golden Bough: A Study in Magic and Religion*; a new abridgement from the 2nd and 3rd editions, ed. and introduction by Robert Fraser, London: Oxford University Press.

Frye, M. (1996) 'The necessity of differences: constructing a positive category of women', *Signs*, 21(4): 991–1010.

Gadon, Elinor (1990) *The Once and Future Goddess: A Symbol for Our Time*, Wellingborough, Northamptonshire: The Aquarian Press.

Gardner, Gerald (1954) *Witchcraft Today*, London: Rider and Company.

Geertz, Clifford (1973) *The Interpretation of Cultures*, New York: Basic Books.

Gimbutas, Marija (1974; 1982) *The Goddesses and Gods of Old Europe 6500–3500 BC: Myths and Cult Images*, London: Thames and Hudson.

—— (1989) *The Language of the Goddess*, San Francisco: Harper and Row.

—— (1991) *The Civilization of the Goddess: The World of Old Europe*, San Francisco: HarperCollins.

—— (1999) *The Living Goddesses*; ed. M. Robbins Dexter, Berkeley, CA: University of California Press.

Ginzburg, Carlo (1983) *The Night Battles: Witchcraft and Agrarian Cults in the Sixteenth and Seventeenth Centuries*, Baltimore, MD: Johns Hopkins University Press.

—— (1990a) *Ecstasies: Deciphering the Witches' Sabbath*, London: Hutchinson Radius.

—— (1990b) 'Deciphering the Sabbath', in B. Ankarloo and G. Henningsen (eds) *Early Modern European Witchcraft: Centres and Peripheries*, Oxford: Clarendon Press, 121–37.

Goldenberg, Naomi (1979) *Changing of the Gods: Feminism and the End of Traditional Religions*, Boston, MA: Beacon Press.

—— (1982) 'Feminist witchcraft: controlling our own inner space', in C. Spretnak (ed.) *The Politics of Women's Spirituality: Essays on the Rise of Spiritual Power within the Feminist Movement*, New York: Anchor Books, 213–18.

Goodison, Lucy (1990) *Moving Heaven and Earth: Sexuality, Spirituality and Social Change*, London: The Women's Press.

Goodison, L. and Morris, C. (1998) 'Introduction: exploring female divinity from modern myths to ancient evidence', in L. Goodison and C. Morris (eds) *Ancient Goddesses: The Myths and the Evidence*, London: British Museum Press, 6–21.

Greenwood, Susan (1996) 'Feminist witchcraft: a transformatory politics', in N. Charles and F. Hughes-Freeland (eds) *Practising Feminism: Identity, Difference, Power*, London: Routledge, 109–34.

—— (2000a) *Magic, Witchcraft and the Otherworld: An Anthropology*, Oxford: Berg.

—— (2000b) 'Gender and power in magical practices', in S. Sutcliffe and M. Bowman (eds) *Beyond New Age: Exploring Alternative Spirituality*, Edinburgh: Edinburgh University Press, 137–54.

—— (2000c) 'Feminist witchcraft', in W. Griffin (ed.) *Daughters of the Goddess: Studies of Healing, Identity and Empowerment*, Walnut Creek, CA: Altamira Press, 136–50.

Griffin, Wendy (1995) 'The embodied Goddess: feminist witchcraft and female divinity', *Sociology of Religion*, 56(1): 35–49.

—— (2000a) (ed.) *Daughters of the Goddess: Studies of Healing, Identity and Empowerment*, Walnut Creek, CA: Altamira Press.

—— (2000b) 'Introduction', in W. Griffin (ed.) *Daughters of the Goddess: Studies of Healing, Identity and Empowerment*, Walnut Creek, CA: Altamira Press, 13–22.

—— (2000c) 'Crafting the boundaries: Goddess narrative as incantation', in W. Griffin (ed.) *Daughters of the Goddess: Studies of Healing, Identity and Empowerment*, Walnut Creek, CA: Altamira Press, 73–88.

Grosz, E. (1989) *Sexual Subversions: Three French Feminists*, Sydney: Allen and Unwin.

—— (1990) 'Conclusion: a note on essentialism and difference', in S. Gunew (ed.) *Feminist Knowledge: Critique and Construct*, London: Routledge, 332–44.

Hackett, J. (1989) 'Can a sexist model liberate us? Ancient Near Eastern "fertility" goddesses', *Journal of Feminist Studies in Religion*, 5(1): 65–76.

Hallen, B. and Sodipo, J. O. (1986) *Knowledge, Belief and Witchcraft: Analytic Experiments in African Philosophy*, London: Ethnographica.

Hamilton, N. (1996) 'The personal is political', *Cambridge Archaeological Journal*, 6(2): 282–5.

Hampson, Daphne (1990) *Theology and Feminism*, Cambridge, MA: Basil Blackwell.

Hardie, Titania (2000) *Hocus Pocus: Titania's Book of Spells*, London: Quadrille.

Harding, Sandra (ed.) (1987) *Feminism and Methodology*, Bloomington and Indianapolis, IN: Indiana University Press.

Hardman, Charlotte (1995) 'Introduction', in C. Hardman and G. Harvey (eds) *Paganism Today*, London: Thorsons, ix–xix.

Harner, Michael (1980, 1990) *The Way of the Shaman*, San Francisco: HarperCollins.

Harris, Marvin (1974) *Cows, Pigs, Wars and Witches: The Riddles of Culture*, New York: Vintage Books.
Harrow, Judy (1996) 'The contemporary neo-Pagan revival' in J. R. Lewis (ed.) *Magical Religion and Modern Witchcraft*, Albany, NY: State University of New York Press, 9–24.
Harvey, Graham (1997) *Listening People, Speaking Earth: Contemporary Paganism*, London: Hurst and Co.
Heliotrope, H. (1999) *God and Goddess in Conflict: The Argument for Modern Paganism*, Christchurch: privately published.
Henningsen, Gustav (1990) '"The Ladies from Outside": an archaic pattern of the witches' sabbath' in B. Ankarloo and G. Henningsen (eds) *Early Modern European Witchcraft: Centres and Peripheries*, Oxford: Clarendon Press, 191–215.
Hester, Marianne (1992) *Lewd Women and Wicked Witches: A Study of the Dynamics of Male Domination*, London and New York: Routledge.
Hoch-Smith, Judith (1978) 'Radical Yoruba female sexuality: the witch and the prostitute', in J. Hoch-Smith and A. Spring (eds) *Women in Ritual and Symbolic Roles*, New York: Plenum Press, 245–67.
Hughes, Pennethorne (1965) *Witchcraft*, Harmondsworth: Penguin.
Hume, Lynne (1997) *Witchcraft and Paganism in Australia*, Melbourne: Melbourne University Press.
Hutton, Ronald (1991) *The Pagan Religions of the Ancient British Isles*, Cambridge, MA: Basil Blackwell.
—— (1994) 'Neo-Paganism, Paganism and Christianity', *Religion Today*, 9(3): 29–32.
—— (1995) 'The roots of modern Paganism', in C. Hardman and G. Harvey (eds) *Paganism Today*, London: Thorsons, 3–15.
—— (1999) 'Modern pagan witchcraft', in B. Ankarloo and S. Clark (eds) *Witchcraft and Magic in Europe: The Twentieth Century*, London: The Athlone Press, 1–79.
—— (2000) *The Triumph of the Moon: A History of Modern Pagan Witchcraft*, Oxford: Oxford University Press.
Irigaray, Luce (1985) *This Sex Which Is Not One*, trans. Catherine Porter, Ithaca, NY: Cornell University Press.
Jackson, Michael (1989) *Paths Toward a Clearing: Radical Empiricism and Ethnographic Inquiry*, Bloomington and Indianapolis, IN: Indiana University Press.
Johnsen, L. (1996) 'Rediscovering Tantra', *Yoga Journal*, January/February: 28–40.
Karlsen, Carol (1987) *The Devil in the Shape of a Woman: Witchcraft in Colonial New England*, New York: W. W. Norton and Co.
Kearney, Céline (1997) *Faces of the Goddess: New Zealand Women Talk about their Spirituality*, Auckland: Tandem Press.
Kelly, Aidan (1991) *Crafting the Art of Magic*, Book I: *A History of Modern Witchcraft, 1939–1964*, St Paul, MN: Llewellyn Publications.
—— (1992) 'An update on Neopagan Witchcraft in America', in J. R. Lewis and J. G. Melton (eds) *Perspectives on the New Age*, Albany, NY: State University of New York Press.
King, Ursula (1989) *Women and Spirituality: Voices of Protest and Promise*, London: Macmillan.
—— (ed.) (1995) *Religion and Gender*, Oxford: Blackwell.
—— (ed.) (1998) *Faith and Praxis in a Postmodern World*, London: Cassell.
Kirby, Vicki (1992) *Addressing Essentialism Differently: Some Thoughts on the Corpo-real*,

University of Waikato Women's Studies Occasional Paper Series, no. 4, Hamilton: University of Waikato.

Kramer, Heinrich and Sprenger, James (1971) *The Malleus Maleficarum*, New York: Dover Publications.

Lather, Patti (1989) 'Deconstructing/deconstructive inquiry: issues in feminist research methodologies', paper presented at New Zealand Women's Studies Association Conference, Christchurch, 25–27 August.

Lehmann, A. C. and Myers, J. E. (2001) *Magic, Witchcraft and Religion: An Anthropological Study of the Supernatural*, 5th edn, Mountain View, CA: Mayfield.

Leland, C. G. (1897, 1974) *Aradia: Gospel of the Witches*, New York: Samuel Weiser.

Levack, Brian (1987) *The Witch-Hunt in Early Modern Europe*, London: Longman.

Lévy-Bruhl, Lucien (1910, 1985) *How Natives Think*, Princeton, NJ: Princeton University Press.

Lewis, Gilbert (1980) *Day of Shining Red: An Essay on Understanding Ritual*, Cambridge: Cambridge University Press.

Lewis, I. M. (1971) *Ecstatic Religions: An Anthropological Study of Spirit Possession and Shamanism*, Harmondsworth: Penguin.

—— (1986) *Religion in Context: Cults and Charisma*, Cambridge: Cambridge University Press.

Lewis, James R. (ed.) (1996) *Magical Religion and Modern Witchcraft*, Albany, NY: State University of New York Press.

—— (1999) *Witchcraft Today: An Encyclopedia of Wiccan and Neopagan Traditions*, Oxford: Clio.

Linn, Denise (1983) *Inner Woman: Initiation into the Mysteries of the Goddess*, cassette tape, Annapolis, MD: Wisdom Books.

Long, A. (1995) 'The Goddess movement in Britain today', *Feminist Theology*, 5: 11–39.

—— (1997) 'The one or the many: the Great Goddess revisited', *Feminist Theology*, 15: 13–29.

Lovell-Smith, Margie *et al.* (eds) (1988) *Women's Ministries and Spirituality Conference: A Resource Book for Women: Reports, Resources and Reflections arising from the Third National Ecumenical Feminist Women's Conference held at Rangi Ruru Girls' School, Christchurch, August 31 to September 4, 1988*, Christchurch: The Planning Group, Women's Ministries and Spirituality Conference.

Lovelock, James (1988) *The Ages of Gaia: A Biography of Our Living Earth*, Oxford: Oxford University Press.

Lozano, Wendy and Foltz, Tanice (1990) 'Into the darkness: an ethnographic study of witchcraft and death', *Qualitative Sociology*, 13(3): 211–34.

Luhrmann, T. M. (1989) *Persuasions of the Witch's Craft: Ritual Magic in Contemporary England*, Cambridge, MA: Harvard University Press.

Lunn, P. (1993) 'Do women need the Goddess? Some phenomenological and sociological reflections', *Feminist Theology*, 4: 17–38.

Macfarlane, Alan (1970a) *Witchcraft in Tudor and Stuart England: A Regional and Comparative Study*, London: Routledge and Kegan Paul.

—— (1970b) 'Witchcraft in Tudor and Stuart Essex', in M. Douglas (ed.) *Witchcraft: Confessions and Accusations*, London: Tavistock Publications.

Marler, J. (ed.) (1997) *From the Realm of the Ancestors: Essays in Honor of Marija Gimbutas*, Manchester, CT: Knowledge, Ideas, and Trends.

Marwick, Max (ed.) (1970) *Witchcraft and Sorcery: Selected Readings*, Harmondsworth: Penguin.
Mascia-Lees, F. E., Sharpe, P. and Cohen, C. B. (1989) 'The postmodernist turn in anthropology: cautions from a feminist perspective', *Signs*, 15(1): 7–33.
Meskell, L. (1995) 'Goddesses, Gimbutas and "New Age" archaeology', *Antiquity*, 69: 74–86.
—— (1998) 'Twin peaks: the archaeologies of Çatalhöyük', in L. Goodison and C. Morris (eds) *Ancient Goddesses: The Myths and the Evidence*, London: British Museum Press, 46–62.
Michelet, Jules (1862, 1952) *La Sorcière*, Paris: Didier.
Midelfort, H. C. Eric (1972) *Witch Hunting in Southwestern Germany, 1562–1684: The Social and Intellectual Foundations*, Stanford, CA: Stanford University Press.
Moore, Sally and Myerhoff, Barbara (eds) (1977) *Secular Ritual*, Amsterdam: Van Gorcum.
Morgan, Robin (1978) *Going Too Far: The Personal Chronicle of a Feminist*, New York: Vintage Books.
Morris, Brian (1987) *Anthropological Studies of Religion: An Introductory Text*, Cambridge: Cambridge University Press.
Mountainwater, Shekhinah (1991) 'Writings on rituals and spells', in D. Stein (ed.) *The Goddess Celebrates*, Freedom, CA: The Crossing Press.
Muchembled, Robert (1990) 'Satanic myths and cultural reality', in B. Ankarloo and G. Henningsen (eds) *Early Modern European Witchcraft: Centres and Peripheries*, Oxford: Clarendon Press, 139–60.
Murray, Margaret (1921, 1971) *The Witch-Cult in Western Europe*, Oxford: Clarendon Press.
Myerhoff, Barbara (1986) '"Life not death in Venice": its second life', in V. Turner and E. Bruner (eds) *The Anthropology of Experience*, Urbana and Chicago, IL: University of Illinois Press, 261–86.
Oldridge, Darren (ed.) (2002) *The Witchcraft Reader*, London: Routledge.
Orion, Loretta (1995) *Never Again the Burning Times: Paganism Revived*, Prospect Heights, IL: Waveland Press.
—— (2001) 'Wicca, a way of working', in A. C. Lehmann and J. E. Myers (eds) *Magic, Witchcraft and Religion: An Anthropological Study of the Supernatural*, Mountain View, CA: Mayfield, 243–52.
Ortner, Sherry B. (1974) 'Is female to male as nature is to culture?', in M. Z. Rosaldo and L. Lamphere (eds) *Women, Culture and Society*, Stanford, CA: Stanford University Press, 67–88.
—— (1996) 'So, is female to male as nature is to culture?', in S. B. Ortner, *Making Gender: The Politics and Erotics of Culture*, Boston, MA: Beacon Press, 173–80.
Parrinder, Geoffrey (1970) *Witchcraft: European and African*, London: Faber and Faber.
Patton, Michael Quinn (1990) *Qualitative Evaluation and Research Methods*, Newbury Park, CA: Sage Publications.
Penny, Noreen (1990) 'Feminist witchcraft', *Broadsheet*, 17: 178–9.
—— (1994) *Women's Rites: An Alternative to Patriarchal Religion*, Christchurch: Waikuku.
Pike, Sarah (2001) *Earthly Bodies, Magical Selves: Contemporary Pagans and the Search for Community*, Berkeley, CA: University of California Press.
Pócs, Éva (1999) *Between the Living and the Dead*, Budapest: Central European University Press.

Raphael, Melissa (1999) *Introducing Thealogy: Discourse on the Goddess*, Sheffield: Sheffield Academic Press.

Reinharz, Shulamit (1992) *Feminist Methods in Social Research*, New York: Oxford University Press.

Rooney, E. (1994) 'In a word: interview, Gayatri Chakravorty Spivak with Ellen Rooney', in N. Schor and E. Weed (eds) *The Essential Difference*, Bloomington, IN: Indiana University Press, 151–84.

Rosaldo, M. Z. (1974) 'Woman, culture, and society: a theoretical overview', in M. Z. Rosaldo and L. Lamphere (eds) *Woman, Culture and Society*, Stanford, CA: Stanford University Press, 17–42.

—— 1980, 'The use and abuse of anthropology: reflections on feminism and cross-cultural understanding', *Signs*, 5(3): 390–417.

Rosaldo, Michelle Z. and Lamphere, Louise (eds) (1974) *Woman, Culture and Society*, Stanford, CA: Stanford University Press.

Rose, Deborah (1992) *Dingo Makes Us Human: Life and Land in an Aboriginal Australian Culture*, Cambridge: Cambridge University Press.

Rountree, Kathryn (1993) 'Re-membering the witch and the Goddess: feminist ritual-makers in New Zealand', unpublished DPhil thesis, University of Waikato, New Zealand.

—— (1999) 'The politics of the Goddess: feminist spirituality and the essentialism debate', *Social Analysis*, 43(2): 142–68.

—— (2001) 'The past is a foreigner's country: Goddess feminists, archaeologists, and the appropriation of prehistory', *Journal of Contemporary Religion*, 16(1): 5–27.

—— (2002a) 'How magic works: New Zealand feminist witches' theories of ritual action', *Anthropology of Consciousness*, 13(1): 42–59.

—— (2002b) 'Goddess pilgrims as tourists: inscribing the body through sacred travel', *Sociology of Religion*, 63(4): 475–96.

Ruby, Jay (ed.) (1982) *A Crack in the Mirror: Reflexive Perspectives in Anthropology*, Philadelphia, PA: University of Pennsylvania Press.

Ruether, Rosemary Radford (1986) *Women-Church*, San Francisco: Harper and Row.

—— (1992) *Gaia and God*, San Francisco: HarperCollins.

—— (1998) *Women and Redemption*, Minneapolis, MN: Fortress Press.

Russell, Jeffrey (1980) *A History of Witchcraft: Sorcerers, Heretics and Pagans*, London: Thames and Hudson.

Russell, Steven (2001) 'Witchcraft, genealogy, Foucault', *British Journal of Sociology*, 52(1): 121–37.

Salomonsen, Jone (2002) *Enchanted Feminism: The Reclaiming Witches of San Francisco*, London: Routledge.

Schechner, Richard (1982) 'Collective reflexivity: restoration of behaviour', in J. Ruby (ed.) *A Crack in the Mirror: Reflexive Perspectives in Anthropology*, Philadelphia, PA: University of Pennsylvania Press, 39–82.

Schechner, Richard and Schuman, Mady (eds) (1976) *Ritual, Play, and Performance: Readings in the Social Sciences/Theatre*, New York: Seabury Press.

Schor, N. (1994) 'This essentialism which is not one: coming to grips with Irigaray', in N. Schor and E. Weed (eds) *The Essential Difference*, Bloomington, IN: Indiana University Press, 40–62.

Sheldrake, Rupert (1988) *The Presence of the Past: Morphic Resonance and the Habits of Nature*, London: Collins.

—— (1991) *The Rebirth of Nature: The Greening of Science and God*, New York: Bantam.
Skorupski, John (1976) *Symbol and Theory: A Philosophical Study of Theories of Religion in Social Anthropology*, Cambridge: Cambridge University Press.
Spretnak, Charlene (ed.) (1982) *The Politics of Women's Spirituality: Essays on the Rise of Spiritual Power within the Feminist Movement*, New York: Anchor Books.
Starhawk (1988) *Dreaming the Dark: Magic, Sex and Politics*, Boston, MA: Beacon Press; first published 1982.
—— (1989) *The Spiral Dance: A Rebirth of the Ancient Religion of the Great Goddess*, San Francisco: Harper and Row; first published 1979.
—— (1990) *Truth or Dare: Encounters with Power, Authority, and Mystery*, San Francisco: HarperCollins.
Stein, Diane (1990) *Casting the Circle: A Women's Book of Ritual*, Freedom, CA: The Crossing Press.
—— (1991) *The Goddess Celebrates: An Anthology of Women's Rituals*, Freedom, CA: The Crossing Press.
Stone, Merlin (1976) *When God Was a Woman*, New York: Harcourt, Brace, Jovanovich.
Strathern, Marilyn (1987) 'An awkward relationship: the case of feminism and anthropology', *Signs*, 12(2): 276–92.
Tambiah, Stanley Jeyaraja (1985) *Culture, Thought, and Social Action: An Anthropological Perspective*, Cambridge, MA: Harvard University Press.
—— (1990) *Magic, Science, Religion and the Scope of Rationality*, Cambridge: Cambridge University Press.
Teish, Luisah (1985) *Jambalaya: The Natural Woman's Book of Personal Charms and Practical Rituals*, San Francisco: Harper and Row.
Thistlethwaite, Susan (1989) *Sex, Race, and God: Christian Feminism in Black and White*, New York: Crossroad.
Thomas, Keith (1970) 'The relevance of social anthropology to the historical study of English witchcraft', in M. Douglas (ed.) *Witchcraft: Confessions and Accusations*, London: Tavistock Publications.
—— (1971) *Religion and the Decline of Magic: Studies in Popular Beliefs in 16th and 17th Century England*, London: Weidenfeld and Nicolson.
Tong, R. (1989) *Feminist Thought: A Comprehensive Introduction*, London: Unwin Hyman.
Trevor-Roper, Hugh (1969) 'The European witch-craze of the 16th and 17th centuries', in H. Trevor-Roper *Religion, the Reformation and Social Change and Other Essays*, London: Macmillan.
Tringham, R. and Conkey, M. (1998) 'Rethinking figurines: a critical view from archaeology of Gimbutas, the "Goddess" and popular culture', in L. Goodison and C. Morris (eds) *Ancient Goddesses: The Myths and the Evidence*, London: British Museum Press, 22–45.
Turner, Edith (1996) *The Hands Feel It: Healing and Spirit Presence among a Northern Alaskan People*, De Kalb, IL: Northern Illinois University Press.
Turner, Victor (1969, 1974a) *The Ritual Process: Structure and Anti-Structure*, Harmondsworth: Penguin.
—— (1974b) *Dramas, Fields and Metaphors*, Ithaca, NY: Cornell University Press.
Tylor, Edward Burnett (1871) *Primitive Culture: Researches into the Development of Mythology, Philosophy, Religion, Art and Custom*, London: John Murray.
Valiente, Doreen (1989) *The Rebirth of Witchcraft*, Custer, WA: Phoenix Publishing.

van Gelder, Lindsy (1989) 'It's not nice to mess with Mother Nature: an introduction to ecofeminism 101, the most exciting new "ism" in eons', *Ms*, 17(7 and 8): 60–3.
van Gennep, Arnold (1960) *The Rites of Passage*, London: Routledge and Kegan Paul.
Walker, Barbara (1985) *The Crone: Woman of Age, Wisdom and Power*, San Francisco: Harper and Row.
—— (1988) *The Woman's Dictionary of Symbols and Sacred Objects*, San Francisco: Harper and Row.
—— (1990) *Women's Rituals: A Sourcebook*, San Francisco: Harper and Row.
Weaver, M. J. (1989) 'Who is the Goddess and where does she get us?', *Journal of Feminist Studies in Religion*, 5(1): 49–64.
Westenholz, J. G. (1998) 'Goddesses of the ancient Near East 3000–1000 BC', in L. Goodison and C. Morris (eds) *Ancient Goddesses: The Myths and the Evidence*, London: British Museum Press, 63–82.
Whitmont, Edward (1983) *Return of the Goddess: Femininity, Aggression and the Modern Grail Quest*, London: Routledge and Kegan Paul.
Winkelman, Michael (2000) *Shamanism: The Neural Ecology of Consciousness and Healing*, Westport, CT: Bergin and Garvey.
Wisewitch, Yolanda (1987) 'Women's rites: a study of fifteen Christchurch women's thoughts and feelings about their involvement in women's spirituality', unpublished MA thesis, University of Canterbury, Christchurch.
Wittig, Monique (1972) *The Guerillères*, London: Picador.
Women's Spirituality Newsletters, available from WSG, PO Box 26–351, Epsom, Auckland, New Zealand.
Wood, J. (1996) 'The concept of the Goddess', in S. Billington and M. Green (eds) *The Concept of the Goddess*, London: Routledge, 8–25.

INDEX